DOMÉSTICA

DOMÉSTICA

Immigrant Workers Cleaning and Caring in the Shadows of Affluence

PIERRETTE HONDAGNEU-SOTELO

University of California Press
Berkeley · Los Angeles · London

All royalties for this book will be donated to the Domestic Workers' Association, a division of the Coalition for Humane Immigrant Rights of Los Angeles (CHIRLA).

University of California Press
Berkeley and Los Angeles, California

University of California Press, Ltd.
London, England

© 2001 by the Regents of the University of California

Library of Congress Cataloging-in-Publication Data

Hondagneu-Sotelo, Pierrette.
    Doméstica : immigrant workers cleaning and caring in
the shadows of affluence / Pierrette Hondagneu-Sotelo.
        p. cm.
    Includes bibliographical references and index.
    ISBN 0-520-21473-0 (cloth : alk. paper)—ISBN 0-520-
22643-7 (pbk. : alk. paper)
        1. Women domestics—California—Los Angeles
Metropolitan Area.   2. Nannies—California—Los
Angeles Metropolitan Area.   3. Hispanic American
women—Employment—California—Los Angeles
Metropolitan Area.   4. Women alien labor—California—
Los Angeles Metropolitan Area.   5. Women immigrants—
California—Los Angeles Metropolitan Area—Economic
conditions.   6. Working class women—California—Los
Angeles Metropolitan Area.   7. Upper class women—
California—Los Angeles Metropolitan Area.   I. Title:
Immigrant workers cleaning and caring in the shadows
of affluence.   II. Title.

HD6072.2.U52 L674 2001
331.4'8164046'08968079494—dc21

                                                00-051171
Manufactured in the United States of America

10   09   08   07   06   05   04   03   02   01
10   9   8   7   6   5   4   3   2   1

The paper used in this publication meets the minimum
requirements of ANSI/NISO Z39.48-1992 (R 1997)
(*Permanence of Paper*).

For Cristina Maria Riegos, 1971–1998,
an inspiration and cherished memory

Contents

Preface   ix

Acknowledgments   xxiii

PART ONE   THE JOB TODAY

1. New World Domestic Order   3

2. Maid in L.A.   29

PART TWO   FINDING HARD WORK ISN'T EASY

3. It's Not What You Know . . .   63

4. Formalizing the Informal:
   Domestic Employment Agencies   92

5. Blowups and Other Unhappy Endings   114

PART THREE   INSIDE THE JOB

6. Tell Me What to Do, But Don't Tell Me How   137

7. Go Away . . . But Stay Close Enough   171

8. Cleaning Up a Dirty Business   210

Notes   245

References   269

Index   279

Preface

Can we conceive of a Los Angeles where there is, as the title of a short film puts it, "A Day without a Mexican"?[1] In fact, as I learned while chatting with domestic workers at parks and bus stops, this is an exercise regularly indulged in by Mexican, Salvadoran, and Guatemalan women who work in middle-class and upper-middle-class homes throughout Los Angeles. "If we called a three-day strike," nannies say to their peers, "How many days would it take before we shut it all down?" Not only would households fall into a state of chaos, but professionals, managers, and office workers of all sorts would find themselves unable to perform their own jobs. Latina domestic workers debate this scenario with humor—some arguing that it might take two days, others chiming in with four. They know that in their job, a general strike is unlikely. Yet their strident humor is bolstered by the resurgence of militant unionism among Latino immigrant janitors and hotel and restaurant employees and by collective organizing among gardeners, day laborers, and drywallers in California. Significantly, their running dialogue speaks to a shared recognition of their own indispensability. In their own conversations, they reclaim what their job experiences often deny them: social recognition and dignity.

Latina immigrant labor, and specifically the work of housecleaners and nanny/housekeepers, constitutes a bedrock of our contemporary U.S. culture and economy, yet the work and the women who do it remain invisible and disregarded. Paid domestic work enjoyed a short-lived flurry of media attention in the early 1990s, when the transgressions of Zoë Baird and Kimba Wood (and several other political nominees and elected officials) came to light, but the public gaze was fleeting.[2] Moreover, attention focused neither on the quality of the jobs nor on the women who do the work but on their employers, who had failed to pay employment taxes.

Private paid domestic work, in which one individual cleans and cares for another individual or family, poses an enormous paradox. In the United States today, these jobs remain effectively unregulated by formal rules and contracts. Consequently, even today they often resemble relations of servitude that prevailed in earlier, precapitalist feudal societies. These contemporary work arrangements contradict American democratic ideals and modern contractual notions of employment. *Doméstica* reveals how these fundamental tensions in American social life are played out in private homes, between the women who do the work and those who employ them.

Paid domestic work is widely recognized as part of the informal "shadow" or "under the table" economy. Although wage and hour regulations do cover the job, scarcely anyone, employee or employer, knows about them. Government regulations remain ineffective, and there are no employee handbooks, unions, or management guidelines to help set wages or job duties or to stipulate how the work should be performed. The jobs are done in isolated, private, widely dispersed households, and typically involve negotiations between two individuals—usually women from radically different backgrounds. Yet despite this laissez-faire context, there are striking regularities in wages, hours, benefits, tasks, and directions; in disputes that arise; and in modes of recruitment, hiring, and firing. In this book, I identify many of these patterns. Relying on primary information gathered in the mid- to late 1990s from more than two hundred people in Los Angeles (in-depth interviews with 68 individuals, a survey of 153 Latina domestic workers, and ethnographic observations in various settings), I examine how the practices and concerns of both employers and employees shape how paid domestic work occurs today.

There are many lived dramas in America today, and among the least visible and most deeply felt are those that unfold behind carefully manicured lawns and residential facades. My book highlights the voices, experiences, and views both of the Mexican and Central American women who care for other people's children and homes and of the women in Los Angeles who employ them. The study of paid domestic work thus offers a key window through which we can view contemporary relations between women whose social positions are in stark contrast: between poor women and affluent families; between foreign-born, immigrant women and U.S.-born citizens; and between members of the growing, but still economically and

racially subordinate, Latino communities and the shrinking population of white suburban residents, many of whom feel increasingly
anxious about these demographic developments. Differences of class,
race, nationality, and citizenship characterize the study's participants, yet this is an occupation in which the chasm of social differences plays out in physical proximity. Unlike the working poor who
toil in factories and fields, domestic workers see, touch, and breath
the material and emotional world of their employers' homes. They
scrub grout, coax reluctant children to nap and eat their vegetables,
launder and fold clothes, mop, dust, vacuum, and witness intimate
and otherwise private family dynamics. Inside the palatial mansion,
the sprawling ranch-style home, or the modest duplex, they do these
activities over and over again.

Ambivalence characterizes the governance of private paid domestic work in the United States. Many contemporary employers of domestic workers feel awkward or ambivalent about the ambiguous
arrangements that they make. In part, this ambivalence reflects
American unease with the whole image of domestic service. Contemporary inequalities notwithstanding, Americans have no titled aristocracy and no feudal past, and the omnipresent ideology of freedom, equality, and democracy clashes with what many American
employers of domestic workers experience in their lives. Some employers try different strategies to address their sense of disquiet. Indeed, most of them think of themselves not as "employers" but
rather as "consumers." Some of them try to not witness the work as
it is performed, deliberately leaving the house when their housecleaners are there even if they have no need to be elsewhere. In casual
conversations, they may refer to the Guatemalan woman who works
in their home as their "baby-sitter," invoking the image of a high
school girl who lives down the street and looks after the kids on
Saturday night. *Nanny*, after all, sounds too unrepentantly British,
and too class marked—though some do flaunt their privilege, grateful at least to be on the employers' side of the fence. *Maid*, a term
that sounds servile, anachronistic, and almost premodern, is rarely
used by anyone. Some employers try to snip off the price tags on
new clothing and home furnishings before the Latina domestic workers read them because they fear the women will compare the prices
of those items with their wages—which they invariably do. While
employers often feel guilty about "having so much" around someone

who "has so little," the women who do the work resent not their affluence but the job arrangements, which generally afford the workers little in the way of respect and living wages.

Domestic work was the single largest category of paid employment for all women in the United States during the late nineteenth and early twentieth centuries, in large part because other opportunities were not available. Although the timing of exit varies by race and region, by the mid–twentieth century the doors to retail, clerical, and professional jobs were opening for many working women, and single and married women walked out of their homes and into formal-sector employment.[3] Paid domestic work declined, a trend leading some commentators to predict the occupation's demise. But instead in the late twentieth century new domestic demands arose and new recruits were found, now crossing the southern border to reach the doorstep of domestic work. The work of cleaning houses and caring for children gradually left the hands of wives and mothers and entered the global marketplace. In the process, it has become the domain of disenfranchised immigrant women of color.

I focus not on the sensationalistic abuses and crimes in domestic work (e.g., the nanny who beats the children, or the employer who holds the housekeeper hostage), but rather on the everyday organization of an occupation and the concerns of the women who do the work. The "L.A. stories" presented here underline that social relationships—among the employees, among the employers, and between the two groups—organize the job. These social relationships, as well-intentioned as some of them may be, sometimes lead to less than desirable job performance and conditions of work. Problems and abuses arise that harm both employers and employees, but especially the latter, primarily because paid domestic work is not treated as employment. Remedying the problems and social injustices of paid domestic work, I argue, will involve bestowing social recognition on the work of caring for homes and for children, and learning to see and treat paid domestic work as employment.

SOCIAL LOCATIONS, RESEARCH LOCATIONS

I wrote this book on time stolen away from teaching and administrative duties at my university, and away from my own housecleaning, grocery shopping, cooking, and child care. Even when blessed with a sabbatical and summer vacations, I struggled to find time when school holidays, or unexpected bouts of chicken pox or flu, would not derail my research and writing momentum. And although I pay a Salvadoran woman to clean my house every other week, I still feel there are not enough hours in the day to do everything I need to do. In this regard, I'm afraid I fit the profile of the harried working mom.

Here's the ironic rub: in this book, I argue that cleaning houses and taking care of children is "real work," yet in the ways I live my life, I still define my real work as my teaching, research, and writing, not the varied activities involved in taking care of my children and home. I love my family and my home, and I spend a good part of each day thinking about, planning, and engaging in family and home activities. Still, if someone asks me, "What do you do?" I tell them what I do for a living. My job as a university professor is privileged work that has been a struggle for me to achieve; I like it, and I don't for a moment take it for granted. The same can truthfully be said of my domestic life, but why don't I claim my own homemaking and care work in the same way? There are many reasons to explain this, and they are primarily social, not individual. They have to do with how we regard—or, more accurately, disregard—the work of running families and households, how we romanticize family as a "natural" arena of expression for women, and how we conceptualize and reward "work," which remains, even as we enter the twenty-first century, something we still think about in terms of nineteenth-century models of production.

Several other biographical features about me frame this study. I am the daughter of a Latina woman who, like many modestly educated women in mid-twentieth-century Latin America, migrated from the countryside to the city to work as a live-in nanny/housekeeper. Eventually, employment in her native Chile for the American family of an Anaconda copper mining engineer was her ticket to California, bought with indentured labor. When the family that brought her to the United States refused to pay her, she found live-in domestic jobs with other well-to-do American families before eventually marrying my father, a French gardener whom she met on the job. I grew up hearing all kinds of stories about *"la señora* Elsa" and *"la* Mrs. Lowe" (the article always prefacing the name, thereby signaling a formidable presence). Throughout my childhood and adolescence, my family maintained close ties with a Chilean family for whom my mother had once worked, well after she had left their employ and migrated to the United States.[4]

Today, my husband and I do laundry, cook, and clean daily, but we also pay a Salvadoran woman to clean our house. Every other Thursday she drives from her apartment near downtown Los Angeles to our suburban home to sweep and mop the hardwood floors, vacuum the carpets, dust the furniture, and scrub, wipe, and polish the bathrooms and kitchen to a blinding gleam. I love the way the house looks after she's done her job; but like many of the employers that I interviewed for this study, I remain deeply ambivalent about the glaring inequalities exposed by this arrangement—and exposed in a particularly visible and visceral way. Capitalist manufacturing misery abounds in this world; but when I purchase Nike shoes or Gap jeans, my reliance on child labor in Mauritania or Pakistan, or on Latina garment workers who toil in sweatshops just a stone's throw away from my office at USC, remains conveniently hidden and invisible in the object of consumption. I take possession of a new item, and no one but the cashier stares back at me. By contrast, my privileges and complicity in a worldwide system of inequalities and exploitation are thrown into relief by the face-to-face relations between me and the woman who cleans my house.

When colleagues and students in my classes have discussed these issues, some of them have argued passionately and compellingly that we cannot have a just society until everyone cleans up and picks up after themselves, regardless of their race, sex, or immigration or class status. They might be right (and I'm certainly in favor of men and boys learning to do their fair share), but I think an abolitionist program smacks of the utopian, not the feasible. Domestic work should not fall disproportionately on the shoulders of any one group (such as Filipina, or Latina, or Caribbean immigrant women); but putting an end to domestic employment is not the answer. Upgrading the occupation, a change ushered in by systemic regulation and by public recognition that this seemingly private activity is a job—one that creates particular obligations in both employees and employers—is our best chance for salvaging paid domestic work, for increasing the opportunities of those who do the work and of their families, and for reclaiming the dignity and humanity of both employees and employers.

Since 1990, well before I began the research for this book, I have worked toward that end with a group of women under the auspices of the Coalition for Humane Immigrant Rights of Los Angeles (CHIRLA). The project began as an information and outreach program organized by immigrant rights attorneys, community organizers, and myself, but today it is a full-fledged, dues-collecting membership organization called the Domestic Workers' Association (DWA), which is part of CHIRLA. All my royalties from the sale of this book will go to the DWA. Similar organizations have sprouted up in other cities around the country, and they have long been common in Latin America. I discuss the DWA in chapter 8; here it is mentioned only to contextualize my relationship to this topic. All research is partial, situated and shaped by who we are. My multiple social locations—as the daughter of a former domestic worker, as a current employer, and as an advocate—have certainly shaped my approach and my emphases. My engagement with previous research and scholarship, particularly that focusing on gender, immigration, and paid domestic work, also situates this study.

RESEARCH DESCRIPTION

I began this project as an interview study, but state and national politics swirling around private domestic work and immigration sometimes made it difficult to find interview participants. From the beginning, I knew I couldn't understand this occupation without understanding those who hire nanny/housekeepers and housecleaners, but some employers turned down my request to come to their home and tape-record them, fearing that I might be an IRS agent posing as a sociologist (the Zoë Baird and Kimba Wood incidents were fresh in their memories). Others said they were too busy. Meanwhile, some Latina immigrant women, in the climate of fear created by California's Proposition 187 (which sought to bar undocumented immigrants and their children from receiving publicly funded health care and public education), suspected I might be an undercover agent for the Immigration and Naturalization Service. I loathed the process of telephoning strangers to ask for interviews, and the rejections made it worse. Still, I persevered and eventually interviewed thirty-seven employers and twenty-three employees.[5] I asked employers and employees alike about their varied experiences with paid domestic work, the specific job terms and how these were set, what they liked and disliked about the job arrangement, and basic demographic information. I conducted nearly all of the interviews in the respondents' homes—which means I drove great distances around Los Angeles County, visiting neighborhoods I might never otherwise see in the course of my daily life and wearing out a set of tires; a few took place at my home. Each interview lasted approximately two and a half hours, and the verbatim transcripts averaged about forty to fifty pages of single-spaced text. I read through them many times, selectively coded portions, and then created computer files to bring together pieces of interviews that addressed themes of interest to me. Nearly all of the interviews with employees were conducted in Spanish, and I translated into English only those portions that appear in the text.

Although I had no illusions about drawing a random sample of a universe about which so little is known, I knew I didn't want to confine interview respondents to self-selected groups, such as feminist university women who employ housecleaners, or Latinas who had already organized in one of Los Angeles' domestic worker organizations or cooperatives. These would have been easy pools of respondents, but I wanted to interview more heterogeneous groups of women. I therefore deliberately sought out women from different social and geographic locations in Los Angeles. For example, when I began to search for employer interviewees, I contacted a friend's mother—a liberal-leaning, Jewish retired teacher living on the Westside of Los Angeles; I subsequently interviewed several of her friends who lived in that vicinity and shared similar characteristics. I also began other small snowball samples that reflected different kinds of diversity by tapping into communities of, for example, young, white, well-to-do homemakers from a nursery school cooperative near the Hollywood Hills; middle-aged women living in a multiracial suburb deep in Los Angeles' San Gabriel Valley; and a younger group of career women, some of whom had children and some of whom didn't. This approach did not produce a representative sample (my method, for example, led me to only one interview with a male employer), but it allowed me to speak with employers from different walks of life, at different life stages, and with diverse opinions and experiences. As I requested interviews with employers, I also looked for a balance among the kinds of arrangement for paid domestic work, including respondents who hired, respectively, live-in nanny/housekeepers, live-out nanny/housekeepers, and weekly housecleaners.

I similarly recruited Latina immigrant domestic workers for the study. I interviewed nannies whom I had met in the park or at bus stops, at presentations that I made in ESL (English as a second language) classes, and through referrals passed to me by friends or other interviewees; I even interviewed a woman who had left her "looking for work" card on my doorstep. These Latina immigrants, as chapter 2 shows, are diverse in their national origins, in their ages, and in the types of domestic work they do. With the exception of two sisters whom I interviewed together, I spoke with each domestic employee privately; and in addition to the questions mentioned above, I also asked them about their work and social lives before migrating to the United States, their family and social lives, and their future occupational aspirations. Cognizant of the precarious financial position of many of these women, and of the substantial time commitment required by my interviews, I initially tried to discreetly pass $25 or $30 in an envelope to each interview participant. Many of the women refused this money. In some cases, I succeeded in prevailing on them; in others, not. Finally, I settled on bringing to each interview a blooming plant, which I purchased at my local supermarket. Most women enjoy receiving flowers, and Latina domestic workers are no exception. In addition to the twenty-three nanny/housekeepers and housecleaners and the thirty-seven employers, I also formally interviewed three attorneys specializing in legal issues surrounding private paid domestic work and five individuals who owned or worked in domestic employment agencies. Altogether, I conducted in-depth, audiotaped interviews with sixty-eight people. And without my tape recorder, I spoke more casually with many more domestic workers, employers, and several organizers and attorneys. Throughout the text, pseudonyms are used for all employers, employees, and agency personnel, but not for the advocacy attorneys.

The interview materials are the most crucial source of information in this book. By using them, I have sought to enable the voices of employers and employees to be heard. To be sure, this is not a kind of ventriloquism, as qualitative, interview research used to be viewed—with the ventriloquist (me) simply mouthing other people's stories. I am deliberately using their words to put forth a specific argument about contemporary paid domestic work. In postmodern anthropology, the illusion is broken, and the power of the ventriloquist to select and form the dialogue is fully revealed: but those in the audience, who hear and interpret the dialogue, also have agency. My position is that this is an interactive process, and the voices that emerge in the interviews, like other sources of information, provide us with only a partial view of the whole. In addition, it is important to note that much of what people reveal in interviews is shaped not only by their relationship to the interviewer but also by particulars and upheavals in their own lives at the time. The salience of these issues changes from day to day, week to week. For this reason, I have tried to avoid taking people's words out of context and to sketch, wherever possible, the proper setting for understanding the interviewee's experiences and perspectives.

Data from a survey questionnaire administered to 153 Latina immigrant domestic workers at a public park, at bus stops, and at evening ESL classes also inform this book. I administered the survey together with two research assistants, Gloria González-López and Ernestine Avila, who were then Ph.D. students. We went to downtown bus stops and to a busy, intracity bus terminal at 6 A.M. on Monday and Tuesday mornings (a time when many live-in workers are returning to their jobs); and we collected other responses at a popular Westside park where nannies bring young children in the middle of weekday mornings and at evening English classes in Hollywood. This was not a random, representative survey. It drew on women employed in the tonier neighborhoods of Los Angeles' Westside, and it left out many Latina domestic workers who speak English well and who drive their own cars to work. Still, it sketches a portrait and provides us with very particular information not available through the census or Labor Department statistics. The survey collected basic demographic information, such as the worker's country of origin, number of years in the United States, marital status, number of children and where they reside, previous occupational experiences, and, most important, information on wages and hours. For this study, I've also consulted the Census Public Use Microdata Sample for Los Angeles, but because both this occupation and the immigrant population generally are largely underrepresented in the census, I do not wholly rely on those indicators.

Finally, the research for this book also draws on limited ethnographic observations made in public and private sites. I spoke to, listened to, and passed time with Latina domestic workers in various settings: at public parks, on buses, at bus kiosks near downtown, in west Los Angeles and in Beverly Hills, at the now-defunct Labor Defense Network legal clinics—where Latina and Latino immigrants doing all kinds of work came to seek legal remedies to job problems—in the waiting rooms of domestic employment agencies, at meetings and informal social gatherings of the Domestic Workers' Association of CHIRLA, and at the information and outreach program that was the DWA's precursor. Rather than limit myself to one method or one source of information, I have explored many different ways of knowing about this occupation.

OVERVIEW

Chapter 1 situates contemporary paid domestic work in place and time and explains why, as the twentieth century ended, paid domestic work became a growth occupation. Besides noting the macrostructural, demographic, and cultural forces that have spurred this occupational growth, the chapter also contrasts historical with contemporary racialization of paid domestic work in the United States, underscoring why the job is still held in low regard. Noting some recent trends in the international migration of labor, I argue that the migration and employment of domestic workers in the United States today is distinctively laissez-faire and forms part of what I call the new world domestic order. Beginning with the observation that paid domestic work is organized in different ways, chapter 2 provides a close-up portrait of some of the domestic employees whom I interviewed. It describes how the job is experienced by live-in nanny/housekeepers, live-out nanny/housekeepers, and housecleaners, focusing on a few of the women and using data from the nonrandom survey of 153 Latina domestic workers to sketch their broader demographic and social profile.

Part 2 includes three chapters that examine the ways in which Latina immigrants enter and exit domestic jobs in Los Angeles. Chapter 3, on informal network hiring, focuses on the formation and inner workings of employer and employee networks. I argue that supply and demand alone are not enough: mechanisms for joining the two must be provided. The labor market for paid domestic work is constructed through the social network reference system, whose processes are important not only in job placement but also in effecting some job standardization, however imperfect. Chapter 4 examines the formalization of recruitment and hiring in domestic employment agencies, and chapter 5 examines the various ways in which domestic jobs end. Both hiring practices and approaches to job termination reveal that paid domestic work is often not recognized or treated as a "real job."

Part 3 examines social relations on the job. Chapter 6 focuses on labor control: the ability of employers to obtain the desired work behavior from their domestic employees, and the ways in which housecleaners and nanny/housekeepers, in turn, comply, resist, and negotiate. While there are broadly shared understandings of these jobs, the tasks are diffuse and there are no written standards to specify which services will be performed, or how they will be executed. Here's the paradox: many domestic workers want clear, fair directives, but their employers often shy away from defining the tasks they want performed. Because of the structure of the different jobs, the approaches of housecleaners and nanny/housekeepers to time and tasks vary; and their employers, of disparate generations and with various relationships to domestic life, also innovate different approaches to matters of labor control.

Chapter 7 concentrates on the topic that has drawn the most attention in the study of paid domestic work, personalism and maternalism. Many Latina immigrants currently employed in private domestic work in Los Angeles express their strong preference for employers who interact personalistically with them, while many of their employers say they would rather not engage in these sorts of relationships. To explain this gap, which contradicts the findings and analyses of previous studies, I distinguish personalism from maternalism and draw attention to the social locations of both employees and their employers. In chapter 8, I review existent labor regulations relevant to paid domestic work, and I explore different pathways to fairer job standards. As an advocate of occupational upgrading, not abolition, I consider how legislation, filing for back wage claims, and collective organizing (in Los Angeles, specifically the DWA), can help achieve this goal.

While this book focuses on private paid domestic work in Los Angeles, California, the occupation is expanding throughout the world. In the newly industrialized nations of Asia, in Europe, and in parts of Africa and Latin America, just as in the United States, many private domestic workers are women who have crossed nation-state borders.[6] For these migrant women, globalization has intensified inequalities that require strategies for change.

This book is not neutral: it is undergirded and motivated by a modernist belief that a fuller appreciation of the experiences and perspectives of both private domestic workers and their employees can lead to positive change. As we come to understand the social world of paid domestic work, which takes form within the context of broader global and legal structures, what is often seen as only private will begin to be made public and thus able to inform efforts to achieve social justice.

Acknowledgments

This is a story about domestic lives, and I owe a deep debt of gratitude to the women who allowed me to probe into the crevices of their lives and homes. They tolerated all sorts of intrusive, nosy questions that I would never consider asking them in other contexts, they sat and talked with me for hours, and they shared incredible stories of human resilience and tragedy. They may not agree with everything I have to say, but I hope that our mutual efforts eventually lead to greater justice.

The book is dedicated to Cristina Riegos, who was working toward that goal until her life was cut short by cancer. She brought tremendous creativity, charisma, and smarts to her job as an organizer among Latina immigrant domestic workers in Los Angeles. Because of her initial efforts, the Domestic Workers' Association, which I detail in the final chapter of this book, is still thriving.

I received research support from several funding sources. Most of the research was supported by a grant from the Social Science Research Council, through their Inter-University Program for Latino Research. At the University of Southern California, the Southern California Studies Center funded the research on domestic employment agencies, and the College of Letters, Arts, and Sciences provided Zumberge grant seed money to get this project off the ground. Funded research allowed me to hire research assistants who took on the monumental task of typing the verbatim transcriptions of the interviews, as well as other chores. For their efforts, I owe big thanks to Kim Huisman, Gloria González-López, Ernestine Avila, José Rodríguez-Pozeilov, Wendy de Boer, Cynthia Cranford, María Elena Espinoza, and Carrie Sutkin. Turning the research into a book became possible because I received in-town, in-residence writing fellowships at the Getty Research Institute and at the UCLA Chicano Studies Research Center.

Public and private conversations with many people furthered my thinking about this topic. Particularly helpful were audience questions and responses to presentations that I made at the Getty Research Institute; the International Sociological Association conference on International Cities at Humboldt University in Berlin; the Care Work, Gender, and Citizenship conference at the University of Illinois; colloquia at the Department of Ethnic Studies at UC San Diego and the Departments of Sociology at UC Berkeley and UC Irvine, as well as the Public Policy Institute at UCLA; the UC-Mexus meetings; seminars at El Colegio de la Frontera campus in Tijuana, El Colegio de Michoacán in Zamora, Michoacan, and at the Center for Working Families at UC Berkeley; American Sociological Association meetings in Toronto, San Francisco, and Chicago; and classroom discussions at UC Santa Barbara, UCLA, the College of William and Mary, and especially with students at USC. I hate being publicly challenged with tough questions, but my exposure to them, in all these settings, greatly helped this book evolve.

Commentary on particular chapters by good friends and colleagues also helped. Conversations with Mike Messner, Barrie Thorne, Laura Pulido, Elaine Bell Kaplan, Vilma Ortiz, Hector Delgado, Sarah Mahler, Barbara Laslett, Mary Romero, Patricia Fernández-Kelly, Gul Ozygin, Pei-Chia Lan, Michael Burawoy, Deborah Stone, and the late Cristina Riegos also moved this project forward. Deborah Stone gave me a big gift when she read the entire manuscript with an eye trained in public policy and politics. When I needed information on Central American immigrants, Louis di Sipio and Cecilia Menjívar moved with the speed of light and graciously shared the results of their own research with me. Warm thanks to Naomi Schneider, my editor at the University of California Press, and to Alice Falk, an amazingly attentive copyeditor. Victor Narro, an attorney who runs the workers' rights program at the Coalition for Humane Immigrant Rights of Los Angeles, helped guide me through what seemed like gobbledygook in the legal codes, enabling me to write chapter 8. Héctor Delgado deserves special recognition because he selflessly read and commented on many early drafts of chapters. He is one of the few professional-class men who actually engages with the nitty-gritty of social reproductive work, and does so with humor.

During the period I worked on this project, I experienced the metamorphosis of my sons Miles and Sasha from nearly preverbal, physically dependent little kids into, respectively, one caring, empathetic electric guitar player and one firecracker of boisterous energy that I siphon to replenish my inner reserves. Life at home with them and Michael Messner—companion, confidant, morning coffee maker, and co-conspirator in all of this—proves that hard work can be lots of fun. It's never seamless, but let's keep those home fires burning.

PART ONE

THE JOB TODAY

Suburban homes are increasingly replacing inner-city factories as the places of economic incorporation for new immigrants. While leafy streets and suburban homes are easier on the eyes than poorly lit sweatshops, it takes a lot of sweat to produce and maintain carefully groomed lawns, homes, and children. Chapters 1 and 2 discuss reasons for the expansion in these kinds of jobs and examine work life for Latina immigrant women who toil in America's new growth industry, paid domestic work. In the United States and elsewhere, the "new economy" not only runs on high-tech information services but also depends on the reorganization of how cleaning and care work are performed.

1

New World Domestic Order

Contemplating a day in Los Angeles without the labor of Latino immigrants taxes the imagination, for an array of consumer products and services would disappear (poof!) or become prohibitively expensive. Think about it. When you arrive at many a Southern California hotel or restaurant, you are likely to be first greeted by a Latino car valet. The janitors, cooks, busboys, painters, carpet cleaners, and landscape workers who keep the office buildings, restaurants, and malls running are also likely to be Mexican or Central American immigrants, as are many of those who work behind the scenes in dry cleaners, convalescent homes, hospitals, resorts, and apartment complexes. Both figuratively and literally, the work performed by Latino and Latina immigrants gives Los Angeles much of its famed gloss. Along the boulevards, at car washes promising "100% hand wash" for prices as low as $4.99, teams of Latino workers furiously scrub, wipe, and polish automobiles. Supermarket shelves boast bags of "prewashed" mesclun or baby greens (sometimes labeled "Euro salad"), thanks to the efforts of the Latino immigrants who wash and package the greens. (In addition, nail parlors adorn almost every corner mini-mall, offering the promise of emphasized femininity for $10 or $12, thanks largely to the work of Korean immigrant women.) Only twenty years ago, these relatively inexpensive consumer services and products were not nearly as widely available as they are today. The Los Angeles economy, landscape, and lifestyle have been transformed in ways that rely on low-wage, Latino immigrant labor.

The proliferation of such labor-intensive services, coupled with inflated real estate values and booming mutual funds portfolios, has given many people the illusion of affluence and socioeconomic mobility. When Angelenos, accustomed to employing a full-time nanny/housekeeper for about $150 or $200 a week, move to Seattle or Durham, they are startled to discover how "the cost of living that way" quickly escalates. Only then do they realize the extent to which their affluent lifestyle and smoothly running household depended on one Latina immigrant woman.

This book focuses on the Mexican and Central American immigrant women who work as nanny/housekeepers and housecleaners in Los Angeles, as well as the women who employ them. Who could have foreseen that at the dawn of the twenty-first century, paid domestic work would be a growth occupation? Only a few decades ago, observers confidently predicted that this occupation would soon become obsolete, replaced by labor-saving household devices such as automatic dishwashers, disposable diapers, and microwave ovens, and by consumer goods and services purchased outside of the home, such as fast food and dry cleaning.[1] Instead, paid domestic work has expanded. Why?

THE GROWTH OF DOMESTIC WORK

The increased employment of women, especially of married women with children, is usually what comes to mind when people explain the proliferation of private nannies, housekeepers, and housecleaners. As women have gone off to work, men have not picked up the slack at home. Grandmothers are also working, or no longer live nearby; and given the relative scarcity of child care centers in the United States, especially those that will accept infants and toddlers not yet toilet trained, working families of sufficient means often choose to pay someone to come in to take care of their homes and their children.

Even when conveniently located day care centers are available, many middle-class Americans are deeply prejudiced against them, perceiving them as offering cold, institutional, second-class child care.[2] For various reasons, middle-class families headed by two working parents prefer the convenience, flexibility, and privilege of having someone care for their children in their home. With this arrangement, parents don't have to dread their harried early-morning preparations before rushing to day care, the children don't seem to catch as many illnesses, and parents aren't likely to be fined by the care provider when they work late or get stuck in traffic. As the educational sociologist Julia Wrigley has shown in research conducted in New York City and Los Angeles, with a private caregiver in the home, parents feel they gain control and flexibility, while their children receive more attention.[3] Wrigley also makes clear that when they hire a Caribbean or Latina woman as their private employee, in either a live-in or live-out arrangement, they typically gain something else: an employee who does two jobs for the price of one, both looking after the children as a nanny and undertaking daily housekeeping duties. I use the term "nanny/housekeeper" to refer to the individual performing this dual job.

Meanwhile, more people are working and they are working longer hours. Even individuals without young children feel overwhelmed by the much-bemoaned "time squeeze," which makes it more difficult to find time for both daily domestic duties and leisure. At workplaces around the nation, women and men alike are pressured by new technology, their own desires for consumer goods, national anxieties over global competition, and exhortations from employers and co-workers to work overtime.[4] As free time shrinks, people who can afford it seek relief by paying a housecleaner to attend to domestic grit and grime once every week or two. Increasing numbers of Americans thus purchase from nanny/housekeepers and housecleaners the work once performed by wives and mothers.

Of course, not everyone brings equal resources to bear on these problems. In fact, growing income inequality has contributed significantly to the expansion of paid domestic work. The mid-twentieth-century trend in the United States toward less income inequality, as many researchers and commentators have remarked, was short-lived. In the years immediately after World War II, a strong economy (based on an increasing number of well-paying unionized jobs in factories), together with growing mass consumption and federal investment in education, housing, and public welfare, allowed many Americans to join an expanding middle class. This upward trend halted in the early 1970s, when deindustrialization, the oil crisis, national inflation, the end of the Vietnam War, and shifts in global trade began to restructure the U.S. economy. Gaps in the occupational structure widened. The college educated began to enjoy greater opportunities in the professions and in corporate and high-technology sectors, while poorly educated workers found their manufacturing jobs downgraded—if they found them at all, as many were shipped overseas. During the 1980s and 1990s, income polarization in the United States intensified, setting the stage for further expansion of paid domestic work.

Specific location is important to this analysis, for the income distribution in some cities is more inequitable than in others, and greater inequality, as an important study directed by UCLA sociologist Ruth Milkman has shown, tends to generate greater concentrations of paid domestic work. When the researchers compared cities around the nation, the Los Angeles–Long Beach metropolitan area emerged as the nation's leader in these jobs (measured by the proportion of all employed women in paid domestic work), followed by Miami-Hialeah, Houston, and New York City.[5]

Los Angeles' dubious distinction is not hard to explain. All of the top-ranked cities in paid domestic work have large concentrations of Latina or Caribbean immigrant women, and Los Angeles remains the number-one destination for Mexicans, Salvadorans, and Guatemalans coming to the United States, most of whom join the ranks of the working poor. Moreover, Los Angeles is a city where capital concentrates. It is a dynamic economic center for Pacific Rim trade and finance—what Saskia Sassen, a leading theorist of globalization, immigration, and transnational capital mobility, refers to as a "global city." Global cities serve as regional "command posts" that aid in integrating the new expansive global economy. Though Los Angeles lacks the financial power of New York or London, it has a large, diversified economy, supported both by manufacturing and by the capital-intensive entertainment industry. The upshot? Los Angeles is home to many people with highly paid jobs. As Southern California businesses bounced back from the recession of the early 1990s, many already handsomely paid individuals suddenly found themselves flush with unanticipated dividends, bonuses, and stock options.[6] And as Sassen reminds us, globalization's high-end jobs breed low-paying jobs.[7]

Many people employed in business and finance, and in the high-tech and the entertainment sectors, are high-salaried lawyers, bankers, accountants, marketing specialists, consultants, agents, and entrepreneurs. The way they live their lives, requiring many services and consuming many products, generates other high-end occupations linked to gentrification (creating jobs for real estate agents, therapists, personal trainers, designers, celebrity chefs, etc.), all of which in turn rely on various kinds of daily servicing that low-wage workers provide. For the masses of affluent professionals and corporate managers in Los Angeles, relying on Latino immigrant workers has become almost a social obligation. After relocating from the Midwest to Southern California, a new neighbor, the homemaker wife of an engineer, expressed her embarrassment at not hiring a gardener. It's easy to see why she felt abashed. In New York, the quintessential service occupation is dog walking; in Los Angeles' suburban landscape, gardeners and domestic workers proliferate. And in fact, as Roger Waldinger's analysis of census data shows, twice as many gardeners and domestic workers were working in Los Angeles in 1990 as in 1980.[8] Mexicans, Salvadorans, and Guatemalans perform these bottom-rung, low-wage jobs; and by 1990 those three groups, numbering about 2 million, made up more than half of the adults who had immigrated to Los Angeles since 1965.[9] Hundreds of thousands of Mexican, Salvadoran, and Guatemalan women sought employment in Los Angeles during the 1970s, 1980s, and 1990s,[10] often without papers but in search of better futures for themselves and for their families. For many of them, the best job opportunity was in paid domestic work.

Mexican women have always lived in Los Angeles—indeed, Los Angeles *was* Mexico until 1848—but their rates of migration to the United States were momentarily dampened by the Bracero Program, a government-operated temporary contract labor program that recruited Mexican men to work in western agriculture between 1942 and 1964. During the Bracero Program, nearly 5 million contracts were authorized. Beginning in the 1970s, family reunification legislation allowed many former bracero workers to legally bring their wives and families from Mexico. Immigration accelerated, and by 1990 there were 7 million Mexican immigrants in the United States, concentrated most highly in Southern California. Structural changes in the economies of both Mexico and the United States also significantly affected this dynamic. Mexico's economic crisis of the 1980s propelled many married women with small children into the labor force, and with the maturation of transnational informational social networks—and especially the development of exclusive women's networks—it wasn't long before many Mexican women learned about U.S. employers eager to hire them in factories, in hotels, and in private homes.[11]

Unlike Mexicans, Central Americans have relatively new roots in Los Angeles. The Salvadoran civil war (1979–92) and the even longer-running conflicts in Guatemala (military campaigns supported by U.S. government aid) drove hundreds of thousands of Central Americans to the United States during the 1980s. Almost overnight, Los Angeles became a second capital city for both Salvadorans and Guatemalans. Estimates of this population, many of whose members cannot speak English and remain undocumented (and hence officially undercounted), vary wildly. The 1990 census counted 159,000 Guatemalans and 302,000 Salvadorans in the Los Angeles region, but community leaders believe that by 1994, the number of Salvadorans in Los Angeles alone had reached 500,000.[12] Central Americans came to the United States fleeing war, political persecution, and deteriorating economic conditions; and though the political violence had diminished by the mid-1990s, few were making plans to permanently return to their old homes.[13] There have been numerous careful case studies of Central American communities in the United States; among their most stunning findings is that wherever Central American women have gone in the United States, including San Francisco, Long Island, Washington, D.C., Houston, and Los Angeles, they predominate in private domestic jobs.[14]

The growing concentration of Central American and Mexican immigrant women in Los Angeles and their entry into domestic service came on the heels of local African American women's exodus from domestic work. The supply of new immigrant workers has helped fuel a demand that, as noted above, was already growing. That is, the increasing number of Latina immigrants searching for work in California, particularly in Los Angeles, has pushed down wages and made modestly priced domestic services more widely available. This process is not lost on the women who do the work. Today, Latina domestic workers routinely complain to one another that newly arrived women from Mexico and Central America are undercutting the rates for cleaning and child care.

As a result, demand is no longer confined to elite enclaves but instead spans a wider range of class and geography in Southern California. While most employers of paid domestic workers in Los Angeles are white, college-educated, middle-class or upper-middle-class suburban residents with some connection to the professions or the business world, employers now also include apartment dwellers with modest incomes, single mothers, college students, and elderly people living on fixed incomes.[15] They live in tiny bungalows and condominiums, not just sprawling houses. They include immigrant entrepreneurs and even immigrant workers. In contemporary Los Angeles, factory workers living in the Latino working-class neighborhoods can and do hire Latino gardeners to mow their lawns, and a few also sometimes hire in-home nanny/housekeepers as well. In fact, some Latina nanny/housekeepers pay other Latina immigrants—usually much older or much younger, newly arrived women—to do in-home child care, cooking, and cleaning, while they themselves go off to care for the children and homes of the more wealthy.

DOMESTIC WORK VERSUS EMPLOYMENT

Paid domestic work is distinctive not in being the worst job of all but in being regarded as something other than employment. Its peculiar status is revealed in many occupational practices, as later chapters will show, and in off-the-cuff statements made by both employers and employees. "Maria was with me for eight years," a retired teacher told me, "and then she left and got a real job." Similarly, many women who do this work remain reluctant to embrace it *as* work because of the stigma associated with it. This is especially true of women who previously held higher social status. One Mexican woman, formerly a secretary in a Mexican embassy, referred to her five-day-a-week nanny/housekeeper job as her "hobby."

As the sociologist Mary Romero and others who have studied paid domestic work have noted, this occupation is often not recognized as employment because it takes place in a private home.[16] Unlike factories or offices, the home serves as the site of family and leisure activities, seen as by their nature antithetical to work. Moreover, the tasks that domestic workers do—cleaning, cooking, and caring for children—are associated with women's "natural" expressions of love for their families. Although Catharine E. Beecher and Harriet Beecher Stowe in the late nineteenth century, like feminist scholars more recently, sought to valorize these domestic activities (in both their paid and unpaid forms) as "real work," these efforts past and present have had little effect in the larger culture.[17] House-cleaning is typically only visible when it is not performed. The work of wives and mothers is not seen as real work; and when it becomes paid, it is accorded even less regard and respect.

Another important factor that prevents paid domestic work from being recognized as real work is its personal, idiosyncratic nature, especially when it involves the daily care of children or the elderly. Drawing on her examination of elder care workers, the public policy analyst Deborah Stone argues that caring work is inherently rela-tional, involving not only routine bodily care, such as bathing and feeding, but also attachment, affiliation, intimate knowledge, pa-tience, and even favoritism. Talking and listening, Stones shows, are instrumental to effective care. Her observation certainly applies to private child care work, as parents want someone who will really "care about" and show preference for their children; yet such per-sonal engagement remains antithetical to how we think about much employment, which, as Stone reminds us, we tend to view on the model of manufacturing.[18] Standardization, and frameworks of effi-ciency and productivity that rely on simplistic notions of labor in-puts and product outputs, simply is irrelevant to paid domestic work, especially when the job encompasses taking care of children as well as cleaning. Since we are accustomed to defining employ-ment as that which does *not* involve emotions and demonstrations of affective preference, the work of nannies and baby-sitters never quite gains legitimacy.

In part because of the idiosyncratic and emotional nature of caring work, and in part because of the contradictory nature of American culture, employers are equally reluctant to view themselves as em-ployers. This, I believe, has very serious consequences for the occu-pation. When well-meaning employers, who wish to voice their grat-itude, say, "She's not just an employee, she's like one of the family," they are in effect absolving themselves of their responsibilities—not for any nefarious reason but because they themselves are confused by domestic work arrangements. Even as they enjoy the attendant privilege and status, many Americans remain profoundly ambiva-lent about positioning themselves as employers of domestic workers. These arrangements, after all, are often likened to master-servant relations drawn out of premodern feudalism and slavery, making for a certain amount of tension with the strong U.S. rhetoric of democracy and egalitarianism.[19] Consequently, some employers feel embarrassed, uncomfortable, even guilty.

Maternalism, once so widely observed among female employers of private domestic workers, is now largely absent from the occupation; its remnants can be found primarily among older homemakers. When employers give used clothing and household items to their employees, or offer them unsolicited advice, help, or guidance, they may be acting, many observers have noted, manipulatively.[20] Such gestures encourage the domestic employees to work harder and longer, and simultaneously allow employers to experience personal recognition and validation of themselves as kind, superior, and altruistic. Maternalism is thus an important mechanism of employer power.

Today, however, a new sterility prevails in employer-employee relations in paid domestic work. For various reasons—including the pace of life that harries women with both career and family responsibilities, as well as their general discomfort with domestic servitude—most employers do not act maternalistically toward their domestic workers. In fact, many of them go to great lengths to minimize personal interactions with their nanny/housekeeper and housecleaners. At the same time, the Latina immigrants who work for them—especially the women who look after their employers' children—crave personal contact. They *want* social recognition and appreciation for who they are and what they do, but they don't often get it from their employers. In chapter 7, I argue that while maternalism serves as a mechanism of power that reinscribes some of the more distressing aspects of racial and class inequality between and among women, the distant employer-employee relations prevalent today do more to exacerbate inequality by denying domestic workers even modest forms of social recognition, dignity, and emotional sustenance. As we will see, personalism, achieved by exchanging private confidences and by recognizing domestic workers as individuals with their own concerns outside of their jobs, partially addresses the problem of social annihilation experienced by Latina domestic workers, offering a tenuous, discursive amelioration of these glaring inequalities.

Ironically, many employers are enormously appreciative of what their Latina domestic workers do for them, but they are more likely to declare these feelings to others than to the women who actually do the work. In informal conversation, they often gush enthusiastically about Latina nanny/housekeepers who care for homes and children, expressing a deep appreciation (or a rationalization?) that one almost never hears from someone speaking about his or her spouse. You might hear someone say, "I don't know what I would do without her," "She's perfect!" or "She's far better with the kids than I am!"; but such sentiments are rarely communicated directly to the employees.

The employers I interviewed did not dwell too much on their status as employers of nanny/housekeepers or housecleaners. They usually identified first and foremost with their occupations and families, with their positions as accountants or teachers, wives or mothers. Like the privilege of whiteness in U.S. society, the privilege of employing a domestic worker is barely noticed by those who have it. While they obviously did not deny that they pay someone to clean their home and care for their children, they tended to approach these arrangements not as employers, with a particular set of obligations and responsibilities, but as consumers.

For their part, the women who do the work are well aware of the low status and stigma attached to paid domestic work. None of the Latina immigrants I interviewed had aspired to the job, none want their daughters to do it, and the younger ones hope to leave the occupation altogether in a few years. They do take pride in their work, and they are extremely proud of what their earnings enable them to accomplish for their families. Yet they are not proud to be domestic workers, and this self-distancing from their occupational status makes it more difficult to see paid domestic work as a real job.

Moreover, scarcely anyone, employer or employee, knows that labor regulations govern paid domestic work. Lawyers that I interviewed told me that even adjudicators and judges in the California Labor Commissioner's Office, where one might go to settle wage disputes, had expressed surprise when informed that labor laws protected housecleaners or nanny/housekeepers working in private homes. This problem of paid domestic work not being accepted as employment is compounded by the subordination by race and immigrant status of the women who do the job.

GLOBALIZATION, IMMIGRATION, AND THE RACIALIZATION OF PAID DOMESTIC WORK

Particular regional formations have historically characterized the racialization of paid domestic work in the United States. Relationships between domestic employees and employers have always been imbued with racial meanings: white "masters and mistresses" have been cast as pure and superior, and "maids and servants," drawn from specific racial-ethnic groups (varying by region), have been cast as dirty and socially inferior. The occupational racialization we see now in Los Angeles or New York City continues this American legacy, but it also draws to a much greater extent on globalization and immigration.

In the United States today, immigrant women from a few non-European nations are established as paid domestic workers. These women—who hail primarily from Mexico, Central America, and the Caribbean and who are perceived as "nonwhite" in Anglo-American contexts—hold various legal statuses. Some are legal permanent residents or naturalized U.S. citizens, many as beneficiaries of the 1986 Immigration Reform and Control Act's amnesty-legalization program.[21] Central American women, most of whom entered the United States after the 1982 cutoff date for amnesty, did not qualify for legalization, so in the 1990s they generally either remained undocumented or held a series of temporary work permits, granted to delay their return to war-ravaged countries.[22] Domestic workers who are working without papers clearly face extra burdens and risks: criminalization of employment, denial of social entitlements, and status as outlaws anywhere in the nation. If they complain about their jobs, they may be threatened with deportation.[23] Undocumented immigrant workers, however, are not the only vulnerable ones. In the 1990s, even legal permanent residents and naturalized citizens saw their rights and privileges diminish, as campaigns against illegal immigration metastasized into more generalized xenophobic attacks on all immigrants, including those here with legal authorization. Immigration status has clearly become an important axis of inequality, one interwoven with relations of race, class, and gender, and it facilitates the exploitation of immigrant domestic workers.

Yet race and immigration are interacting in an important new way, which Latina immigrant domestic workers exemplify: their position as "foreigners" and "immigrants" allows employers, and the society at large, to perceive them as outsiders and thereby overlook the contemporary racialization of the occupation. Immigration does not trump race but, combined with the dominant ideology of a "color-blind" society, manages to shroud it.[24]

With few exceptions, domestic work has always been reserved for poor women, for immigrant women, and for women of color; but over the last century, paid domestic workers have become more homogenous, reflecting the subordinations of both race and nationality/immigration status. In the late nineteenth century, this occupation was the most likely source of employment for U.S.-born women. In 1870, according to the historian David M. Katzman, two-thirds of all nonagricultural female wage earners worked as domestics in private homes. The proportion steadily declined to a little over one-third by 1900, and to one-fifth by 1930. Alternative employment opportunities for women expanded in the mid– and late twentieth century, so by 1990, fewer than 1 percent of employed American women were engaged in domestic work.[25] Census figures, of course, are notoriously unreliable in documenting this increasingly undocumentable, "under-the-table" occupation, but the trend is clear: paid domestic work has gone from being *either* an immigrant woman's job *or* a minority woman's job to one that is now filled by women who, as Latina and Caribbean immigrants, embody subordinate status both racially and as immigrants.[26]

Regional racializations of the occupation were already deeply marked in the late nineteenth and early twentieth centuries, as the occupation recruited women from subordinate racial-ethnic groups. In northeastern and midwestern cities of the late nineteenth century, single young Irish, German, and Scandinavian immigrants and women who had migrated from the country to the city typically worked as live-in "domestic help," often leaving the occupation when they married.[27] During this period, the Irish were the main target of xenophobic vilification. With the onset of World War I, European immigration declined and job opportunities in manufacturing opened up for whites, and black migration from the South enabled white employers to recruit black women for domestic jobs in the Northeast. Black women had always predominated as a servant caste in the South, whether in slavery or after, and by 1920 they constituted the single largest group in paid domestic work in both the South and the Northeast.[28] Unlike European immigrant women, black women experienced neither individual nor intergenerational mobility out of the occupation, but they succeeded in transforming the occupation from one characterized by live-in arrangements, with no separation between work and social life, to live-out "day work"— a transformation aided by urbanization, new interurban transportation systems, and smaller urban residences.[29]

In the Southwest and the West of the late nineteenth and early twentieth centuries, the occupation was filled with Mexican American and Mexican immigrant women, as well as Asian, African American, and Native American women and, briefly, Asian men. Asian immigrant men were among the first recruits for domestic work in the West.[30] California exceptionalism—its Anglo-American conquest from Mexico in 1848, its ensuing rapid development and overnight influx of Anglo settlers and miners, and its scarcity of women— initially created many domestic jobs in the northern part of the territory for Chinese "houseboys," laundrymen, and cooks, and later for Japanese men, followed by Japanese immigrant women and their U.S.-born daughters, the nisei, who remained in domestic work until World War II.[31] Asian American women's experiences, as Berkeley sociologist Evelyn Nakano Glenn has demonstrated, provide an intermediate case of intergenerational mobility out of domestic work between that of black and Chicana women who found themselves, generation after generation, stuck in the occupational ghetto of domestic work and that of European immigrant women of the early twentieth century who quickly moved up the mobility ladder.[32]

For Mexican American women and their daughters, domestic work became a dead-end job. From the 1880s until World War II, it provided the largest source of nonagricultural employment for Mexican and Chicana women throughout the Southwest. During this period, domestic vocational training schools, teaching manuals, and Americanization efforts deliberately channeled them into domestic jobs.[33] Continuing well into the 1970s throughout the Southwest, and up to the present in particular regions, U.S.-born Mexican American women have worked as domestics. Over that time, the job has changed. Much as black women helped transform the domestic occupation from live-in to live-out work in the early twentieth century,

Chicanas in the Southwest increasingly preferred contractual house-cleaning work—what Romero has called "job work"—to live-in or daily live-out domestic work.[34]

While black women dominated the occupation throughout the nation during the 1950s and 1960s, there is strong evidence that many left it during the late 1960s. The 1970 census marked the first time that domestic work did not account for the largest segment of employed black women; and the proportion of black women in domestic work continued to drop dramatically in the 1970s and 1980s, falling from 16.4 percent in 1972 to 7.4 percent in 1980, then to 3.5 percent by the end of the 1980s.[35] By opening up public-sector jobs to black women, the Civil Rights Act of 1964 made it possible for them to leave private domestic service. Consequently, both African American and Mexican American women moved into jobs from which they had been previously barred, as secretaries, sales clerks, and public-sector employees, and into the expanding number of relatively low-paid service jobs in convalescent homes, hospitals, cafeterias, and hotels.[36]

These occupational adjustments and opportunities did not go unnoticed. In a 1973 *Los Angeles Times* article, a manager with thirty years of experience in domestic employment agencies reported, "Our Mexican girls are nice, but the blacks are hostile." Speaking very candidly about her contrasting perceptions of Latina immigrant and African American women domestic workers, she said of black women, "you can feel their anger. They would rather work at Grant's for $1.65 an hour than do housework. To them it denotes a lowering of self."[37] By the 1970s black women in the occupation were growing older, and their daughters were refusing to take jobs imbued with servitude and racial subordination. Domestic work, with its historical legacy in slavery, was roundly rejected. Not only expanding job opportunities but also the black power movement, with its emphasis on self-determination and pride, dissuaded younger generations of African American women from entering domestic work.

It was at this moment that newspaper reports, census data, and anecdotal accounts first register the occupation's demographic shift toward Latina immigrants, a change especially pronounced in areas with high levels of Latino immigration. In Los Angeles, for example, the percentage of African American women working as domestics in private households fell from 35 percent to 4 percent from 1970 to 1990, while foreign-born Latinas increased their representation from 9 percent to 68 percent.[38] Again, since census counts routinely underestimate the poor and those who speak limited or no English, the women in this group may represent an even larger proportion of private domestic workers.

Ethnographic case studies conducted not only in Los Angeles but also in Washington, D.C., San Francisco, San Diego, Houston, El Paso, suburban areas of Long Island, and New York City provide many details about the experiences of Mexican, Caribbean, and Central American women who now predominate in these metropolitan centers as nanny/housekeepers and housecleaners.[39] Like the black women who migrated from the rural South to northern cities in the early twentieth century, Latina immigrant women newly arrived in U.S. cities and suburbs in the 1970s, 1980s, and 1990s often started as live-ins, sometimes first performing unpaid household work for kin before taking on very low paying live-in jobs for other families.[40] Live-in jobs, shunned by better-established immigrant women, appeal to new arrivals who want to minimize their living costs and begin sending their earnings home. Vibrant social networks channel Latina immigrants into these jobs, where the long hours and the social isolation can be overwhelming. As time passes, many of the women seek live-out domestic jobs. Despite the decline in live-in employment arrangements at the century's midpoint, the twentieth century ended in the United States much as it began, with a resurgence of live-in jobs filled by women of color—now Latina immigrants.

Two factors of the late twentieth century were especially important in creating this scenario. First, as many observers have noted, globalization has promoted higher rates of immigration. The expansion of U.S. private investment and trade; the opening of U.S. multinational assembly plants (employing mostly women) along the U.S.-Mexico border and in Caribbean and Central American nations, facilitated by government legislative efforts such as the Border Industrialization Program, the North American Free Trade Agreement, and the Caribbean Basin Initiative; the spreading influence of U.S. mass media; and U.S. military aid in Central America have all helped rearrange local economies and stimulate U.S.-bound migration from the Caribbean, Mexico, and Central America. Women from these countries have entered the United States at a propitious time for families looking to employ housecleaners and nannies.[41]

Second, increased immigration led to the racialized xenophobia of the 1990s. The rhetoric of these campaigns shifted focus, from attacking immigrants for lowering wages and competing for jobs to seeking to bar immigrants' access to social entitlements and welfare. In the 1990s, legislation codified this racialized nativism, in large part taking aim at women and children.[42] In 1994 California's Proposition 187, targeting Latina immigrants and their children, won at the polls; and although its denial of all public education and of publicly funded health care was ruled unconstitutional by the courts, the vote helped usher in new federal legislation. In 1996 federal welfare reform, particularly the Immigration Reform Act and Individual Responsibility Act (IRAIRA), codified the legal and social disenfranchisement of legal permanent residents and undocumented immigrants. At the same time, language—and in particular the Spanish language—was becoming racialized; virulent "English Only" and anti–bilingual education campaigns and ballot initiatives spread.

Because Latina immigrants are disenfranchised as immigrants and foreigners, Americans can overlook the current racialization of the job. On the one hand, racial hostilities and fears may be lessened as increasing numbers of Latina and Caribbean nannies care for tow-headed children. As Sau-ling C. Wong suggests in an analysis of recent films, "in a society undergoing radical demographic and economic changes, the figure of the person of color patiently mothering white folks serves to allay racial anxieties."[43] Stereotypical images of Latinas as innately warm, loving, and caring certainly round out this picture. Yet on the other hand, the status of these Latinas as immigrants today serves to legitimize their social, economic, and political subordination and their disproportionate concentration in paid domestic work.

Such legitimation makes it possible to ignore American racism and discrimination. Thus the abuses that Latina domestic workers suffer in domestic jobs can be explained away because the women themselves are foreign and unassimilable. If they fail to realize the American Dream, according to this distorted narrative, it is because they are lazy and unmotivated or simply because they are "illegal" and do not merit equal opportunities with U.S.-born American citizens. Contemporary paid domestic work in the United States remains a job performed by women of color, by black and brown women from the Caribbean, Central America, and Mexico. This racialization of domestic work is masked by the ideology of "a color-blind society" and by the focus on immigrant "foreignness."

GLOBAL TRENDS IN PAID DOMESTIC WORK

Just as paid domestic work has expanded in the United States, so too it appears to have grown in many other postindustrial societies—in Canada and in parts of Europe—in the "newly industrialized countries" (NICs) of Asia, and in the oil-rich nations of the Middle East. Around the globe Caribbean, Mexican, Central American, Peruvian, Sri Lankan, Indonesian, Eastern European, and Filipina women— the latter in disproportionately great numbers—predominate in these jobs. Worldwide, paid domestic work continues its long legacy as a racialized and gendered occupation, but today divisions of nation and citizenship are increasingly salient. Rhacel Parreñas, who has studied Filipina domestic workers, refers to this development as the "international division of reproductive labor," and Anthony Richmond has called it part of a broad, new "global apartheid."[44]

In the preceding section, I highlighted the inequalities of race and immigration in the United States, but we must remember that the inequality of nations is a key factor in the globalization of contemporary paid domestic work. This inequality has had three results. First, around the globe, paid domestic work is increasingly performed by women who leave their own nations, their communities, and often their families of origin to do it. Second, the occupation draws not only women from the poor socioeconomic classes but also women of relatively high status in their own countries—countries that colonialism made much poorer than those countries where they go to do domestic work. Thus it is not unusual to find middle-class, college-educated women working in other nations as private domestic workers. Third, the development of service-based economies in postindustrial nations favors the international migration of women laborers. Unlike in earlier industrial eras, today the demand for gendered labor favors migrant women's services.

Nations use vastly different methods to "import" domestic workers from other countries. Some countries have developed highly regulated, government-operated, contract labor programs that have institutionalized both the recruitment and working conditions of migrant domestic workers. Canada and Hong Kong exemplify this approach. Since 1981 the Canadian federal government has formally recruited thousands of women to work as live-in nanny/housekeepers for Canadian families. Most come from third world countries, the majority in the 1980s from the Caribbean and in the 1990s from the Philippines; and once in Canada, they must remain in live-in domestic service for two years, until they obtain their landed immigrant status, the equivalent of the U.S. "green card."[45] During this period, they must work in conditions reminiscent of formal indentured servitude and they may not quit their jobs or collectively organize to improve job conditions.

Similarly, since 1973 Hong Kong has relied on the formal recruitment of domestic workers, mostly Filipinas, to work on a full-time, live-in basis for Chinese families. Of the 150,000 foreign domestic workers in Hong Kong in 1995, 130,000 hailed from the Philippines, with smaller numbers drawn from Thailand, Indonesia, India, Sri Lanka, and Nepal.[46] Just as it is now rare to find African American women employed in private domestic work in Los Angeles, so too have Chinese women vanished from the occupation in Hong Kong. As Nicole Constable reveals in her detailed study, Filipina domestic workers in Hong Kong are controlled and disciplined by official employment agencies, employers, and strict government policies.[47] Filipinas and other foreign domestic workers recruited to Hong Kong find themselves working primarily in live-in jobs and under two-year contracts that stipulate job rules, regulations for bodily display and discipline (no lipstick, nail polish, or long hair; submission to pregnancy tests; etc.), task timetables, and the policing of personal privacy.

In the larger global context, the United States remains distinctive, as it follows a more laissez-faire approach to incorporating immigrant women into paid domestic work.[48] Unlike in Hong Kong and Canada, here there is no formal government system or policy to legally contract with foreign domestic workers. In the past, private employers in the United States were able to "sponsor" individual immigrant women working as domestics for their green cards, sometimes personally recruiting them while they were vacationing or working in foreign countries, but this route is unusual in Los Angeles today.[49] For such labor certification, the sponsor must document that there is a shortage of labor able to perform a particular, specialized job—and in Los Angeles and many other parts of the country, demonstrating a shortage of domestic workers has become increasingly difficult. And it is apparently unnecessary, as the significant demand for domestic workers in the United States is largely filled not through formal channels but through informal recruitment from the growing number of Caribbean and Latina immigrant women who are already living (legally or illegally) in the United States. The Immigration and Naturalization Service, the federal agency charged with stopping illegal migration, has historically served the interest of domestic employers and winked at the hiring of undocumented immigrant women in private homes.

As we compare the hyperregulated employment systems in Hong Kong and Canada with the U.S. approach to domestic work, we must distinguish between the regulation of labor and the regulation of foreign domestic workers. As Sedef Arat-Koc puts it in discussing the labor conditions of Filipina and Caribbean domestic workers in Canada, "while their conditions of work have been under-regulated, domestic workers themselves, especially those from the 'least desirable' backgrounds, have become over-regulated."[50] Here, the United States is again an exception. U.S. labor regulations *do* cover private domestic work—but no one knows about them. As I describe in detail in chapter 8, domestic workers' wages and hours are governed by state and federal law, and special regulations cover such details as limits on permissible deductions for breakage and for boarding costs of live-in workers. These regulations did not fall from the sky: they are the result of several important, historic campaigns organized by and for paid domestic workers. Most U.S. employers now know, after the Zoë Baird incident, about their obligations for employment taxes—though these obligations are still widely ignored—but few employers and perhaps fewer employees know about the labor laws pertaining to private domestic work. It's almost as though these regulations did not exist. At the same time, the United States does not maintain separate immigration policies for domestic workers, of the sort that mandate live-in employment or decree instant deportation if workers quit their jobs.

This duality has two consequences. On the one hand, both the absence of hyperregulation of domestic workers and the ignorance about existing labor laws further reinforce the belief that paid domestic work is not a real job. Domestic work remains an arrangement that is thought of as private: it remains informal, "in the shadows," and outside the purview of the state and other regulating agencies. On the other hand, the absence of state monitoring of domestic job contracts and of domestic workers' personal movement, privacy, and bodily adornment suggests an opening to upgrade domestic jobs in the United States. Unlike in Hong Kong and Canada, for example, where state regulations prevent Filipina domestic workers from quitting jobs that they find unsatisfactory or abusive, in Los Angeles, Latina immigrant domestic workers can—and, as we'll see in chapter 5, *do*—quit their jobs. Certainly they face limited options when they seek jobs outside of private homes, but it is important to note that they are not yoked by law to the same boss and the same job.

The absence of a neocolonialist, state-operated, contractual system for domestic work thus represents an opportunity to seek better job conditions. The chance of success might be improved if existing labor regulations were strengthened, if domestic workers were to work at collective organizing, and if informational and educational outreach to the domestic workers were undertaken. But to be effective, these efforts must occur in tandem with a new recognition that the relationships in paid domestic work are relations of employment.

SOCIAL REPRODUCTION AND NEW REGIMES OF INEQUALITY: TRANSNATIONAL MOTHERHOOD

Sometimes it is necessary to state the obvious. In employer households, women are almost exclusively in charge of seeking and hiring domestic workers. This social fact speaks to the extent to which feminist, egalitarian goals of sharing household cleaning and care work remain unachieved. Even among wealthy white women born and raised in the United States in the late twentieth century, few escape the fetters of unpaid social reproductive labor. As many observers have noted, their reliance on housecleaners and nannies allows well-to-do women to act, in effect, as contractors.[51] By subcontracting to private domestic workers, these women purchase release from their gender subordination in the home, effectively transferring their domestic responsibilities to other women who are distinct and subordinate by race and class, and now also made subordinate through language, nationality, and citizenship status. The work performed by Latina, Caribbean, and Filipina immigrant women today subsidizes the work of more privileged women, freeing the latter to join the productive labor force by taking jobs in business and the professions, or perhaps enabling wealthier women to become more active consumers and volunteers and to spend more time culturally grooming their children and orchestrating family recreation. Consequently, male privilege within homes and families remains uncontested and intact, and new inequalities are formed.

Some feminist theorists, especially those influenced by Marxist thought, have used the term "social reproduction" or "reproductive labor" to refer to the myriad of activities, tasks, and resources expended in the daily upkeep of homes and people. Taking care of ourselves, raising the next generation, and caring for the sick and elderly are projects requiring constant vigilance and dedication. As the sociologists Barbara Laslett and Joanna Brenner put it, "renewing life is a form of work, a kind of production, as fundamental to the perpetuation of society as the production of things."[52] More recently, feminist scholars influenced by feminist Scandinavian research on social welfare have shifted their focus to "caring" and "care work." Regardless of specific theoretical underpinnings, two important points must be emphasized.

First, the way we socially organize reproductive labor has varied historically, and across culture and class. Different arrangements bring about different social consequences and different forms of inequality. Second, our definitions of what are appropriate forms and goals of social reproduction also vary. What passes today as a clean house or proper meal? What behavioral or educational expectations do we hold for our children? The proliferation of fast, frozen, and already prepared foods, and of women's magazines that promise to reveal how to make family meals in ten minutes, suggests that standards for what constitutes a proper American middle-class meal have dropped. (Meal preparation is a task rarely assigned to contemporary domestic workers; perhaps convenience foods have made it trivial, or perhaps meal preparation remains too symbolic of family life to assign to an outsider.)[53] Simultaneously, standards of hygiene and home cleanliness, like the size of the average American home, have increased throughout the twentieth century. And perhaps nowhere has the bar been raised more than regarding what constitutes proper child rearing, especially among middle-class professionals. Parents (mostly mothers) study books and attend classes on how to provide babies and toddlers with appropriate developmental stimulation, and middle-class children today are generally expected to perform grueling amounts of homework, participate in a variety of organized sports and social clubs, take music lessons, and exhibit prescribed stages of emotional literacy and sensitivity. In any society, raising children is work that requires tremendous expenditures of manual, mental, spiritual, and emotional energy, but enormous amounts of money and work are now invested in developing middle-class and upper-class children, presumably so that they can assume or better their parents' social status.[54] Paid domestic work, especially the work of nanny/housekeepers, occurs in this context of diminished expectations for preparing meals and heightened standards for keeping homes clean and rearing children.

Inequalities of race, class, and gender have long characterized private, paid domestic work, and as we have seen, globalization is creating new regimes of inequality. We must remember that the immigrant women who are performing other people's private reproductive work are women who were themselves socially reproduced in other societies. The costs of their own social reproduction—everything that it took to raise them from infants to working adults—were shouldered by families, governments, and communities in Mexico and in Central American and Caribbean nations. For this reason, their employment as domestic workers represents a bargain for American families and American society. The inequalities of social reproduction in these Latinas' contemporary family and work lives, however, are even more glaringly apparent when we consider their own children.

Today, many of these domestic workers care for the homes and children of American families while their children remain "back home" in their societies of origin. This latter arrangement, which I call transnational motherhood, signals new international inequalities of social reproduction.[55] A continuing strain of contemporary xenophobia in California protests the publicly funded schooling for the children of Mexican undocumented immigrants (e.g., Proposition 187 in 1994 and the 1999 attempt by the Anaheim School Board to "bill" the Mexican federal government for the schooling of Mexican children in Orange County), but this same logic might be used to promote an alternative view, one emphasizing that the human investment and reaping of benefits occurs in precisely the opposite direction. Though the children (themselves U.S. citizens) of undocumented immigrants are later likely, as adults, to work and reside in the same society in which they were raised (the United States), Central American and Mexican immigrant women enter U.S. domestic jobs as adults, already having been raised, reared, and educated in another society. Women raised in another nation are using their own adult capacities to fulfill the reproductive work of more privileged American women, subsidizing the careers and social opportunities of their employers. Yet the really stinging injury is this: they themselves are denied sufficient resources to live with and raise their own children.

Since the early 1980s, thousands of Central American women and Mexican women in increasing numbers have left their children behind with grandmothers, with other female kin, with the children's fathers, and sometimes with paid caregivers while they themselves migrate to work in the United States. The subsequent separations of time and distance are substantial; ten or fifteen years may elapse before the women are reunited with their children. Feminist scholarship has shown us that isolationist, privatized mothering, glorified and exalted though it has been, is just one historically and culturally specific variant among many; but this model of motherhood continues to inform many women's family ideals.[56] In order to earn wages by providing child care and cleaning for others, many Latina immigrant women must transgress deeply ingrained and gender-specific spatial and temporal boundaries of work and family.

One precursor to these arrangements is the mid-twentieth-century Bracero Program, discussed above. This long-standing arrangement of Mexican "absentee fathers" coming to work in the United States as contracted agricultural laborers is still in force today, though the program has ended. When these men come north and leave their families in Mexico, they are fulfilling masculine obligations defined as breadwinning for the family. When women do so, they are entering not only another country but also a radical, gender-transformative odyssey. As their separations of space and time from their communities of origin, homes, children, and sometimes husbands begin, they must cope with stigma, guilt, and others' criticism.

The ambivalent feelings and new ideological stances accompanying these new arrangements are still in flux, but tensions are evident. As they wrestle with the contradictions of their lives and beliefs, and as they leave behind their own children to care for the children of strangers in a foreign land, these Latina domestic workers devise new rhetorical and emotional strategies. Some nanny/housekeepers develop very strong ties of affection with the children in their care during their long workweeks, and even more grow critical of their employers. Not all nanny/housekeepers bond tightly with their employers' children (and they do so selectively among the children), but most of them sharply criticize what they perceive as their employers' neglectful parenting—typically, they blame the biological mothers. They indulge in the rhetoric of comparative mothering, highlighting the sacrifices that they themselves make as poor, legally disenfranchised, racially subordinate working mothers and setting them in contrast to the substandard mothering provided by their multiply privileged employers.

Notions of childhood and motherhood are intimately bound together, and when the contrasting worlds of domestic employers and employees overlap, different meanings and gauges of motherhood emerge. In some ways, the Latina transnational mothers who work as nanny/housekeepers sentimentalize their employers' children more than their own. This strategy enables them to critique their employers, especially the homemakers who neither leave the house to work nor care for their children every day. The Latina nannies can endorse motherhood as a full-time vocation for those able to afford it, while for those suffering financial hardships they advocate more elastic definitions of motherhood—including forms of transnational motherhood that may force long separations of space and time on a mother and her children. Under these circumstances, and when they have left suitable adults in charge, they tell themselves that "the kids are all right."

These arrangements provoke new debates among the women. Because there is no universal or even widely shared agreement about what constitutes "good mothering," transnational mothers must work hard to defend their choices. Some Latina nannies who have their children with them in the United States condemn transnational mothers as "bad women." In response, transnational mothers construct new measures to gauge the quality of mothering. By setting themselves against the negative models of mothering that they see in others—especially the models that they can closely scrutinize in their employers' homes—transnational mothers redefine the standards of good mothering. At the same time, selectively developing motherlike ties with other people's children allows them to enjoy the affectionate, face-to-face interactions that they cannot experience on a daily basis with their own children.

Social reproduction is not simply the secondary outcome of markets or modes of production. In our global economy, its organization among privileged families in rich nations has tremendous repercussions for families, economies, and societies around the world. The emergence of transnational motherhood underscores this point, and shows as well how new inequalities and new meanings of family life are formed through contemporary global arrangements in paid domestic work.

POINT OF DEPARTURE

As we have seen, no single cause explains the recent expansion of paid domestic work. Several factors are at work, including growing income inequality; women's participation in the labor force, especially in professional and managerial jobs; the relatively underdeveloped nature of day care in the United States—as well as middle-class prejudices against using day care; and the mass immigration of women from Central America, the Caribbean, and Mexico. We have also examined the cultural and social perceptions that prevent paid domestic work from being seen and treated as employment, and have observed how contemporary racialization and immigration affect the job. Yet simply understanding the conditions that have fostered the occupation's growth, the widely held perceptions of the job, or even the important history of the occupation's racialization tells us little about what is actually happening in these jobs today. How are they organized, and how do employers and employees experience them? The remainder of this book draws on interviews, a survey, and limited ethnographic observations made in Los Angeles to answer these questions.

Jobs in offices, in factories, or at McDonald's are covered by multiple regulations provided by government legislation, by corporate, managerial strategies, by employee handbooks, and sometimes by

labor unions; but paid domestic work lacks any such formal, institutionalized guides. It is done in the private sphere and its jobs are
usually negotiated, as Judith Rollins puts it, "between women."
More broadly, I argue, paid domestic work is governed by the parallel and interacting networks of women of different classes, ethnic-
ities, and citizenship statuses who meet at multiple work sites in
isolated pairs. While employer and employee individually negotiate
the job, their tactics are informed by their respective social networks.
Today, many employers in Los Angeles and many Latina immigrants
are, generationally speaking, new to the occupation. Rather than relying on information passed down from their mothers, both employers and employees draw on information exchanged within their
own respective networks of friends, kin, and acquaintances and, increasingly, on lessons learned from their own experiences to establish the terms of private, paid domestic work (hiring practices, pay
scales, hours, job tasks, etc.). That employers rarely identify themselves as employers, just as many employees hesitate to embrace
their social status as domestic workers, means that the job is not
always regarded as a job, leading to problematic relations and terms
of employment.

   Although there are regularities and patterns to the job, contemporary paid domestic work is not monolithic. I distinguish three
common types of jobs:[57] (1) *Live-in nanny/housekeeper*. The live-in employee works for and lives with one family, and her responsibilities
generally include caring for the children and the household. (2) *Live-
out nanny/housekeeper*. The employee works five or six days a week
for one family, tending to the children and the household, but returns
to her apartment, her own community, and sometimes her own family at night. (3) *Housecleaner*. The employee cleans houses, working
for several different employers on a contractual basis, and usually
does not take care of children as part of her job. Housecleaners, as
Mary Romero's research emphasizes, work shorter hours and receive
higher pay than do other domestic workers, enjoying far greater job
flexibility and autonomy; and because they have multiple jobs, they
retain more negotiating power with their employers.[58] The following chapter profiles some of the women who do these jobs in Los
Angeles.

2

Maid in L.A.

The title of this chapter was inspired by Mary Romero's 1992 book, *Maid in the U.S.A.*, but I am also taking the pun to heart: most Latina immigrant women who do paid domestic work in Los Angeles had no prior experience working as domestics in their countries of origin. Of the 153 Latina domestic workers that I surveyed at bus stops, in ESL classes, and in parks, fewer than 10 percent reported having worked in other people's homes, or taking in laundry for pay, in their countries of origin. This finding is perhaps not surprising, as we know from immigration research that the poorest of the poor rarely migrate to the United States; they simply cannot afford to do so.

Some of the Latina immigrant women who come to Los Angeles grew up in impoverished squatter settlements, others in comfortable homes with servants. In their countries of origin, these women were housewives raising their own children, or college students, factory workers, store clerks, and secretaries; still others came from rural families of very modest means. Regardless of their diverse backgrounds, their transformation into housecleaners and nanny/housekeepers occurs in Los Angeles. I emphasize this point because images in popular culture and the media more or less identify Latinas with domestic workers—or, more precisely, as "cleaning gals" and "baby-sitters," euphemisms that mask American discomfort with these arrangements. Yet they take on these roles only in the United States, at various points in their own migration and settlement trajectories, in the context of private households, informal social networks, and the larger culture's racialized nativism.

Who are these women who come to the United States in search of jobs, and what are those jobs like? Domestic work is organized in different ways, and in this chapter I describe live-in, live-out, and housecleaning jobs and profile some of the Latina immigrants who do them and how they feel about their work. The chapter concludes with a discussion of why it is that Latina immigrants are the primary recruits to domestic work, and I examine what they and their employers have to say about race relations and domestic work.

LIVE-IN NANNY/HOUSEKEEPER JOBS

For Maribel Centeno, newly arrived from Guatemala City in 1989 at age twenty-two and without supportive family and friends with whom to stay, taking a live-in job made a lot of sense. She knew that she wouldn't have to spend money on room and board, and that she could soon begin saving to pay off her debts. Getting a live-in job through an agency was easy. The *señora*, in her rudimentary Spanish, only asked where she was from, and if she had a husband and children. Chuckling, Maribel recalled her initial misunderstanding when the *señora*, using her index finger, had drawn an imaginary "2" and "3" in the palm of her hand. "I thought to myself, well, she must have two or three bedrooms, so I said, fine. 'No,' she said. 'Really, really big.' She started counting, 'One, two, three, four . . . two-three rooms.' It was twenty-three rooms! I thought, *huy!* On a piece of paper, she wrote '$80 a week,' and she said, 'You, child, and entire house.' So I thought, well, I have to do what I have to do, and I happily said, 'Yes.' "

"I arrived on Monday at dawn," she recalled, "and I went to the job on Wednesday evening." When the *señora* and the child spoke to her, Maribel remembered "just laughing and feeling useless. I couldn't understand anything." On that first evening, the *señora* put on classical music, which Maribel quickly identified. "I said, 'Beethoven.' She said, 'Yeah,' and began asking me in English, 'You like it?' I said 'Yes,' or perhaps I said, '*Sí,*' and she began playing other cassettes, CDs. They had Richard Clayderman and I recognized it, and when I said that, she stopped in her tracks, her jaw fell open, and she just stared at me. She must have been thinking, 'No schooling, no preparation, no English, how does she know this music?' " But the *señora*, perhaps because of the language difficulty, or perhaps because she felt upstaged by her live-in's knowledge of classical music, never did ask. Maribel desperately wanted the *señora* to respect her, to recognize that she was smart, educated, and cultivated in the arts. In spite of her best status-signaling efforts, "They treated me," she said, "the same as any other girl from the countryside." She never got the verbal recognition that she desired from the *señora*.

Maribel summed up her experiences with her first live-in job this way: "The pay was bad. The treatment was, how shall I say? It was cordial, a little, uh, not racist, but with very little consideration, very little respect." She liked caring for the little seven-year-old boy, but keeping after the cleaning of the twenty-three-room house, filled with marble floors and glass tables, proved physically impossible. She eventually quit not because of the polishing and scrubbing, but because being ignored devastated her socially.

Compared to many other Latina immigrants' first live-in jobs, Maribel Centeno's was relatively good. She was not on call during all her waking hours and throughout the night, the parents were engaged with the child, and she was not required to sleep in a child's bedroom or on a cot tucked away in the laundry room. But having a private room filled with amenities did not mean she had privacy or the ability to do simple things one might take for granted. "I had my own room, with my own television, VCR, my private bath, and closet, and a kind of sitting room—but everything in miniature, Thumbelina style," she said. "I had privacy in that respect. But I couldn't do many things. If I wanted to walk around in a T-shirt, or just feel like I was home, I couldn't do that. If I was hungry in the evening, I wouldn't come out to grab a banana because I'd have to walk through the family room, and then everybody's watching and having to smell the banana. I could never feel at home, never. Never, never, never! There's always something invisible that tells you this is not your house, you just work here."

It is the rare California home that offers separate maid's quarters, but that doesn't stop families from hiring live-ins; nor does it stop newly arrived Latina migrant workers from taking jobs they urgently need. When live-ins cannot even retreat to their own rooms, work seeps into their sleep and their dreams. There is no time off from the job, and they say they feel confined, trapped, imprisoned.

"I lose a lot of sleep," said Margarita Gutiérrez, a twenty-four-year-old Mexicana who worked as a live-in nanny/housekeeper. At her job in a modest-sized condominium in Pasadena, she slept in a corner of a three-year-old child's bedroom. Consequently, she found herself on call day and night with the child, who sometimes went several days without seeing her mother because of the latter's schedule at an insurance company. Margarita was obliged to be on her job twenty-four hours a day; and like other live-in nanny/housekeepers I interviewed, she claimed that she could scarcely find time to shower or brush her teeth. "I go to bed fine," she reported, "and then I wake up at two or three in the morning with the girl asking for water, or food." After the child went back to sleep, Margarita would lie awake, thinking about how to leave her job but finding it hard to even walk out into the kitchen. Live-in employees like Margarita literally have no space and no time they can claim as their own.

Working in a larger home or staying in plush, private quarters is no guarantee of privacy or refuge from the job. Forty-four-year-old Elvia Lucero worked as a live-in at a sprawling, canyon-side residence, where she was in charge of looking after twins, two five-year-old girls. On numerous occasions when I visited her there, I saw that she occupied her own bedroom, a beautifully decorated one outfitted with delicate antiques, plush white carpet, and a stenciled border of pink roses painstakingly painted on the wall by the employer. It looked serene and inviting, but it was only three steps away from the twins' room. Every night one of the twins crawled into bed with Elvia. Elvia disliked this, but said she couldn't break the girl of the habit. And the parents' room lay tucked away at the opposite end of the large (more than 3,000 square feet), L-shaped house.

Regardless of the size of the home and the splendor of the accommodations, the boundaries that we might normally take for granted disappear in live-in jobs. They have, as Evelyn Nakano Glenn has noted, "no clear line between work and non-work time," and the line between job space and private space is similarly blurred.[1] Live-in nanny/housekeepers are at once socially isolated and surrounded by other people's territory; during the hours they remain on the employers' premises, their space, like their time, belongs to another. The sensation of being among others while remaining invisible, unknown and apart, of never being able to leave the margins, makes many live-in employees sad, lonely, and depressed. Melancholy sets in and doesn't necessarily lift on the weekends.

Rules and regulations may extend around the clock. Some employers restrict the ability of their live-in employees to receive telephone calls, entertain friends, attend evening ESL classes, or see boyfriends during the workweek. Other employers do not impose these sorts of restrictions, but because their homes are located on remote hillsides, in suburban enclaves, or in gated communities, their live-in nanny/housekeepers are effectively kept away from anything resembling social life or public culture. A Spanish-language radio station, or maybe a *telenovela*, may serve as their only link to the outside world.

Food—the way some employers hoard it, waste it, deny it, or just simply do not even have any of it in their kitchens—is a frequent topic of discussion among Latina live-in nanny/housekeepers. These women are talking not about counting calories but about the social meaning of food on the job. Almost no one works with a written contract, but anyone taking a live-in job that includes "room and board" would assume that adequate meals will be included. But what constitutes an adequate meal? Everyone has a different idea, and using the subject like a secret handshake, Latina domestic workers often greet one another by talking about the problems of managing food and meals on the job. Inevitably, food enters their conversations.

No one feels the indignities of food more deeply than do live-in employees, who may not leave the job for up to six days at a time. For them, the workplace necessarily becomes the place of daily sustenance. In some of the homes where they work, the employers are out all day. When these adults return home, they may only snack, keeping on hand little besides hot dogs, packets of macaroni and cheese, cereal, and peanut butter for the children. Such foods are considered neither nutritious nor appetizing by Latina immigrants, many of whom are accustomed to sitting down to meals prepared with fresh vegetables, rice, beans, and meat. In some employers' homes, the cupboards are literally bare. Gladys Villedas recalled that at one of her live-in jobs, the *señora* had graciously said, " 'Go ahead, help yourself to anything in the kitchen.' But at times," she recalled, "there was nothing, nothing in the refrigerator! There was nothing to eat!" Even in lavish kitchens outfitted with Subzero refrigerators and imported cabinetry, food may be scarce. A celebrity photographer of luxury homes that appear in posh magazines described to a reporter what he sees when he opens the doors of some of Beverly Hills' refrigerators: "Rows of cans of Diet Coke, and maybe a few remains of pizza."[2]

Further down the class ladder, some employers go to great lengths to economize on food bills. Margarita Gutiérrez claimed that at her live-in job, the husband did the weekly grocery shopping, but he bought things in small quantities—say, two potatoes that would be served in half portions, or a quarter of a watermelon to last a household of five all week. He rationed out the bottled water and warned her that milk would make her fat. Lately, she said, he was taking both her and the children to an upscale grocery market where they gave free samples of gourmet cheeses, breads, and dips, urging them all to fill up on the freebies. "I never thought," exclaimed Margarita, formerly a secretary in Mexico City, "that I would come to this country to experience hunger!"

Many women who work as live-ins are keenly aware of how food and meals underline the boundaries between them and the families for whom they work. "I never ate with them," recalled Maribel Centeno of her first live-in job. "First of all, she never said, 'Come and join us,' and secondly, I just avoided being around when they were about to eat." Why did she avoid mealtime? "I didn't feel I was part of that family. I knew they liked me, but only because of the good work I did, and because of the affection I showered on the boy; but apart from that, I was just like the gardener, like the pool man, just one more of their staff." Sitting down to share a meal symbolizes membership in a family, and Latina employees, for the most part, know they are not just like one of the family.

Food scarcity is not endemic to all of the households where these women work. In some homes, ample quantities of fresh fruits, cheeses, and chicken stock the kitchens. Some employer families readily share all of their food, but in other households, certain higher-quality, expensive food items may remain off-limits to the live-in employees, who are instructed to eat hot dogs with the children. One Latina live-in nanny/housekeeper told me that in her employers' substantial pantry, little "DO NOT TOUCH" signs signaled which food items were not available to her; and another said that her employer was always defrosting freezer-burned leftovers for her to eat, some of it dating back nearly a decade.

Other women felt subtle pressure to remain unobtrusive, humble, and self-effacing, so they held back from eating even when they were hungry. They talked a lot about how these unspoken rules apply to fruit. "Look, if they [the employers] buy fruit, they buy three bananas, two apples, two pears. So if I eat one, who took it? It's me," one woman said, "they'll know it's me." Another nanny/housekeeper recalled: "They would bring home fruit, but without them having to say it, you just knew these were not intended for you. You understand this right away, you get it." Or as another put it, "*Las Americanas* have their apples counted out, one for each day of the week." Even fruits growing in the garden are sometimes contested. In Southern California's agriculture-friendly climate, many a residential home boasts fruit trees that hang heavy with oranges, plums, and peaches, and when the Latina women who work in these homes pick the fruit, they sometimes get in trouble.[3] Eventually, many of the women solve the food problem by buying and bringing in their own food; early on Monday mornings, you see them walking with their plastic grocery bags, carting, say, a sack of apples, some chicken, and maybe some prepared food in plastic containers.

The issue of food captures the essence of how Latina live-in domestic workers feel about their jobs. It symbolizes the extent to which the families they work for draw the boundaries of exclusion or inclusion, and it marks the degree to which those families recognize the live-in nanny/housekeepers as human beings who have basic human needs. When they first take their jobs, most live-in nanny/ housekeepers do not anticipate spending any of their meager wages on food to eat while on the job, but in the end, most do—and sometimes the food they buy is eaten by members of the family for whom they work.

Although there is a wide range of pay, many Latina domestic workers in live-in jobs earn less than minimum wage for marathon hours: 93 percent of the live-in workers I surveyed in the mid-1990s were earning less than $5 an hour (79 percent of them below minimum wage, which was then $4.25), and they reported working an average of sixty-four hours a week.[4] Some of the most astoundingly low rates were paid for live-in jobs in the households of other working-class Latino immigrants, which provide some women their first job when they arrive in Los Angeles. Carmen Vasquez, for example, had spent several years working as a live-in for two Mexican families, earning only $50 a week. By comparison, her current salary of $170 a week, which she was earning as a live-in nanny/housekeeper in the hillside home of an attorney and a teacher, seemed a princely sum.

Many people assume that the rich pay more than do families of modest means, but working as a live-in in an exclusive, wealthy neighborhood, or in a twenty-three-room house, provides no guarantee of a high salary. Early one Monday morning in the fall of 1995, I was standing with a group of live-in nanny/housekeepers on a corner across the street from the Beverly Hills Hotel. As they were waiting to be picked up by their employers, a large Mercedes sedan with two women (a daughter and mother or mother-in-law?) approached, rolled down the windows, and asked if anyone was interested in a $150-a-week live-in job. A few women jotted down the phone number, and no one was shocked by the offer. Gore Vidal once commented that no one is allowed to fail within a two-mile radius of the Beverly Hills Hotel, but it turns out that plenty of women in that vicinity are failing in the salary department. In some of the most affluent Westside areas of Los Angeles—in Malibu, Pacific Palisades, and Bel Air—there are live-in nanny/housekeepers earning $150 a week. And in 1999, the *Los Angeles Times* Sunday classified ads still listed live-in nanny/housekeeper jobs with pay as low as $100 and $125.[5] Salaries for live-in jobs, however, do go considerably higher. The best-paid live-in employee whom I interviewed was Patricia Paredes, a Mexicana who spoke impeccable English and who had legal status, substantial experience, and references. She told me that she currently earned $450 a week at her live-in job. She had been promised a raise to $550, after a room remodel was finished, when she would assume weekend housecleaning in that same home. With such a relatively high weekly salary she felt compelled to stay in a live-in job during the week, away from her husband and three young daughters who remained on the east side of Los Angeles. The salary level required that sacrifice.

But once they experience it, most women are repelled by live-in jobs. The lack of privacy, the mandated separation from family and friends, the round-the-clock hours, the food issues, the low pay, and especially the constant loneliness prompt most Latina immigrants to seek other job arrangements. Some young, single women who learn to speak English fluently try to move up the ranks into higher-paying live-in jobs. As soon as they can, however, the majority attempt to leave live-in work altogether. Most live-in nanny/housekeepers have been in the United States for five years or less; among the live-in nanny/housekeepers I interviewed, only two (Carmen Vasquez and the relatively high-earning Patricia Paredes) had been in the United States for longer than that. Like African American women earlier in the century, who tired of what the historian Elizabeth Clark-Lewis has called "the soul-destroying hollowness of live-in domestic work,"[6] most Latina immigrants try to find other options.

Until the early 1900s, live-in jobs were the most common form of paid domestic work in the United States, but through the first half of the twentieth century they were gradually supplanted by domestic "day work."[7] Live-in work never completely disappeared, however, and in the last decades of the twentieth century, it revived with vigor, given new life by the needs of American families with working parents and young children—and, as we have seen, by the needs of newly arrived Latina immigrants, many of them unmarried and unattached to families. When these women try to move up from live-in domestic work, they see few job alternatives. Often, the best they can do is switch to another form of paid domestic work, either as a live-out nanny/housekeeper or as a weekly housecleaner. When they do such day work, they are better able to circumscribe their work hours, and they earn more money in less time.[8]

LIVE-OUT NANNY/HOUSEKEEPERS

When I first met twenty-four-year-old Ronalda Saavedra, she was peeling a hard-boiled egg for a dog in the kitchen of a very large home where I was interviewing the employer. At this particular domestic job, the fifth she had held since migrating from El Salvador in 1991, she arrived daily around one in the afternoon and left after the children went to bed. On a typical day, she assisted the housekeeper, a middle-aged woman, with cleaning, laundry, and errands, and at three o'clock she drove off in her own car to pick up the children—a nine-year-old boy, whom she claimed was always angry, and his hyperactive six-year-old brother.

Once the children were put to bed, Ronalda Saavedra drove home to a cozy apartment that she shared with her brother in the San Fernando Valley. When I visited her, I saw that it was a tiny place, about half the size of the kitchen where we had first met; but it was pleasantly outfitted with new bleached oak furniture, and the morning sunshine that streamed in through a large window gave it a cheerful, almost spacious feel. Ronalda kept a well-stocked refrigerator, and during our interview she served me *pan dulce*, coffee, and honeydew melon.

Like many other women, Ronalda had begun her work stint in

the United States with a live-in job, but she vastly preferred living out. She slept through the night in peace, attended ESL classes in the morning, ate what she wanted when she wanted it, and talked daily on the phone with her fiancé. All this was possible because live-out jobs are firmly circumscribed. Even when women find it difficult to say no to their employers when they are asked, at the last minute, to stay and work another hour or two, they know they will eventually retreat to their own places. So while the workday tasks and rhythms are similar to those of live-ins, the job demands on live-outs stop when they exit the houses where they work and return to their own homes, usually small and sometimes crowded apartments located in one of Los Angeles' many Latino neighborhoods. For such women with husbands or with children of their own, live-out jobs allow them to actually live with their family members and see them daily.

Live-out nanny/housekeepers also earn more money than live-ins. Most of them work eight or nine hours a day, and of those I surveyed, 60 percent worked five days a week or fewer. Their mean hourly wages were $5.90—not an exorbitant wage by any means, but above the legal minimum, unlike the wages of their peers in live-in jobs. Ronalda earned $350 for her forty-hour workweek, making her hourly wage $8.75. On top of this, her employer gave her an additional $50 to cover gasoline expenses, as Ronalda spent a portion of each afternoon driving on errands, such as going to the dry cleaners, and ferrying the children home from school and then to and from soccer practices, music lessons, and so on. In the suburban landscape of Los Angeles, employers pay an extra premium for nanny/housekeepers who can provide this shuttling service. Only Latina nanny/housekeepers with experience, strong references, English skills, and an impressive array of certificates and licenses enjoy earnings that reach Ronalda's level.

Today, most Americans who hire a domestic worker to come into their homes on a daily basis do so in order to meet their needs for *both* housecleaning and child care. Most Latina nanny/housekeepers work in households where they are solely responsible for these tasks, and they work hard to fit in the cleaning and laundry (most of them don't cook) while the children are napping or at school. Some of them feel, as one woman said, that they need to be "octopuses," with busy arms extended simultaneously in all directions. A big part of their job requires taking care of the children; and various issues with the children present nanny/housekeepers with their greatest frustrations. Paradoxically, they also experience some of their deepest job satisfaction with these children with whom they spend so much time.

After what may be years of watching, feeding, playing with, and reprimanding the same child from birth to elementary school, day in and day out, some nanny/housekeepers grow very fond of their charges and look back nostalgically, remembering, say, when a child took her first steps or first learned nursery rhymes in Spanish. Ronalda, an articulate, highly animated woman who told stories using a lot of gestures and facial expressions, talked a great deal about the children she had cared for in her various jobs. She imitated the voices of children she had taken care of, describing longingly little girls who were, she said, "*muy* nice" or "*tan* sweet," and recalled the imaginary games they would play. Like many other nanny/housekeepers, she wept freely when she remembered some of the intimate and amusing moments she had spent with children she no longer saw. She also described other children who, she said, were dour, disrespectful, and disobedient.

Many live-out nanny/housekeepers made care work—the work of keeping the children clean, happy, well nourished, and above all safe—a priority over housecleaning duties. This sometimes created conflicts with their employers, who despite saying that their children should come first still expected a spotless house. "The truth is," explained Teresa Portillo, who looked after a child only on the weekends, "when you are taking care of children, you can't neglect anything, absolutely nothing! Because the moment you do, they do whatever little *travesura*, and they scrape their knees, cut themselves or whatever." Nanny/housekeepers fear they will be sent to jail if anything happens to the children.

Feeding the children is a big part of the job. Unlike their live-in peers, when live-out nanny/housekeepers talk about food, they're usually concerned with what the children eat or don't eat. Some of them derive tremendous pleasure and satisfaction from bringing the children special treats prepared at their own homes—maybe homemade flan or *pan con crema*, or simply a mango. Some nanny/housekeepers are also in charge, to their dismay, of feeding and cleaning the children's menagerie of pets. Many feel disgusted when they have to bathe and give eyedrops to old, sick dogs, or clean the cages of iguanas, snakes, lizards, and various rodents. But these tasks are trivial in comparison to the difficulties they encounter with hard-to-manage children. Mostly, though, they complain about permissive, neglectful parents.

Not all nanny/housekeepers bond tightly with their employers' children, but most are critical of what they perceive as their employers' careless parenting—or, more accurately, mothering, for their female employers typically receive the blame. They see mothers who may spend, they say, only a few minutes a day with their babies and toddlers, or who return home from work after the children are asleep. Soraya Sanchez said she could understand mothers who work "out of necessity," but all other mothers, she believed, hired nanny/housekeepers because they just didn't like being with their own kids. "*La Americana* is very selfish, she only thinks about herself," she said. "They prefer not to be with their children, as they find it's much easier to pay someone to do that." Her critique was shared by many nanny/housekeepers; and those with children of their own, even if they didn't live with them, saw their own mothering as far superior. "I love my kids, they don't. It's just like, excuse the word, 'shitting kids,' " said Patricia Paredes. "What they prefer is to go to the salon, get their nails done, you know, go shopping, things like that. Even if they're home all day, they don't want to spend time with the kids because they're paying somebody to do that for them." For many Latina nanny/housekeepers, seething class resentments find expression in the rhetoric of comparative mothering.

When Latina immigrant women enter the homes of middle-class and upper-middle-class Americans, they encounter ways of raising children very different from those with which they are familiar. As Julia Wrigley's research has shown, the child-rearing values of many Latina and Caribbean nannies differ from those of their employers, but most are eager to do what middle-class parents want—to adopt "time out" discipline measures instead of swatting, or to impose limits on television viewing and Nintendo.[9] Some of them not only adapt but come to genuinely admire and appreciate such methods of child rearing. Yet they, too, criticize the parenting styles they witness close up in the homes where they work.

Some nanny/housekeepers encounter belligerent young children, who yell at them, call them names, and throw violent temper tantrums; and when they do, they blame the parents. They are aghast when parents, after witnessing a child scratch or bite or spit at them, simply shrug their shoulders and ignore such behavior. Parents' reactions to these incidents were a litmus test of sorts. Gladys Villedas, for example, told me that at her job, a five-year-old "grabbed my hair and pulled it really hard. Ay! It hurt so much I started crying! It really hurt my feelings because never in my own country, when I was raising my children, had this happened to me. Why should this happen to me here?" When she complained to her employer, she said the employer had simply consulted a child-rearing manual and explained that it was "a stage." Not all nanny/housekeepers encounter physically abusive children, but when they do, they prefer parents who allow them the authority to impose discipline, or who back them up by firmly instructing their children that it is not okay to kick or slap the nanny. Nanny/housekeepers spoke glowingly about these sorts of employers.

When nanny/housekeepers see parent-child interactions in the homes where they work, they are often put off and puzzled by what they observe. In these moments, the huge cultural gulf between Latina nanny/housekeepers and their employers seems even wider than they had initially imagined. In the home where Maribel Centeno was working as a live-out nanny/housekeeper, she spent the first few hours of her shift doing laundry and housecleaning, but when a thirteen-year-old boy, of whom she was actually very fond, arrived home from school, her real work began. It was his pranks, which were neither malicious nor directed at her, and parental tolerance of these, that drove her crazy. These adolescent pranks usually involved items like water balloons, firecrackers, and baking soda made to look like cocaine. Recently the boy had tacked up on his parents' bedroom door a condom filled with a small amount of milk and a little sign that read, "Mom and Dad, this could have been my life." Maribel thought this was inappropriate behavior; but more bewildering and disturbing than the boy's prank was his mother's reaction—laughter. Another nanny/housekeeper had reacted with similar astonishment when, after a toddler tore apart a loaf of French bread and threw the pieces, balled like cotton, onto the floor, the father came forward not to reprimand but to record the incident with a camcorder. The regularity with which their employers waste food astounds them, and drug use also raises their eyebrows. Some nanny/housekeepers are instructed to give Ritalin and Prozac to children as young as five or six, and others tell of parents and teens locked in their separate bedrooms, each smoking marijuana.

Nanny/housekeepers blame permissive and neglectful parents, who they feel don't spend enough time with their own children, for the children's unruly behavior and for teen drug use. "The parents, they say 'yes' to everything the child asks," complained one woman. "Naturally," she added, "the children are going to act spoiled." Another nanny/housekeeper analyzed the situation this way: "They [the parents] feel guilty because they don't spend that much time with the kids, and they want to replace that missed time, that love, with toys."

Other nanny/housekeepers prided themselves on taming and teaching the children to act properly. "I really had to battle with these children just to get them to pay attention to me! When I started with them, they had no limits, they didn't pick up their toys, and they couldn't control their tempers. The eldest—oof! He used to kick and hit me, and in public! I was mortified," recalled Ronalda Saavedra. Another woman remarked of children she had looked after, "These kids listened to me. After all, they spent most of the time with me, and not with them [the parents]. They would arrive at night, maybe spend a few moments with the kids, or maybe the kids were already asleep." Elvia Areola highlighted the injustice of rearing children whom one will never see again. Discussing her previous job, she said, "I was the one who taught that boy to talk, to walk, to read, to sit! Everything! She [the child's mother] almost never picked him up! She only picked him up when he was happy." Another nanny/housekeeper concluded, "These parents don't really know their own children. Just playing with them, or taking them to the park, well, that's not raising children. I'm the one who is with them every day."

Nanny/housekeepers must also maneuver around jealous parents, who may come to feel that their children's affections have been displaced. "The kids fall in love with you and they [the parents] wonder, why? Some parents are jealous of what the kids feel toward you," said Ronalda Saavedra, "I'm not going to be lying, 'I'm your mommy,' but in a way, children go to the person who takes care of them, you know? That's just the way it is." For many nanny/housekeepers, it is these ties of affection that make it possible for them to do their job by making it rewarding. Some of them say they can't properly care for the children without feeling a special fondness for them; others say it just happens naturally. "I fall in love with all of these children. How can I not? That's just the way I am," one nanny/housekeeper told me. "I'm with them all day, and when I go home, my husband complains that that's all I talk about, what they did, the funny things they said." The nanny/housekeepers, as much as they felt burdened by disobedient children, sometimes felt that these children were also a gift of sorts, one that parents—again, the mothers—did not fully appreciate. "The babies are so beautiful!" gushed Soraya Sanchez. "How is it that a mother can lose those best years, when their kids are babies. I mean, I remember going down for a nap with these little babies, how we'd cuddle. How is it that a person who has the option of enjoying that would prefer to give that experience to a stranger?" Precisely because of such feelings, many Latina immigrants who have children try to find a job that is compatible with their own family lives. Housecleaning is one of those jobs.

HOUSECLEANERS

Like many working mothers, every weekday morning Marisela Ramírez awoke to dress and feed her preschooler, Tomás, and drive him to school (actually, a Head Start program) before she herself ventured out to work, navigating the dizzying array of Los Angeles freeways. Each day she set off in a different direction headed for a different workplace. On Mondays she maneuvered her way to Pasadena, where she cleaned the stately home of an elderly couple; on Tuesdays she alternated between cleaning a home in the Hollywood Hills and a more modest-sized duplex in Glendale; and Wednesdays took her to a split-level condominium in Burbank. You had to keep alert, she said, to remember where to go on which days and how to get there!

By nine o'clock she was usually on the job, and because she zoomed through her work she was able to finish, unless the house was extremely dirty, by one or two in the afternoon. After work, there were still plenty of daylight hours left for Marisela to take Tomás to the park, or at least to take him outside and let him ride down the sidewalk on his kid-sized motorized vehicle before she started dinner. Working as a housecleaner allowed Marisela to be the kind of wife and mother she wanted to be. Her job was something she did, she said, "because I have to"; but unlike her peers who work in live-in jobs, she enjoyed a fairly regular family life of her own, one that included cooking and eating family meals, playing with her son, bathing him, putting him to bed, and then watching *telenovelas* in the evenings with her husband and her sister. On the weekends, family socializing took center stage, with *carne asadas* in the park; informal gatherings with her large Mexican family, which extended throughout Los Angeles; and music from her husband, who worked as a gardener but played guitar in a weekend *ranchera* band.

Some might see Marisela Ramírez as just another low-wage worker doing dirty work, but by her own account—and gauging by her progress from her starting point—she had made remarkable occupational strides. Marisela had begun working as a live-in nanny/ housekeeper in Los Angeles when she was only fifteen years old. Ten years later, the move from live-in work to housecleaning had brought her higher hourly wages, a shorter workweek, control over the pace of work, and flexibility in arranging when she worked. Cleaning different houses was also, she said, less boring than working as a nanny/housekeeper, which entailed passing every single day "in just one house, all week long with the same routine, over and over."

For a while she had tried factory work, packaging costume jewelry in a factory warehouse located in the San Fernando Valley, but Marisela saw housecleaning as preferable on just about every count. "In the factory, one has to work very, very fast!" she exclaimed. "And you can't talk to anybody, you can't stop, and you can't rest until it's break time. When you're working in a house, you can take a break at the moment you wish, finish the house when you want, and leave at the hour you decide. And it's better pay. It's harder work, yes," she conceded, "but it's better pay."

"How much were you earning at the factory?" I asked.

"Five dollars an hour; and working in houses now, I make about $11, or even more. Look, in a typical house, I enter at about 9 A.M., and I leave at 1 P.M., and they pay me $60. It's much better [than factory work]." Her income varied, but she could usually count on weekly earnings of about $300. By pooling these together with her husband's and sister's earnings, she was able to rent a one-bedroom bungalow roofed in red tile, with a lawn and a backyard for Tomás's sandbox and plastic swimming pool. In Mexico, Marisela had only studied as far as fifth grade, but she wanted the best for Tomás. Everyone doted on him, and by age four he was already reading simple words.

Of the housecleaners I surveyed, the majority earned, like Marisela, between $50 and $60 per housecleaning, which usually took about six hours. This suggests an average hourly wage of about $9.50, but I suspect the actual figure is higher.[10] Women like Marisela, who drive their own cars and speak some English, are likely to earn more than the women I surveyed, many of whom ride the buses to work. Marisela was typical of the housecleaners whom I surveyed in having been in the United States for a number of years. Unlike nanny/housekeepers, most of the housecleaners who were mothers themselves had all their children with them in the United States. Housecleaning, as Mary Romero has noted, is a job that is quite compatible with having a family life of one's own.

Breaking into housecleaning is tough, often requiring informal tutelage from friends and relatives. Contrary to the image that all women "naturally" know how to do domestic work, many Latina domestic workers discover that their own housekeeping experiences do not automatically transfer to the homes where they work. As she looked back on her early days in the job, Marisela said, "I didn't know how to clean or anything. My sister taught me." Erlinda Castro, a middle-aged women who had already run her own household and raised five children in Guatemala, had also initially worked in live-in jobs when she first came to Los Angeles. Yet despite this substantial domestic experience, she recalled how mystified she was when she began housecleaning. "Learning how to use the chemicals and the liquids" in the different households was confusing, and, as friends and employers instructed her on what to do, she began writing down in a little notebook the names of the products and what they cleaned. Some women learn the job by informally apprenticing with one another, accompanying a friend or perhaps an aunt on her housecleaning jobs.

Establishing a thriving route of *casas* requires more than learning which cleaning products to use or how to clean quickly and efficiently. It also involves acquiring multiple jobs, which housecleaners typically gain by asking their employers if they have friends, neighbors, or acquaintances who need someone to clean their houses; and because some attrition is inevitable, they must constantly be on the lookout for more *casas*. Not everyone who wants to can fill up her entire week.

To make ends meet when they don't have enough houses to clean, Latina housecleaners in Los Angeles find other ways to earn income. They might prepare food—say, tamales and *crema*—which they sell door-to-door or on the street; or they might sell small amounts of clothing that they buy wholesale in the garment district, or products from Avon, Mary Kay cosmetics, and Princess House kitchenware. They take odd jobs, such as handing out flyers advertising dental clinics or working at a swap meet; or perhaps they find something more stable, such as evening janitorial work in office buildings. Some housecleaners work swing shift in garment factories, while others work three days a week as a nanny/housekeeper and try to fill the remaining days with housecleaning jobs. Some women supplement their husband's income by cleaning only one or two houses a week, but more often they patch together a number of jobs in addition to housecleaning.

Housecleaning represents, as Romero has written, the "modernization" of paid domestic work. Women who clean different houses on different days sell their labor services, she argues, in much the same way that a vendor sells a product to various customers.[11] The housecleaners themselves see their job as far preferable to that of a live-in or live-out nanny/housekeeper. They typically work alone, during times when their employers are out of the home; and because they are paid "by the job" instead of by the hour, they don't have to remain on the job until 6 or 7 P.M., an advantage much appreciated by women who have families of their own. Moreover, because they work for different employers on different days, they are not solely dependent for their livelihood on one boss whom they see every single day. Consequently, their relationships with their employers are less likely to become highly charged and conflictual; and if problems do arise, they can leave one job without jeopardizing their entire weekly earnings. Since child care is not one of their tasks, their responsibilities are more straightforward and there are fewer points of contention with employers. Housecleaning is altogether less risky.

Housecleaners also see working independently and informally as more desirable than working for a commercial cleaning company. "The companies pay $5 an hour," said Erlinda Castro, whose neighbor worked for one, "and the women have to work their eight hours, doing up to ten, twenty houses a day! One does the vacuuming, the other does the bathroom and the kitchen, and like that. It's tremendously hard work, and at $5 an hour? Thank God, I don't have to do that." Two of the women I interviewed, one now a live-out nanny/housekeeper and the other a private housecleaner, had previously worked for cleaning services, and both of them complained bitterly about their speeded-up work pace, low pay, and tyrannical bosses.

Private housecleaners take enormous pride in their work. When they finish their job, they can see the shiny results, and they are proud of their job autonomy, their hours, their pay, and, most important, what they are able to do with their pay for themselves and for their families. Yet housecleaning brings its own special problems. Intensive cleaning eventually brings physical pain, and sometimes injury. "Even my bones are tired," said fifty-three-year-old Lupe Vélez; and even a relatively young woman like Celestina Vigil at age thirty-three was already reporting back problems that she attributed to her work. While most of them have only fleeting contact with their employers, and many said they work for "good people," just about everyone has suffered, they said, "inconsiderate persons" who exhort them to work faster, humiliate them, fail to give raises, add extra cleaning tasks without paying extra, or unjustly accuse them of stealing or of ruining a rug or upholstery. And the plain old hard work and stigma of cleaning always remain, as suggested by the answer I got when I asked a housecleaner what she liked least about her job. "The least?" she said, with a wry smile. "Well, that you have to clean."

DOMESTIC JOB TRAJECTORIES
AND TRANSNATIONAL MOTHERHOOD

As we have seen, private paid domestic work is organized into sub-occupations, each with different pay scales, tasks, and hours.[12] Although they share many similarities, each job arrangement has its

Table 1
Type of Domestic Work, Length of Residence
in the United States, and Mean Hourly Wages

	Live-ins (percent) (n=30)	Live-outs (percent) (n=64)	Housecleaners (percent) (n=59)
Five years or less in United States	60	31	17
More than five years in United States	40	69	83
Mean hourly wage	$3.80	$5.90	$9.50

own different problems and rewards. In this section I discuss the movement between the three suboccupations and some of the family characteristics of the women who fill these jobs.

Some researchers have called live-in domestic work "the bridging occupation," because in various periods and places, it allowed rural migrant women to acculturate to the city and learn new ways of living.[13] Unlike Irish immigrant women or the black women who went from the South to the North to work as domestics in the early twentieth century, and unlike many private domestics in Europe and Latin America in the past, most Latina immigrants doing paid domestic work in the United States are *not* new to the city. Yet for many of them in Los Angeles today, especially those who are single and have very limited options for places to work and live, live-in jobs do serve as an initial occupational step. As table 1 shows, new arrivals and women who have lived in the United States five years or less concentrate in live-in jobs (60 percent). In contrast, the majority of housecleaners (83 percent) and live-out nanny/housekeepers (69 percent) have lived in the United States for more than five years. Some begin their live-in jobs literally within forty-eight hours after arriving in Los Angeles, while some housecleaners have lived in the United States for twenty years or more. For newly arrived immigrant women without papers, a live-in job in a private home may feel safer, as private homes in middle- and upper-middle-class neighborhoods are rarely, if ever, threatened by Immigration and Naturalization Service raids.[14]

As the years pass, the women who took live-in jobs learn some English, gain knowledge of other job possibilities, and learn to use their social networks to their occupational advantage. Most of them eventually move out of live-in work. Some return to their countries of origin, and others look to sales, factory work, or janitorial work. But given the low pay of those jobs—in 1999, garment workers in Los Angeles were earning $5.00 an hour, and nonunion janitors with six years of experience were earning $6.30 an hour—many of them transition into some form of domestic day work.[15] As they abandon their live-in positions for live-out nanny/housekeeper and house-cleaner jobs, their wages increase. For these women, the initial misery suffered in their live-in jobs makes other domestic work look if not good then at least tolerable—and certainly better than where they started.

For Latina immigrants in Los Angeles today, live-in domestic work does serve as an occupational bridge of sorts, but it often leads only to other types of domestic jobs. These individual trajectories match historical transformations in the occupation. Much as live-in jobs were once the dominant form of paid domestic work, and then gave way to arrangements in which domestics continued to work daily for one employer but lived with their own families, and finally to modernized "job work" or periodic housecleaning, so many Latina immigrants today traverse these three different types of jobs. Some roughly follow the historical order, moving from live-in to live-out nanny/housekeeper jobs, and then to housecleaning, but their modest occupational mobility does not always follow such a linear course.

As Mexican and Central American immigrant women move into live-out and housecleaning jobs, their family lives change. With better pay and fewer hours of work, they become able to live with their own family members. Among those I surveyed, about 45 percent of the women doing day work were married, but only 13 percent of the live-ins were married. Most women who have husbands and children with them in Los Angeles do not wish to take live-in jobs; moreover, their application for a live-in job is likely to be rejected if they reveal that they have a husband, a boyfriend, or children living in Los Angeles. As one job seeker in an employment agency waiting room put it, "You can't have a family, you can't have anyone [if you

Table 2
Type of Domestic Work, Marital Status,
and Location of Children

	Live-ins (percent) (n=30)	Live-outs (percent) (n=64)	Housecleaners (percent) (n=59)
Single (includes the widowed, divorced, or separated)	87	55	54
Married	13	45	46
Domestic Workers with Children	*(n=16)*	*(n=53)*	*(n=45)*
All children in United States	18	58	76
At least one child "back home"	82	42	24

want a live-in job]." Live-out nanny/housekeepers often face this family restriction too, as employers are wary of hiring someone who may not report for work when her own children come down with the flu.

Their subminimum wages and long hours make it impossible for many live-in workers to bring their children to Los Angeles; other live-ins are young women who do not have children of their own. Once they do have children who are either born in or have immigrated to Los Angeles, most women try to leave live-in work to be with them. Not all the women can do so, and sometimes their finances or jobs force them to send the children "back home" to be reared by grandmothers. Clearly, performing domestic work for pay, especially in a live-in job, is often incompatible with caring for one's own family and home.[16]

The substantial proportion of Latina domestic workers in Los Angeles whose children stay in their countries of origin are in the same position as many Caribbean women working in domestic jobs on the East Coast, and as the Filipinas who predominate in domestic jobs in many cities around the globe. This is what I labeled "transnational motherhood" in chapter 1; in a 1997 article Ernestine Avila and I coined this term as we examined how Latina immigrant domestic workers are transforming their own meanings of motherhood to accommodate these spatial and temporal separations.[17] As table 2 suggests, these arrangements are most common among women with live-in jobs, but live-in domestic workers and single mothers are not the only ones who rely on them.[18]

These transnational arrangements are not altogether new. The United States has a long history of incorporating people of color through coercive systems of labor that do not recognize family rights, including the right to care for one's own family members. As others have pointed out, slavery and contract labor systems were organized to maximize economic productivity, and offered few supports to sustain family life.[19] Today, international labor migration and the job characteristics of paid domestic work, especially live-in work, virtually impose transnational motherhood on many Mexican and Central American women who have children of their own.

At the other end of the spectrum are the housecleaners, who earn higher wages than live-ins (averaging $9.50 an hour vs. $3.80) and who work fewer hours per week than live-ins (twenty-three vs. sixty-four). The majority of them (76 percent) have all their children in the United States, and they are the least likely to experience transnational spatial and temporal separations from their children. Greater financial resources and more favorable job terms enhance housecleaners' abilities to bring their children to the United States. As we have seen, weekly housecleaning is dominated by relatively well-established women with more years of experience in the United States, who speak some English, who have a car, and who have job references. Because their own position is more secure, they are also more likely to have their children here. And because they tend to work fewer hours per week, have greater flexibility in scheduling, and earn higher wages than the live-ins, they can live with and care for their children.

With respect to their ability to care for their own children, live-out nanny/housekeepers fall between live-ins and weekly cleaners—predictably, since they are also in an intermediate position in their earnings, rigidity of schedule, and working hours. Live-out domestic workers, according to the survey, earn $5.90 an hour and work an average workweek of thirty-five hours, and 42 percent of those who are mothers reported having at least one of their children in their country of origin.

THE DOMINANCE OF CENTRAL AMERICAN
AND MEXICAN IMMIGRANT WOMEN

Paid domestic work has long been a racialized and gendered occupation, but why today are Central American women hugely overrepresented in these jobs in Los Angeles in comparison with Mexicans (whose immigrant population is of course many times larger)? In the survey I conducted of 153 Westside Latina domestic workers, 75 percent of the respondents were from Central America; of those, most were from El Salvador and Guatemala. And in census counts, Salvadoran and Guatemalan women are, respectively, twelve times and thirteen times more likely than the general population to be engaged in private domestic work in Los Angeles.[20] Numerous studies paint a similar picture in other major U.S. cities, such as Washington, D.C., Houston, and San Francisco; one naturally wonders why this should be so.[21]

In Los Angeles, the heavy concentration of Central American women in paid domestic work is partially explained by the location of L.A.'s primary Central American immigrant neighborhood, the Pico-Union/Westlake area, just west of the small, high-rise downtown. As UCLA sociologist David Lopez and his colleagues explain, "A large proportion of Central Americans tend to reside closer to the middle-class neighborhoods of the Westside and the San Fernando Valley . . . while Mexicans are concentrated in the more isolated areas east and south of Downtown Los Angeles."[22] It is certainly quicker to drive or take a bus to the Westside from the Pico Union area than it is from East L.A. But there is more to this story than spatial location and L.A. transportation systems: distinct migration patterns have also influenced these occupational concentrations.

Mexican migration to the United States goes back over a hundred years, initially driven by labor recruitment programs designed to bring in men to work in agriculture. Since the late 1960s, it has shifted from a primarily male population of temporary or sojourner workers to one that includes women and entire families; these newcomers have settled in rural areas, cities, and suburbs throughout the United States, but disproportionately in California. Many Mexican women who migrated in the 1970s and 1980s were accompanied by their families and were aided by rich social networks; the latter helped prevent the urgency that leads new immigrants to take live-in jobs. Even those unmarried Mexican women who did migrate on their own, despite being opposed and sometimes stigmatized by their family and community, were often assisted by friends and more sympathetic family members. By the 1990s, more unmarried Mexican women were going north, encouraged in part by help from female friends and kin. When Mexican women arrive in the United States, many of them enjoy access to well-developed, established communities whose members have long been employed in various industries, particularly agriculture, construction, hotels, food-processing plants, and garment factories. Compared to their Central American peers, Mexican women are more likely to have financial support from a husband; because fewer Mexican immigrant women *must* work outside their home, they have lower rates of overall participation in the labor force than do Central American women.[23] Their social networks also give Mexican women greater variety in their employment options; paid domestic work is only one of their alternatives.

Salvadoran and Guatemalan women migrating to the United States have done so under different circumstances than Mexican women. For Central Americans coming to *el norte*, there was no long-standing labor program recruiting men who could then bring, or encourage the migration of, their wives and daughters. In fact, as Terry Repak's study shows, some of the early pioneers of Salvadoran migration to Washington, D.C., were women, themselves informally recruited by individual members of the diplomatic corps precisely because they were desired as private domestics.[24] More significantly, Salvadoran and Guatemalan women and men left their countries in haste, often leaving their children behind, as they fled the civil wars, political violence, and economic upheaval of the 1980s. Theirs are immigrant communities that subsisted without legal status for nearly two decades, grew rapidly, and remain very poor. Even Guatemalan and Salvadoran women who arrived in the United States in the late 1980s and early 1990s could not count on finding communities of well-established compatriots who could quickly and efficiently situate them in jobs in restaurants, hotels, factories, or other industries. In fact, as some of the most compelling ethnographies of Salvadorans in San Francisco and on Long Island have shown, Central Americans' relatively shallow U.S. roots have left their social

networks extremely impoverished and sometimes fractured.[25] For
Central American women arriving on their own, without husbands
and children in tow, desperate and lacking information about jobs—
and at a crucial historical moment when American families were
seeking to resolve their own child care and housekeeping problems—live-in jobs were both attractive and available.

Family structures and marriage patterns may have also contributed to the preponderance of Central American women in paid domestic work. El Salvador has traditionally had one of the lowest
marriage rates in the hemisphere, especially among the urban poor,
where common-law marriages and legacies of internal and intra–
Central America labor migration—mostly for work on coffee plan-
tations—have encouraged the formation of female-headed households.[26] Thus Salvadoran women have been more likely to migrate
on their own and accept live-in jobs.[27] Their large numbers in this
lowest rung of domestic work would then explain their eventual
disproportionate concentration in all types of private paid domestic
work, following the pattern discussed above.

The experience of Central American women might also be compared to that of Asian immigrant women, who have been entering
the United States at increasing rates. The latter are an extremely heterogeneous group, but on average—and this is particularly true of
Chinese, Indian, and Filipina women—they arrive with much higher
levels of education, better English language skills, and more professional credentials than do their Latina peers. They are also more
likely to have legal status; and members of some groups, especially
Korean immigrant women, enjoy access to jobs in family businesses
and ethnic enclaves.[28] At the same time, the generally poorer and
less-educated women from Vietnam, Laos, and Cambodia have been
able to withstand periods of underemployment and unemployment
because they are officially sanctioned political refugees and therefore
enjoy access to welfare and resettlement assistance from the federal
government. While some individual Asian immigrant women are
working in paid domestic work, they have not developed social networks that channel them into this niche.

It is particularly striking that Filipina immigrants predominate in
this occupation elsewhere around the globe, but not in the United
States. Worldwide, about two-thirds of Filipina migrants in countries
as different as Italy, Canada, Hong Kong, Taiwan, Singapore, Saudi
Arabia, and Jordan, do paid domestic work; but in the United States,

their high levels of education and fluent English enable most of them to enter higher status occupations that require more skills than does domestic work. In 1990, 71 percent of the Filipinas in the United States were working in managerial, professional, technical/sales, and administrative support jobs, and only 17 percent were employed in service jobs.[29] They are disproportionately concentrated in the health professions, the result of formal recruitment programs designed to fill U.S. nursing shortages.[30] Experience in the health professions leads many Filipinas to take jobs in elder care; and though some work as nanny/housekeepers in Los Angeles, many of them as live-ins, in my numerous discussions with employers, Latina employees, attorneys, and owners and employees of domestic employment agencies, no one ever mentioned Filipina housecleaners.

Nevertheless, Filipina immigrants are doing paid domestic work in the United States. Interviews conducted by Rhacel Parreñas with twenty-six Filipina domestic workers in Los Angeles reveal that many of these women have college diplomas and are working in homes because they are older and face age discrimination; they tend to earn more as care providers for the elderly ($425 per week) and more as nanny/housekeepers ($350 per week) than do Latina immigrants in these same jobs.[31] When it comes to caring for their children, some employers prefer Filipina nanny/housekeepers because they speak English well (English is the official language of schools and universities in the Philippines), and because they tend to be highly educated. Paradoxically, these qualities may predispose some employers to *not* choose Filipinas as domestic employees. At three domestic employment agencies, the owners told me that they rarely placed Filipina job applicants, because they were deemed "uppity," demanding, and likely to lie about their references. Racial preferences, as the next section suggests, shape the formation of Latina domestic workers and their employment in Los Angeles.

NARRATIVES OF RACIAL PREFERENCES

In a race-conscious society, everyone has racial preferences and prejudices, and Latina domestic workers and the women who employ them are no exception. When choosing someone to work in their homes, many employers prefer Latinas, because as "others" in language, race-ethnicity, and social class, they are outside white,

English-speaking, middle-class social circles and are thus seen as unlikely to reveal family secrets and intimacies. If they do tell someone about the family fight they witnessed, that someone is likely to be another Latina nanny or a member of their own family—in either case, no one who matters to the employers. This fear of exposure sometimes prevents employers from choosing white, English-speaking job candidates. "She was non-Hispanic, and I wasn't sure if I could trust her," said one woman of a prospective employee. Another employer had been advised not to hire a white woman as a nanny/housekeeper because an immigrant would be less likely to recognize her philanthropic family's name and to engage in bribery or kidnapping. Other women told me that they did not want a European au pair or midwestern (white) teenager taking care of their children because they would probably be young, irresponsible teens, more interested in cavorting with boyfriends, cruising the beach, and stargazing in Hollywood than in doing their job. Employers may also prefer to hire Latina nannies, as research conducted by Julia Wrigley suggests, because they view them as more submissive than whites.[32]

While some of the older employers I interviewed had hired African American housecleaners and domestics in the past, none were now doing so. Of the relatively few black women working in paid domestic work in contemporary Los Angeles, most are immigrants from Belize and Brazil, and some employers remain adamantly opposed to hiring black women to work in their homes. One domestic employment agency owner told me that some clients had requested that he never send black women to interview for a job. And at an informal luncheon, arranged by one of the employer interviewees, one of them cleared her throat and then offered, with some awkward hesitation, "Uhm, ah, I would never hire a black woman. I'd be too scared to, and I'd be especially scared if her boyfriend came around." The women, all of them relatively upper-class white matrons, had nodded in silent agreement. The old stereotype of the bossy black maid is apparently alive and well, now joined by newer terrifying images associated with young black men; but since African American women are not pursuing domestic work jobs in Los Angeles, most employers need never confront their own racial fears directly. It is, after all, Latina immigrant women who are queuing up for domestic jobs in private homes.

When I talked with them, most employers expressed genuine appreciation for the effort, dedication, and work that these women put into their homes and children. They viewed Latina domestic workers as responsible, trustworthy, and reliable employees who have "a really strong work ethic." And while plenty of employers spoke at length about Latina women as ideally suited to caring for children, relying on images of Latinas as exceptionally warm, patient, and loving mothers, there was no similar racialized image of cleanliness. No one said, for instance, "She cleans like a Mexican." Such a phrase may sound offensive, but the absence of any such generalization is striking when nearly everyone hired to do cleaning in Los Angeles is Mexican or Central American.

Indeed, some of the employers I interviewed did make this kind of statement—to associate their own northern European heritage with superior cleaning and hygiene. A few of them offered remarks such as "People associate very clean homes with Dutch people," or "My mother's German and she cleans, you know, like Germans clean." These women did not necessarily claim that they were excellent cleaners, only that they belonged to racial-ethnic groups associated with cleanliness. None of them described their domestic employees as "dirty," but the adjective has been commonly featured in racial epithets directed at Mexicans in the Southwest and at domestic workers just about everywhere. The historian Phyllis Palmer, who has written compellingly about dirt, domesticity, and racialized divisions among women, notes that while dirt and housework connote inferior morality, white middle-class women transcend these connotations by employing women different from themselves to do the work. "Dirtiness," Palmer notes, "appears always in a constellation of the suspect qualities that, along with sexuality, immorality, laziness, and ignorance, justify social rankings of race, class and gender. The 'slut,' initially a shorthand for 'slattern' or kitchen maid, captures all of these personifications in a way unimaginable in a male persona."[33]

Employers are not the only ones who hold strong racial-ethnic preferences and prejudices. Latina domestic workers at the bus stops, at the agencies, and in the public parks readily agreed on who were their worst employers: Armenians, Iranians, Asians, Latinos, blacks, and Jews, especially Israeli Jews. "I'll never work again for *un chino!*" or "*Los armenios* [Armenians] are the worst," they tell each other.

These statements were echoed in the individual interviews, as well as by the preferences job candidates register at employment agencies, and they seem to mirror what Latino men who work as day laborers think about their similarly racialized employers in Los Angeles.[34] Anyone marked as "nonwhite," it seems, is at risk of being denounced as a cheap, abusive, and oppressive employer, one to be avoided at all costs.

There are a number of factors at work here. Many of the employers in these racial-ethnic groups are immigrants themselves, albeit entrepreneurial and professional immigrants with substantially more resources than the Latinas they hire to care for their homes and children. Many had belonged to elites in their countries of origin, accustomed to having servants in their homes who would be expected to perform all sorts of jobs on demand. Some of them bring these expectations with them when they come to the United States. When Latina domestic workers are expected to massage the *señora's* feet with oil, or scrub the kitchen floor on their hands and knees, they take offense. Others are wholly unprepared to iron Hindu saris, or to follow kosher food preparation and serving practices in the homes of Orthodox Jews. At the same time, the immigrant and ethnic employers may have been accustomed in their countries of origin to paying slave wages, and the tenuous financial situations of some makes them unable to pay minimum wage. Some newly arrived women who find their first job working as a live-in for other working-class Latino immigrant families may receive as little as $25 or $50 a week in exchange for their round-the-clock services.

Latina immigrants also operate under racist assumptions, many of which they learn in the United States. They quickly pick up the country's racial hierarchies and racist stereotypes. "Jews are cheap," "Mexican Americans and blacks are lazy," or "*Los chinos* are too bossy," they say. The regional racial hierarchy also fixes Jews, Armenians, and Iranians in low positions. "*Los Americanos*," the term they typically use to refer to employers marked only "white," are almost never singled out by ethnicity and are rarely criticized or negatively labeled as a group.

Conversely, Latina domestic workers single out the race of particular employers who happen to be both "bad employers" and "racialized" as nonwhite. One Mexican housecleaner who maintained that Latino employers were among the most exploitative was Lupe

Vélez. When I probed why she felt this way, she cited as evidence her experiences with one employer, a man from Monterrey, Mexico. A large, verbally abusive man, he had called her a pig, he went out of his way to deny her food when he sat down to eat with his family, and he had unfairly accused her of scratching and ruining a stove top. These deeply felt, painful experiences were recounted tearfully.

Yet as we talked longer, I discovered that in Los Angeles, Lupe had worked in three different Latino homes; she spoke of a Mexican American teacher who had treated her well and paid her fairly. Mutual fondness, respect, and closeness had grown between the two, who had unsuccessfully conspired at matchmaking between their young adult children. How could she maintain that Latinos were the "worst" employers when in fact a Mexican American had been among her best employers? In recalling her bad experience with the Mexican man, Lupe Vélez singled out his racial-ethnic identity. As she recalled that painful experience, his being Mexican and consistently acting abusively toward her became the most salient features about him. She applied "Latino," a racial marker, to this man, labeled an abusive, bad employer, but not to the teacher whom she had favored.

I suspect that when Latina domestic workers denounce Jewish employers, a similar process is at work. In those cases, they may only identify as Jewish those employers who are abusive and who are, as Orthodox Jews or recently emigrated Israeli Jews, unambiguously marked as Jewish. They might not recognize the other Jews for whom they work. Or perhaps Latina domestic workers' disdain for Jewish employers is testimony to the force of contemporary anti-Semitism. It is no small irony that a major provider of legal services for Latina domestic workers in Los Angeles is a Jewish nonprofit organization.[35]

Some Latina domestic workers related counternarratives, criticizing their peers for relying on racial stereotypes and hasty racial judgments. One Salvadoran housecleaner cited her Moroccan employer as one of the most gracious because she always served her a hot lunch, sitting down to chat with her; another related her appreciation of an African American bachelor, an ex-basketball player, who kept a messy house but paid her very generously; still another felt warmly toward her Korean employer who did not pay well, but who passed many choice housecleaning jobs on to her. Yet the voices of these women were drowned out by the louder, frequently blanket condemnations that other Latina domestic workers offered about their racially marked minority and immigrant employers. Amid the public clamor of racialized nativism that propelled California ballot initiatives against health and education services for undocumented immigrants and their children, against affirmative action, and against bilingual education (Propositions 187, 209, and 227 respectively), Latina immigrant domestic workers learn their own version of regional racism.

In this chapter, I conveyed briefly some of the life textures and the daily trials and triumphs experienced by Latina immigrants who work as housecleaners, live-out nanny/housekeepers, and live-in nanny/housekeepers. The Mexican, Salvadoran, and Guatemalan women who occupy these jobs come from diverse class, regional, and cultural locations, and they bring different expectations to their jobs. Once in the United States, however, they share a set of similar experiences, in part because of the way that their domestic work is structured. In the following three chapters, I analyze the processes through which these Latina immigrant women get in and out of jobs doing paid domestic work.

PART TWO

FINDING HARD WORK ISN'T EASY

The three chapters in this section examine Latina immigrant women's ex-periences as they enter and exit jobs as private housecleaners and nanny/ housekeepers. I focus on the inner workings of two spheres, informal social networks and the domestic employment agencies, as these are the principal arenas for locating jobs and recruiting employees. In the survey of 153 Latina domestic workers, 88 percent reported finding their current jobs through personal contacts with friends, family members, or other employers; only 9 percent relied on a domestic employment agency. Full-time live-in and live-out domestic workers were slightly more likely to have used an agency than were weekly housecleaners. For this reason, and because the agencies are instrumental in placing both low-end and high-end nanny/ housekeepers, the domestic employment agencies are worthy of our atten-tion.

Informal social networks and domestic employment agencies do more than facilitate recruitment and hiring. They are important because they create a labor market and they serve to regulate the occupation. In this regard, both the informal networks and the agencies fulfill two require-ments, intended (recruiting and hiring) and unintended (structuring the job). While written employment contracts are rare, the jobs exhibit some standardization with respect to wages, hours, tasks, and the lack of benefits; these similarities derive, in part, from the exchange of key information through the networks and the agencies. Tensions within the networks and the agencies may result in the occupation being downgraded or, as I am advocating, upgraded. Chapter 3 concentrates on informal networks, chap-ter 4 looks at the agencies, and chapter 5 examines the ways in which nanny/housekeepers and cleaners exit jobs. White lies and excuses are used by both employees and employers, and many nanny/housekeepers simply and sometimes loudly quit after emotionally explosive blowups with their employers.

3

It's Not What You Know . . .

At first you think, "How will I ever find someone?" But
then you talk to your neighbor, whose housekeeper has a
friend or a sister looking for a job, and then it's like you
just fall into this whole other world.

There is a parallel universe of women doing paid domestic work; it
remains invisible, out of the sight and consciousness of employers,
until the moment when it is tapped. Then, the network linkages act
like dye to make visible the points of connection that socially and
spatially link women of different groups and different needs.

Most prospective employers looking for paid domestic workers
in Los Angeles bypass employment agencies, newspaper ads, or
other formal job announcements, which they find expensive, slow,
and unreliable. Instead, the majority rely on their co-workers, neighbors, friends, and relatives when they seek domestic help. Latina
immigrant women seeking domestic jobs do the same, relying on
their friends, acquaintances, and relatives.

ENTRY-LEVEL EXPERIENCES

Imagine that you are a young woman, newly arrived in the United
States. You are penniless—no, hugely in debt from making the trip—
you do not speak English, and you are without a passport or any
other legitimizing documents. Vilified in political campaigns as an
"illegal," or simply scorned as a "Mexican," you live as a fugitive.
You know only a distant cousin, a childhood friend, or perhaps an
older brother whose wife is determined to cut your stay in their
already-crowded apartment to a minimum. What do you do? You
take a live-in job; or as the women say, *te encierras*. You lock yourself up.

As noted in chapter 2, live-in jobs are a typical point of occupational entry for Latina immigrants in Los Angeles, as they were for

earlier generations of women in U.S. cities.[1] Today, the first job in paid domestic work is both the hardest and the easiest job search that Latina immigrant women face. It is hard because references from past employers are key credentials for obtaining all but the most undesirable jobs (i.e., live-in arrangements, with their low pay and long hours). But it is precisely workers in live-in jobs that are in greatest demand, so landing one of these bottom-of-the-barrel jobs is relatively easy.

Although some newly arrived Latina immigrant women are warned by their friends to avoid live-in jobs, such work remains the best route to rapid employment and to quick if modest earnings. Most use personal contacts that put them in touch with employer networks. Central Americans in Los Angeles routinely comment on how easy it is for women to find live-in employment. Social networks connecting remote villages or urban neighborhoods in El Salvador with jobs in suburban L.A. homes seem to offer Latina women who are seeking jobs information superior to that available to their male peers. Many women know before leaving their homes in El Salvador or Guatemala that they have a good chance of beginning to earn money within days of arrival, but their male counterparts may search for weeks before securing jobs even as casual day laborers. Consider Ronalda Saavedra, who arrived in Los Angeles from El Salvador in 1991: her aunt immediately found a placement for her as a live-in nanny/housekeeper. Soon after, when Ronalda expressed dissatisfaction with the low pay and heavy workload, her sister found her another live-in job. Similarly, when Erlinda Castro left her five children in Guatemala and joined her husband in Los Angeles, her cousin found her a live-in job. In both of these cases, female kin knew of prospective employers and vouched for the more recently arrived women's reputations, thus removing their need for references from a former employer. In other instances, newly arrived women will work alongside a friend or relative already employed as a housecleaner or nanny, thereby gaining both experience and access to employer referrals. When the referrals fail them, they turn to the agencies or newspaper ads.

Informal apprenticeships sometimes develop. That was how Celestina Vigil, formerly a university student and insurance sales representative in El Salvador, began her career in paid domestic work in 1988. Soon after arriving in Los Angeles at age twenty-six, she began accompanying her friend Marta to her five-day-a-week, live-out housekeeper job. Marta then took Celestina, now armed with some modest experience and a credible reference from Marta's employer, an *Americana*, to a domestic employment agency. Still, Marta and other Salvadoran friends warned Celestina to stay clear of live-in jobs. "From the very beginning, they advised me not to take a live-in job, because it's really sad," she recalled. "They had become really depressed, and they hadn't lasted long at their jobs for that reason. It's depressing to be with people you don't know, recently arrived in this country, and well, you know, people abuse you!" she exclaimed, referring to the typical experience that includes daily indignities, social isolation, morning-to-midnight work schedules, and additions to cleaning tasks without commensurate raises in pay. Unlike many other new job seekers, Celestina was able to secure a live-out position as her first job, but it did not last long. She was abruptly fired when she refused the employer's request to work as a live-in.

Only 2 percent of the 153 Latina women that I surveyed reported finding their current job through a newspaper ad. Still, some women who lack personal contacts locate their first live-in job with surprising speed through radio or newspaper ads. When Gladys Vargas joined her brothers in Los Angeles in 1988, she had to resort to the newspaper for her first job search. She answered a private ad placed in the Spanish-language newspaper *La Opinión*, interviewed on Sunday, and began the live-in job the next day, working for a Filipina single mother with two young children. She recalled her interview: "She asked me, 'How old are you? Do you like children?' Well, I've always liked children, so the moment I saw the girls, I started playing with them. They [the girls] wouldn't let me get up!" When the employer saw how Gladys interacted with the children, she hired her on the spot. Gladys now recognizes that she took a low-paying job, but looking back she notes that at the time, "I thought $90 was plenty. Especially compared to what I had been earning in my country, when I worked at Texas Instruments, right?"

Newly arrived immigrant workers are initially willing to take low-paying jobs not only because of their urgent need to begin sending money home but also because they use their society of origin as their point of comparison. Though they recognize that their new wages are lower than those of their peers, the low pay may seem acceptable when they compare it to what they had previously earned in Mexico or El Salvador. Less widely noted is the special attraction that live-in jobs hold for newly arrived immigrant women who need a place to live as desperately as they need income. Like the employers who pay them, newly arrived immigrant women who take live-in jobs may rationalize their subminimum wages by arguing that the job includes "free" room and board.

The women rarely stay at their first live-in job for more than a year or two, even if they are offered raises. With job experience and a reference in hand, as well as the knowledge that better-paying jobs exist, most Latina immigrants will try to locate a better domestic job. Gladys Vargas recalled her treatment by the Filipina single mother for whom she worked as "magnificent"; but when the woman married a man who Gladys believed was sexually molesting the little girls, she quit. By that time, she had brought her youngest daughter from El Salvador; and though she was grateful that her daughter could live with her in the employer's home, she began to fear for her daughter's safety with the employer's new husband in the home. Live-in housekeepers leave their jobs for various reasons—lack of privacy and respect, low wages, long hours, social isolation, disputes, and sexual harassment or the threat of it.

At this point in their job trajectory as domestic workers in Los Angeles, most Latina women try to move up in their careers by finding a nanny/housekeeper job that offers higher pay, better treatment, and shorter workdays. Toward that end, they may consult friends and relatives, newspaper ads, or domestic employment agencies. In the search for better-quality work, there are no guarantees; sometimes they regret leaving a bad job for one that turns out to be worse. Erlinda Castro left her first live-in job after two years—not because of the hours and wages, she said, but because she could no longer withstand the cold, impersonal treatment from her employers. Day and night, she often stood right next to them while they barely acknowledged her existence. A friend told her about an Evangelical family who was searching for a live-in nanny/housekeeper to care for their home and three young children. "It was only $15 more a week, but she told me they [the employers] are really good, they're Evangelicals." This appealed to Erlinda, who had been raised as an Evangelical in Guatemala. She took the job with the understanding that she would primarily be caring for the children, but she found herself in charge of full housecleaning as well; living in a house with almost no food, she said, except for Cheerios and canned tuna fish; and working without limits to her hours. She hated the job, but she felt compelled to remain so that she could build up her references, knowing well that her future earnings would depend on their consistency. "I don't like to just take a job, try it out, and then leave, because then my record is no good," she explained. "I couldn't stand that job, but I put up with it for a year and two months."

Employers, too, view this hiring process as difficult and risky. Families often cannot informally locate full-time nanny/housekeepers, in either live-in or live-out arrangements, as easily as weekly housecleaners. Friends and neighbors can share the same weekly housecleaner, who may clean at one person's home on Monday and at another's on Tuesday, but they cannot share a full-time nanny/housekeeper, who by definition does that job for only one employer at a time. Informal recruitment of nanny/housekeepers therefore may take longer and may require accepting sketchy referrals from strangers. When child care is involved, as it usually is in full-time housekeeper jobs, hiring becomes more complex and trust becomes even more important. Complicating matters further is the scarcity of Latina women looking for live-in jobs. After a few years of working as a live-in, most immigrant women try to move up to better positions, and those who continue to work as live-ins will seek improvements in their wages, hours, and duties. Still, informality prevails in the hiring process.

Employers are more nervous about hiring women to look after their children than to just clean, as parents may imagine the worst. They fear that their children might be physically abused by the nannies (as surveillance videotapes too often displayed on evening news programs demonstrate), that the children might be kidnapped, or that the children will simply languish in front of the television set without proper care. Given these concerns, they put great weight on procuring references from other employers known to them. As one mother put it, if you obtain a nanny reference from a stranger, then "you're calling someone for a reference and you don't know the person's values, right?"

Often the personal references are supplemented with direct observation of the prospective employee's interactions with the children. "You know, with the cleaning lady, I wouldn't say, 'Well go clean my bathroom and I'll see you in half an hour,'" explained Tara

Mostrianni, a homemaker who employed a housecleaner and a nanny/housekeeper, both located through referrals from friends. "But with the children, I really watched the interactions to see how much initiative the person would take in both reaching out to the child and also about being creative in playing with them. You know, if this toy wasn't working, did she reach for another one? Does she sing songs to them? You know, just how much versatility did they show in interacting with the kids?"

Employers prefer informed references supplemented by direct observations when hiring someone for this "labor of love." Like other parents, Tara wanted to hire a warm, loving, creative, enthusiastic woman to care for her children and her home. Most mothers in her situation state that their primary concern is child care, but they are usually interested in hiring a Latina who will also care for their home and clean. Even when they euphemistically refer to employees as "baby-sitters," it is clear that the position involves much more than looking after children. In fact, the ideal baby-sitter may be the energetic cleaner. Tara made this point very directly. "Personality factors are paramount in the baby-sitting situation. I mean, Nilda happens also to love to clean," she clarified. "The personality to me is everything, and Nilda is a good cleaner and has that personality where she doesn't rest. If Monroe is asleep, she washes my kitchen floor or wipes out my refrigerator shelves. There's always something done I can point to. She also doesn't mind folding laundry for me." The right personality for this job is one that is driven to clean. When employers hire Latina immigrants to care for their children in their home, they want trustworthy, loving, enthusiastic care providers who will also be energetic, thorough, versatile cleaners and will do laundry and perhaps some cooking too. Ideally, they want a person who speaks English and can read, but those abilities may be less important.

Regardless of their specific criteria, parents who know other people who hire nanny/housekeepers have a distinct advantage in meeting them. When Karla Steinheimer, a busy executive in the entertainment industry, began looking for a nanny/housekeeper, she was still pregnant. She knew of a friend who would soon be sending her own child to nursery school and laying off her nanny, Filomina. While her friend was shooting a movie in Italy for six weeks, she left her child home with the nanny, and during this period Karla visited several times. She implicitly trusted her friend's judgment, but she also wanted to see firsthand how the nanny/housekeeper acted with the child. When she saw that "the little girl was in her arms and crawling all over her as Filomina was talking to me," she decided to hire her. The referral from her friend and, just as important, her personal observation of the nanny engaged in affectionate play and care made her decide that Filomina was "the one."

Even employers with incomes in the stratosphere, people for whom agency fees were no concern, often preferred to recruit by informal word of mouth. One such employer, Bonnie Feinstein, who had substantial experience in hiring domestic help, agreed that "The best way to do it is to have a personal reference, you know, where people know them." She too, however, wanted to observe these women closely before hiring them, adding that it was important to see "their manners and their warmth."

For those looking for child care, going outside of one's personal social network is seen as risky, but at times it is necessary. Ellen Maxson, who worked part-time, turned up no leads when she began using her neighborhood contacts to find a part-time nanny/house-keeper to work Monday through Friday, for four hours each day. No one seemed willing to work part-time for hours that would preclude other employment, at what was perceived as a relatively low wage ($5 an hour, the same as her neighbors paid their full-time help). Most Latina immigrants know that they can earn more than twice that hourly wage by cleaning houses. Frustrated, Ellen reluctantly placed a newspaper ad and hired a young Mexican woman. Without a recommendation from a trusted source, brief direct observations of the employee playing with the children may not be enough to quash parental fears; new strategies for protection may seem necessary. "One of my concerns is hiring people who might steal my baby and if you're not falling through a network and you're going anonymous in a newspaper," she said, "how do you assure yourself?" As she rhetorically posed this question in our interview, Ellen began crying. Tearfully, she disclosed the surveillance measures she had devised to protect herself and her family in the absence of the trust inspired by informal networks.

"I got all her information . . . and I took her picture," she laughed, with embarrassment. "I handed her a glass of water and I kept it and didn't wash it so I'd have her fingerprints, and I drove her home to her house where she was staying with her sister, so I knew where she lived." She also took photos of her holding the baby, claiming that she was just finishing up a roll of film, but all the while intending to save the photos for criminal identification, should the need arise. Ellen Maxson worked in her home office while the nanny was there, but she remained cautious. "I wouldn't let her take the baby out of the house for the first two weeks. She couldn't go for a walk around the block." These surveillance measures did not go unnoticed by the nanny/housekeeper. "Later, she said to her sister and repeated it for me, 'This lady thinks I'm gonna steal her baby.' But what could I do? I just felt panic about it, even though I was gonna be there." In the culture of fear that permeates parenthood in the United States today, even parents who are home when the nanny is with the children feel apprehensive and vulnerable when they lack referrals from their network.

As already noted, most Latina immigrants in Los Angeles do not remain in their first live-in job for long. With job experience, some English language facility, and good employer references in hand, those searching for better nanny/housekeeper jobs may turn to a domestic employment agency. Over time, many women, especially those with their own families in Los Angeles, seek alternatives to full-time domestic work.[2] Job options for Latina immigrants in Los Angeles, where factory employment may bring in less money than domestic work, are scarce and unappealing. For this reason, many women who begin as live-in nanny/housekeepers try to move into weekly housecleaning. The potential earnings in housecleaning are higher than the average pay in live-in and live-out jobs, and usually the work hours are fewer and far more flexible.

HOUSECLEANERS: FINDING *CASAS*

Breaking into housecleaning work and getting enough *casas* (houses) to fill the workweek is difficult and sometimes takes several years. Unlike the job search for a live-in or live-out position, which requires securing only one job, the search for housecleaning jobs is an unending process, as full employment requires numerous *casas*. Here, too, network resources are crucial, and successful housecleaners are constantly drawing on their network affiliations. Below, I discuss cleaners who successfully tapped the employer networks to ensure a full-time income from cleaning different houses, and several others who were struggling to achieve a full route of *casas*. I also examine the networks from the perspective of the employers.

Women who seek housecleaning jobs need employer referrals, but finding that first job is a challenge. Some women who decide to stop doing domestic work for only one employer turn to the domestic employment agencies as they seek enough houses to support them, but the agencies are rarely helpful.[3] Housecleaners also report that a woman who is leaving the occupation or perhaps returning to her country of origin may charge someone beginning the job for access to her clientele. "Not long ago," reported Erlinda Castro, "a woman asked me if I didn't want to buy a route of five or six houses, and she wanted $500!" Although Latino and Asian immigrant men working as private gardeners and landscapers engage in similar practices, relatively few women, especially Latina immigrant women leaving live-in jobs, have $500 to invest in the promise of future employment. In all my interviews and informal conversations with housecleaners, I never met anyone who had purchased an entire route of houses. Still, breaking into housecleaning may require some initial financial resources, including other sources of income or family support until full employment is reached.

Once a woman obtains a steady employer, she benefits from the possibility—but no guarantee—that the job will snowball into more referrals and more jobs. Most women wish to maximize their earnings by maximizing their number of jobs. In part because the turnover of employers was unpredictable, few women had as many jobs as they could handle. An exception in this regard was Lupe Vélez, a fifty-three-year-old Mexicana who had a thriving route of houses to clean. The shape of her career was slightly different from that of the newer cohorts of immigrant women. She came to Los Angeles in the 1970s, and before marrying she had worked on a crew that cleaned brand-new tract homes. Later, to accommodate family obligations when her children were young, she had worked in the evenings, cleaning high-rise offices for a janitorial firm. With all her children in school, she decided to break into housecleaning, where she might earn much more money but would need to secure multiple employers. Although she initially faced some obstacles to becoming an independent housecleaner, she now had plenty of jobs. Monday through Saturday, she drove her Toyota to clean homes all over the sprawling San Gabriel Valley, earning approximately $300 a week as a *limpiadora,* or cleaner. She and her husband, a welder, were homeowners in East Los Angeles, and her five children were attending high school and college. "My biggest dream," she said, "is that they study so they won't have to work as I do."

For Lupe, getting referrals through the employer networks ensured both the quality and the quantity of her jobs. When she was first starting out, she learned from experience the risks of taking jobs from complete strangers. "At that time, I was only working two days, and I was desperate. So I decided to have some cards printed up," she recalled. She had placed these on doorsteps in middle-class and upper-middle-class neighborhoods. "Yes," she sighed, "some call you, but you get inside strangers' houses. Once, I got into this house where the *señora* didn't know me, but she trusted me. I went, and she told me to return tomorrow, that she would leave the key under the mat and $40. I went, but as soon as I stepped in the door, I couldn't clean the house. It was so dirty! The bathrooms had old bottles of shampoo, left since God knows when, dirty papers by the toilets, mountains of it! It was just exaggeratedly dirty!" she exclaimed. "I went, but couldn't do it, so I left the money and came home."

"Another time," she continued, "I went to a house where the people had their hair dyed all different colors, purple, orange. You know which kind I mean, right? Well, I thought, '*Ay Señor!* No!' And I began thinking that it's really dangerous to go to a house where you don't know the people, to leave cards who knows where." Reliance on the employer networks contributes to financial as well as personal security. Lupe told me, "I've never had problems with people not paying me. Since I only take jobs with people who've been recommended to me, they are known persons (*personas conocidas*)." Just as employers suspected that new housecleaners without references from their acquaintances might be unreliable or even dangerous, so too successful housecleaners such as Lupe Vélez avoided taking jobs from new employers who lacked connections to known employers. After her initial forays with the cards, Lupe had always relied on referrals, never radio or newspaper ads, agencies, or her own friends or relatives. Over time, she had become adept at using the employer networks. "It's easy to find new houses. I've figured it out by now," she explained. "When I see that I'm losing a house, and that I need another, I ask my employers if they know someone they can refer me to." She was currently facing the loss of her Tuesday house, but she had already put the word out; and one evening while we talked in her living room, I overheard three telephone inquiries from prospective employers, which her teenage daughter, fluent in English, helped mediate.

Lupe faced the enviable and almost unheard-of prospect of having a surplus of *casas*. Her thorough, expert cleaning, her strategy of rarely turning down a job, and her constant cultivation of employer referrals had brought her such success that the only way for her to expand her earnings would have been to take on a helper. Her teenage daughters urged her to do so; but though jobless and underemployed friends often asked to clean alongside her or to pass along a house referral, she refused because she did not want to risk damaging her good reputation among the employers. "I talk to my friends a lot about my work, and many have said, 'Oh, pass me a house! Invite me to work alongside you!' But I don't like to bring along someone to help me because it's not that much money for two people," she said. "I also don't like to recommend other people," she added, "because you don't know what's going to happen, and you are the one responsible. So they may have the need, but I'm not going to recommend them, because then I'm going to look bad."

Other women who were desperately searching for new housecleaning jobs complained about people like Lupe Vélez. Gladys Villeda, a Salvadoran nanny/housekeeper who had briefly tried getting into weekly housecleaning, recalled her frustrations: "It's really difficult [to find *casas*]. We ourselves, Latinos, we're eating each other up! Perhaps someone has the opportunity to tell someone about a job, but no, they prefer to see that person lose an opportunity, so they say nothing. No, nothing!" But she also recognized the dynamics of references and reputations. As she continued to speak, she shifted her narrative perspective to empathize with a housecleaner who doesn't wish to risk her reputation. "Perhaps people do that also because they don't really know that person's background, and how they work, right? Because they can't honestly say [to the employer], 'I know how this person works.' Then when that person is on the job, they'll call you to say that the person is not working out, and then what do you say? See, how do you explain that?"

Erlinda Castro, a Guatemalan woman and mother of five children, four of whom still lived in Guatemala, had been in Los Angeles for nine years. She initially worked as live-in nanny/housekeeper, but she had spent the previous three years building up a housecleaning route. When I interviewed her, she was finally enjoying an abundance of jobs. Women who are just beginning work as a housecleaner are in a precarious position; like many others, Erlinda had covered herself during this period both by relying on her husband's income and by improvising various other income-earning activities. On days when there were no houses to clean, she kept busy working, but as an undocumented immigrant her opportunities were limited. She had bought and sold cosmetics, Tupperware, and crystal in various pyramid schemes, and she had purchased women's clothing and lingerie wholesale in the downtown garment district, which she then sold door-to-door. On Sundays, she had cooked huge batches of tamales and phoned friends and acquaintances to see who might want to purchase one or two dozen, which she would then deliver, driven by her husband. Even though she was now reaping the benefits of her carefully cultivated informal job-finding networks, she still clung circumspectly to a part-time job working at a child care center two evenings a week. Erlinda maintained that "the best jobs you can find are those recommended by friends. Through the agencies, no. At the agencies, you need letters of reference, this thing and the other, Social Security cards, and all that. When you're recommended [through employer acquaintances], it's enough for them to say, 'She cleans for me. She's been cleaning for me for one year. She's honest.' And there you go!"

Network contacts, or lack of them, can make you or break you. Erlinda attributed her recent success in finding houses to luck, but she also talked at length about her affiliation with one employer, a Korean woman. Although Young Song paid only the relatively modest sum of $40, she provided the extremely valuable service of referring Erlinda to many different housecleaning jobs. Consequently, each day Erlinda boarded public buses bound for the homes of Korean families living throughout the sprawl of Los Angeles County, from the San Gabriel Valley to the bluffs overlooking the Pacific Ocean. Erlinda cherished her job with Young, not because she paid particularly well but because she was friendly to her and, equally important, because she regularly passed along the choicest referrals.

She explained that Young went out of her way to help Erlinda do better at new jobs. "Well, she is really good, because she never, never says to the others [employers] how much she pays me. Never. And she said this to me, 'You charge for your work.' Ay, and then she'll tell me, 'Oh, this one is a millionaire,' she'll say. 'You'll go work with my friend, and she has a lot of money. You charge for your work.'"

But Erlinda Castro was well aware of how referrals through employer network could quickly make the already bad conditions of housecleaning jobs worse. She lived with her cousin and the two spoke frequently about their jobs. Erlinda described at length her cousin's lamentable housecleaning jobs, for which she blamed both her cousin and one particular employer in her cousin's network. "Last night I told her," she explained, "you're to blame, because you say to her, 'Oh, *Señora* Susan, I really urgently need the money.' But no! One shouldn't say those things. We're all here out of necessity. But if you tell her, 'Ay, I really need the money,' then she's going to take advantage of you. And then she tells someone else that."

Erlinda also faulted her cousin for allowing her employer to pass along information about her pay when referring her to new housecleaning jobs. "A Mexican American woman gave her her first house. ... Then she said to another friend, an Anglo-Saxon, 'Oh, Soñia needs houses. She washes clothes, irons, and cleans, all for $40.' 'Okay, send Soñia.' So then Soñia goes with that one. That other friend says to another Anglo-Saxon, 'The girl I have working for me washes, irons, cooks, and charges $40,'" she mimicked in a sing-songy voice. "Well, in one month, she got together seven houses!" Erlinda tried to advise her cousin and put her on the right path. "So I said to her, 'You should have told her that she doesn't have to put a price on your work. If someone tells me they want me to work for $40 for them, well, okay, it's up to me to take it or not, right?'"

While Erlinda Castro strongly urged her cousin and other women to work against such exchanges of information in the employer networks, they were in no position to insist on silence. The jobs are volatile, and domestic workers remain vulnerable to employers' whims; jobs may disappear when employers go on vacation, remodel their house, or decide that they can no longer afford to pay for the service. At the same time, Latina domestic workers have bills that need to be paid. Housecleaners accommodate themselves to these conditions by constantly seeking and maintaining a sufficient number of jobs. For them the job search is not an occasional chore or a finite precursor to work, but an ongoing part of the job itself.[4]

THE EMPLOYERS' SEARCH

"I really depended on the recommendations from people who I respected, and I wanted somebody," said one employer, "who I could trust in the house." As we have seen, people looking to hire someone to clean their house typically do so by approaching friends, kin, coworkers, or neighbors who are currently employing a housecleaner. Employers pursue referrals in various settings. Describing their searches, they said, "If you need somebody, then you get on the phone," or "You run into somebody in the grocery store"; or perhaps they tried "just asking friends if they knew of somebody who was good and available."

Such informal referrals are certainly cheaper and often faster than placing an ad or going through an employment agency. I found that domestic employment agencies in Los Angeles generally charge the employers, at minimum, the equivalent of one month of the employee's pay for their placement services. Some people turn to commercial cleaning services, but many find these unsatisfactory. Informal referrals and individual cleaners are preferred because they offer less expensive and more customized cleaning than do the established businesses.[5] The employers also prefer personal referrals because they believe this the best method for ensuring that they find a reliable, trustworthy cleaner.

In these searches, people rely on what they know about the integrity and personal characteristics of the person who is making the referral. They look particularly at the referring employer's home, which is also an indicator of how the domestic worker handles her job at the work site; simply looking at the children also provides important information about the housecleaner or housekeeper/ nanny. Some have even met the domestic worker at the home of the referring employer. Although such encounters are more common when child care is involved, Heidi Gustaf reported that when searching for a new housecleaner, she will casually arrange to "stop by and meet them" at her friend's home. "I had gotten to know Erma little by little," recounted Alice McCoy-Fishman, "so I just chitchatted with her while she was house-sitting next door. And I met Elena a couple of times up at the Morgans because she helps when they have parties." On these "drop by" visits, the employer is most interested in observing the prospective employee's demeanor and appearance. They do not watch the woman scrub or vacuum, both because they already have information on her job performance and because they feel uncomfortable and sometimes guilty at watching the housecleaner work.

As many who have studied private, paid domestic work have observed, employers are keenly interested in the personalities of their employees.[6] I found that regardless of whether they are looking for child care or solely for housecleaning, employers take into account the character not only of the employee but also of the referring employer, as they believe that this information will help them predict the domestic worker's job performance. Kathy Kelly, a forty-two-year-old homemaker with three young children, recalled obtaining a cleaning referral from a German woman whom she barely knew, but whom she described as a "very demanding and just a big pain-in-the-neck lady." As she put it, "She's the one I asked because I thought, 'Well, if they can put up with her, they can put with any amount of anything.' " At the time, she implied, she could not afford to pay well or otherwise be accommodating as an employer. "I was pregnant and I was very desperate, but I also didn't have a lot of money."

Conversely, Kathy recalled her shock that others did not pay such careful attention to the referring employer's character, child-rearing practices, and household: "I've had people stop me on the street. This lady was new in the neighborhood, came over and said she liked my car or something. She asked me if I knew of a housekeeper and I gave her the name of that lady that was slow but loved the kids and she said great and called her up. She started working like the next day. That was weird! She [the neighbor] didn't even go in my house. She had no idea what my life was like." In this case, despite the lack of information on the "known employer" and her home, the employer referral system was still effective. Kathy's story and those of other employers make it clear that what matters most is the personal contact (however fleeting) with the "known employer," who appears to vouch for the domestic worker's integrity and performance.

In part, contact with the known employer becomes so significant because of the context and the conditions in which the employee will perform her work—not in, say, a manufacturing firm or restaurant, but in private homes. For employers of weekly housecleaners, who typically work unsupervised and alone, trust and honesty emerged as key themes. When asked, "What is the most important quality you look for in hiring someone to clean your home?" most employers said something like, "Making sure you can trust her—that's the highest priority on my list." They were particularly worried about the theft of household items.

Employers of housecleaners emphasized that personal referrals enabled them to almost take for granted the trustworthiness and honesty of the domestic worker. As Rosamaria Stranski, a Mexican American administrator who had recently hired a housecleaner, said, "I would never hire anyone for cleaning who had not been recommended because of course, you know, they can be [cleaning] there when you're not [home] and there is always the fear that you're going to come home and there'll be nothing left." These women recognize that references from strangers might very well be bogus. "You have no way of knowing who it is you're phoning," noted a skeptical Julie Thompson-Ahib. "You phone, you ask how long they've worked, and you get all the right answers. I don't think people are up-front in the blind referrals." And Rita Hamilton, a veteran employer who had been hiring housecleaners for forty years, said, "I have never called an agency because I have always preferred working with people where I know the [person providing the] reference. People can walk into your house and say, 'Here are my references,' but it's like hiring anybody. You have to be very alert.

Network hires inspire automatic trust. At the point of hiring and when employment first begins, this trust—so necessary when a housecleaner works unsupervised and alone—derives more from familiarity between employers than familiarity between employer and employee. The only male employer interviewed, Jeffrey Weinstock, underscored this point in describing the hiring of his housecleaner. "We were sold on her right away, just from the reference we got and we needed someone," he recalled. "We were told that she was very trustworthy, and that's actually an interesting thing to me," he reflected. "There is a high level of trust. I mean, you give people, basically strangers, a key to your home—and we didn't even know her last name for the first four years that she worked for us." He was not alone in this. "I've talked to a lot of other people who are in a similar situation. They don't know where their housekeeper lives or their full name. Sometimes they don't even have a phone number and yet they turn over the key to the house and everything."

Here the personal referral from the known employer assumes tremendous significance precisely because the domestic worker remains relatively anonymous, perhaps even nameless, to her employers. Although Jeffrey spoke of the efforts of his housecleaner with genuine appreciation, and concretely expressed more concern about his housecleaner's well-being than had other employers I interviewed, his comment emphasizes the odd pairing of trust and distance. Referrals through employer networks make possible this seeming contradiction.

KEY CREDENTIALS: NETWORK REFERRALS

In the formal sector of the labor market, employee referrals are uncommon; the "references" for prospective employees typically come from strangers—usually former employers—who are themselves not known by the new employer. The integrity of the reference is verified by the position that the employer holds within a company or business. Since paid domestic work occurs in private residential settings, where the employers have no standard occupational status or institutional titles, this kind of anonymous reference is not feasible.

Employers who had had negative experiences with domestic workers not hired from known employers felt very strongly that the referral system protected them from the transgressions of housecleaners. Tara Mostrianni, a homemaker with two young children, recalled the first time that she hired a housecleaner, when she had responded to a flyer left in her mailbox by an Eastern European woman. She ultimately fired the woman when she suspected her of stealing jewelry. Tara said that now she would hire only through what she called a "personal referral." "The second time, I wanted to be really sure I had a referral," she explained. "With the personal referral you have some insight into their honesty and work habits. You know, do they show up on time? Do they work hard? Do they know not to put oven cleaner on your range top, not to put Brillo on a shining, clear, polished chrome surface?" She believed that "that referral gets you a long way. You have another satisfied customer who's already saying they're pleased with this person's work." Currently she employed both a Mexican woman who cleaned weekly and a Guatemalan woman who came three days a week to look after her two boys and do general housekeeping. She had found both through personal contacts: The referral for the cleaner came, she said, from "someone who I'd only met at a couple of parties but I had been to their home and I knew that she would be extremely particular."

Having worked for a known employer emerges as a key credential of a potential job candidate. The new employer knows little about the employee at the point of hiring, and indeed may not learn much even after several years of continuous employment; it is the trustworthiness of the known employer, transferred to the employee, that forms the basis for trust in the new employer-employee relationship.

CROSS-CLASS LATINA LINKAGES

Latina employers may bypass both the "known employer" hiring route and more formal recruitment because they can reach a wide range of prospective employees directly. Despite their relatively high socioeconomic status, the five Latina employers whom I interviewed still maintained ties with communities of lower-income Latinas, which enabled more immediate access to networks of housecleaners than that enjoyed by the Anglo-American or Jewish employers. The Latinas I interviewed found domestic workers through family, work, church, and community contacts; and once they employed someone, they usually passed along referrals to neighbors and co-workers.

"She was a friend of my aunt's who is very involved with her church that has a lot of Hispanic members," reported a young, single Chicana lawyer who had her house cleaned biweekly. Virginia Lopez, a Mexican American retired teacher who had taught English as a second language to immigrants, said that she had used her classroom to find and screen housecleaners for herself and for her adult daughters and friends. Cross-class interactions and community ties among Mexican American women and Mexican immigrant women facilitated recruitment and hiring.

EMPLOYERS' INFORMATIONAL EXCHANGES AND OMISSIONS: STRUCTURING THE "GOING RATE"

Employers told me that they devoted little time to discussing among friends their paid housecleaners or their cleaning arrangements, citing various reasons that typically derived from their social positions and identities. Some women, especially those holding liberal or progressive political views, seemed too embarrassed or ashamed to discuss the topic. "We don't talk about it a lot," said Eleanor Zabrinsky. "We talk about it as little as possible—'our help,' you know?" Homemakers, too, rarely spoke of it among friends. As one put it, "Really, there's not much reference to housekeeping. . . . I mean, we don't sit around and talk about the housekeeper."

Women who worked as teachers, nurses, or administrative assistants said they felt "a bit embarrassed" to disclose to less-affluent colleagues that they employed housecleaners. Vicki Gosset, an African American nurse married to a physician, recalled what happened at the hospital where she worked: "I mentioned it once, and I felt like I was bragging or boastful. [Afterward] I felt like I couldn't really talk about that, that I hired somebody to come in and clean my house." More affluent women also said they didn't discuss it much, but for different reasons. Louise Lowinger, an art gallery owner and mother of three grown children, said flatly: "I hate to say this to you, but it really isn't a subject that [we discuss] unless I'm in need or they're in need. . . . I mean, as long as somebody does it, I don't want to think about it."

When new housecleaners or nanny/housekeepers are needed, then employers break this pattern and actually discuss "the help." The referral system requires that people talk at the point of recruitment and hiring about things usually not mentioned; once the domestic workers are hired, employers again retreat to silence, murmuring only occasionally about the personal lives or betrayals (theft or quitting) of their employees. Approaching the topic instrumentally, employers discuss what they perceive to be the essential subjects when referring a housecleaner: the price, the quality of her work, and her reliability. As Ann Evans explained, "We would simply discuss whether they were good cleaners, whether they were pretty reliable people, if they would show up when they said, and what they cost." Honesty and integrity are taken for granted, as qualities embedded in the employer referral system itself.

As Kathy Kelly listed the kinds of information exchanged in a staccato, no-nonsense style, tapping one index finger into the palm of her other hand for emphasis, she stressed the practical: "Everybody always tells you how much they pay—always. It's like right up there in the first four questions or the first four statements or something. 'Yeah, I have a great person. I pay her *x*. She's wonderful. She does this, this, this.'" Other women echoed that when they or their friends were searching for new housecleaners, they would seek similar information. Evelyn Potts summarized, "They would say, 'What does she do for you? How often does she come? What do you pay her? Is her English adequate to communicate with her?' That's about it." Nelly Foster said that if she were looking for someone to hire and heard "somebody say 'I've got an awfully good girl,' well, [I'll ask] 'How much does she charge?'" And Norine Christophe said that how much the referring employer was paying "would always be one of my first questions. I'd ask them because then that gave me a base of what she expected to receive."

These employer referrals thus do more than help provide cleaning services: the employers are sharing information that is vital to structuring the job, as the hiring decisions of individuals are informed by what their friends tell them about their own domestic arrangements. People who are hiring full-time nanny/housekeepers also make it a point to find out what their peers are paying, even if they have been unable to locate the job applicants via an employer network. Candace Ross, for example, recalled how she had set pay when she first hired a live-in nanny/housekeeper: "I checked that [what neighbors were paying] out, and um, I found a real range. I found a range that went $125 a week on up to like $200, so we started her at $150, which would have been, in my opinion, a very good deal."

Contributing to low pay levels is a general assumption that those who work more days will tolerate a lower hourly pay. Carolyn Astor told me that she had initially paid her nanny/housekeeper $65 a day, two days a week, because that is what her in-laws paid the same woman; but when she added a third day a week, she lowered the daily pay to $60. Although Ellen Maxson had not gone through an employer network to hire her nanny/housekeeper, she did go to the employer network to counter the employee's request for a raise. "I had gone to all the neighbors and all my friends and said, 'What do you do, how many hours do you work, what do you make?' And I wrote it all down for her, handed it to her, and said, 'You know, I want to do what's fair and I fall in this line, so I think, you know, I'm fair.'"

Payment is one key area of job standardization. By exchanging information, employers actively create what comes to be known as the "going rate." Although the rates themselves are never uniform, employers share the perception that a set of particular practices and pay level constitute a correct "standard." Typically, a new employer follows the payment guidelines provided by the referring employer. "It was standard in the neighborhood, what everyone was paying then," recalled Eleanor Zabrinsky. "You know, we compared notes and that's what people got." Even Rita Hamilton, who believed that she deliberately paid on the high end of the range, explained that inquiring about pay, tasks, and hours was important in determining her own arrangements, because "then you have some kind of metric." I asked the interviewees if their friends had recommended that they pay a certain level. Nearly all said "No," no one in their circle had advised a specific rate; nor had anyone urged them to pay below or above a particular wage ceiling. They claimed that they paid the same as their friends because "it just happens." In fact, "it happens" because their shared information creates and legitimizes the going rate.

When I interviewed them in the mid-1990s, most employers were paying $50 to $60 per housecleaning. Only one of the respondents, the one man interviewed, said he offered a regular, annual raise. Most respondents who had employed domestic workers over many years had gradually increased the pay; but other than Jeffrey Weinstock, none did so at regular intervals—and two admitted to never offering pay raises. Pay increases sometimes resulted from requests and negotiations by the domestic workers, and sometimes were initiated by the employers.[7]

In most jobs in the formal sector, long employment tenure is rewarded with higher pay. In domestic work, on the contrary, because of the absence of regular pay increases, lower pay rates may prevail precisely *because* employees stay in the same job. Moreover, the network hiring processes helps keep earnings low for the newly hired as well. A domestic worker who takes a new job in 1999 often carries with her a pay rate inherited from a job that began in 1989. In effect, a long-term employer may receive a discount as a reward for providing steady employment, and the employer's friend who has received information about the employee's pay may enjoy this discount as well. To be sure, the employer referral system does not reproduce pay scales precisely. The new employer may elect to pay slightly more or less than the referring employer, and the domestic worker may agree to these terms. Two employers who share the same employee may also deliberately raise her pay after the second hires her, though this practice appears to be rare, since employers prefer not to discuss these matters unless soliciting or offering a referral.

Not all employers follow the implicit guidelines embedded in the shared information, and those who offered pay considered too generous sometimes faced social sanctions from other employers in their social circle. None of the respondents told me of resenting or sanctioning their friends for paying too well, but such behavior, if they were not too embarrassed to admit it, may have conveniently slipped their mind. Several employers vividly recalled being accused of pushing upward the pay rates or benefits. For example, Rita Hamilton recalled that "One friend stopped me after church and said, 'You are ruining it for everybody else.' And I said, innocently, 'Why, what do mean, Joan?' She said, 'You're paying them more than anybody else and you're giving them two weeks' [vacation] pay and nobody else is doing that.' And I said, 'Well, I'm not going to not do it, so why don't you all think about doing it?'" Other employers shared memories of similar incidents:

> I have one friend who thinks we are outrageous because we pay too much, and that doesn't influence what we pay. I have another acquaintance who has someone who works twice a week and I finally got the courage up to ask how much she pays and she pays a third less for somebody who works two days a week and I thought that was awful and they aren't such good friends anymore. They were probably on the verge of not being good friends anyway.
>
> Louise Lowinger

> My sister used to get bent out of shape because she really can't afford to have a housekeeper. . . . She [my sister] thought that if she worked for four hours, then she should give her twenty dollars. . . .

We had many discussions about that and I was like, "I don't care if it takes her five minutes, if she does it that good, she gets paid."

Kathy Kelly

Well she [the landlady] confronted me with this bad behavior on my part, that [by paying two or three times more after moving from the Northeast to the South] I was upsetting the status quo and that I was doing something that would be very uncomfortable to contend with. Oh, she was angry!

Eleanor Zabrinsky

When an employer raises pay beyond the norm, she risks incurring the wrath of friends, neighbors, and relatives who also employ domestic workers. In the most extreme cases, friendships—usually casual ones—were jeopardized. Rita Hamilton proudly told me, "We always paid more, and we still do. . . . And so if somebody is working for me who is working for other friends, I'm in trouble with friends." While offering higher pay may pressure others to pay more, deliberately withholding key information or referrals may be even more effective.

The information that the employers do not share among themselves is nearly as important as what they do. When I asked if they knew about the legal status of the housecleaners, a topic treated at length in national media only months before our interviews, one woman said, "I don't think anyone really cares"; indeed, with two exceptions, the others agreed. An employer seeking a full-time nanny/housekeeper will ask about her language facility and her family situation because these factors can directly affect her ability to perform her work and keep her job schedule. The employers also said that they and their peers generally do not describe racial or ethnic markers, though the dominance of Latina immigrant women in the occupation in Los Angeles makes any mention of race irrelevant. As Virginia Lopez said, "It's a foregone conclusion" [that they will be Latina]; an Anglo homemaker echoed, "The assumption is she will be Hispanic," while another offered: "Well, let's see, her name is Maria Luz. Okay, I kind of figured it out." The question of years of experience on the job, standard information given to prospective employers in other fields, was also ignored. Such disinterest both derives from and fuels the notion of paid domestic work as a low-skilled, low-status job without prerequisites—an unskilled job that "anyone can do."

But an even more significant omission is the failure to disclose how the referring employers act in their capacity as employers. The only information shared (and then only at the point of hiring) pertains to payment; in all other respects, the vast majority of people know nothing about the practices of others. They often do not know if their friends are home or out while the cleaning occurred, or how they go about asking for or scheduling special cleaning tasks. Most important, they do not know how their friends define and fulfill their obligations as employers. As they refer housecleaners to one another, the employers rarely mention the employer's obligations and the employee's benefits.

Paying employment taxes is one such obligation. Four of the employers interviewed, who were either likely to fall under public scrutiny or who were vaguely connected to federal politics, filed Social Security, workers' compensation, and federal income tax payments after the Zoë Baird debacle; one other had done so in the past, when she was married to an attorney. Many of the other respondents offered more immediate, informal benefits, of the sort that are traditional in the occupation—Christmas presents, paid vacation days, leftover food as well as special food items, and used clothes or furniture.[8] Most of them, however, reported that they did not tell other employers about these practices, even when making referrals.

In some cases, they suggested that they were reluctant to set precedents. When I asked Laura Jaspers, "Has there ever been any information about a cleaning woman that you consciously withheld from one of your friends when you've given a referral?" she said, "With Goya, I just withheld that I got so involved with it [helping her] because that's a topic that might scare somebody away. 'Well, on every weekend you have to take her here and there and the other place.' I probably didn't mention that." Later, when I asked if she omitted information about gifts, she implied that this was a personal choice, and that it might be too maternalistic to pass along such information: "No, I would never discuss that with anybody. That's my thing. You know, if Josefa wants to work for somebody else who doesn't give her a Christmas present, that's between them. That's not my business. I've never said anything about that kind of stuff." Emma Toledo Wilson routinely gave "a bag of goodies" (food items), but she didn't mention this practice when passing along referrals to other employers because she saw it as a personal decision: "That's up to them."

Employers saw these as private matters, not topics for open discussion. Eleanor Zabrinsky paid one or two vacation days a year to her weekly housecleaner, but when I asked if this was discussed in referral exchanges, she said, "No, I don't ask and they don't say. I don't know. I think some people are stingy and some people are generous." In her view, the decision to pay vacation days reflected the employer's personality not a business practice. Similarly, Candace Ross did not tell other employers that she paid for holidays and vacations: "No, I figured that was a private matter." Evelyn Potts mentioned to her friends that she had sponsored her housecleaner for legal permanent residency and offered paid vacation, but she did not advise that prospective employers make vacation pay part of the job arrangement.

There were a few significant exceptions to this practice of omitting information about job benefits. Alice McCoy-Fishman and her husband Barry, both full-time employed professionals, began paying the legally mandated withholding tax after Baird's failed nomination. A discussion at a dinner party with two neighbors, men who worked in high-profile, public positions—one as a judge and the other as a well-known newspaper columnist—had helped motivate them. Alice told me, "He [the judge] just said you have to do it . . . that was a conversation between Barry and him. So I didn't really have anything to do with it." As we talked about employment taxes, many interviewees quipped, "Well, I guess I can never be attorney general"; but Alice, her husband, and her neighbors were possible future candidates for high-level federal posts or potential targets of media attention.

The selective exchanges and omissions among employers have significant effects. By circulating information on pay and on the character of domestic workers, employer networks help standardize wages and enable employers to screen housecleaners for honesty, initiative, and reliability. Yet their routine failure to discuss employer practices ultimately helps reproduce the notion that employers of domestic workers do not have the same obligations as other kinds of employers.

WITHHOLDING REFERRALS AND PAY INFORMATION:
HELPING THE WORKER OR SAVING FACE?

Not all employers traded so freely in information about employees. A minority of those interviewed told me that when referring domestic workers to their friends, they had deliberately withheld pay information, or they had selectively refrained from passing referrals to people they believed to be abusive employers.

One woman who adamantly and consistently withheld pay information from her friends was Erin Caldwell, a white lesbian who had been active in the civil rights movement in the South during the 1960s. When Erin's friends needed to hire someone, they knew they could approach her for a referral, but she disclosed information sparingly: "In trying to come up with other positions for Lita, I tell people that she's a very good businesswoman, that she will negotiate her own price, and that she will prefer to be paid in cash." She emphasized that she never disclosed what she herself was paying, even if asked.

Another woman who also withheld pay information when referring her housecleaner to others worked part-time giving private piano lessons. Dorine Weismann explained that her own pay had been reduced when the parents of her pupils told prospective clients of her rates. Her own experiences working as a piano teacher, she said, encouraged her to keep such information to herself: "It's really up to me to say this is what I charge rather than somebody maybe coming and saying, 'Now I understand you charge such and such amount.' . . . It gives me the leeway to raise my rates. . . . So if I was recommending somebody [for housecleaning] I'd prefer to say, 'She'll look at your house and she'll tell you what she'll charge.'"

Perhaps it is significant that Dorine was among the lowest-paying employers that I interviewed; she paid $40 to have her roomy (2,800-square-foot) home cleaned. She had paid that rate to the same housecleaner for ten years, and she may have withheld this information from her peers to spare herself shame and embarrassment. Yet her silence kept her own cleaning costs low without passing on the disadvantage to her housecleaner. Another woman, Emma Toledo Wilson, said that in referring one housecleaner, she had deliberately inflated the pay, in order to increase the housecleaner's future earnings. Rosamaria Stranski, when referring a housecleaner to a coworker, said, "I knew she would charge them more than she charged me so I would just tell them that uh . . . 'I don't know what she'll charge you. It all depends on the size of your house and what you want her to do.' " These respondents expressed their appreciation for their housecleaners by selectively preventing information from circulating in the employer referral system. Their avowed efforts to give the housecleaners a chance at higher earnings also kept down their own housecleaning payments while enabling them to save face in front of their peers.

It is possible that housecleaners submit to these lower rates because they know that these employers will help them find jobs that pay better. Thus indirect benefits for the employees could be won at no financial cost to the employers. There may have been social costs, however; potential employers who received referrals minus the important pay information sometimes felt cheated by their friends. "When I asked her, 'How much are you paying her [the maid],' she said, 'Well, I don't know what she's gonna want to ask you so why don't you negotiate it on your own.' . . . You know, there was some solidarity there with the cleaning woman and that was nice, but I was also a little pissed," Nora Polansky remarked. "Why isn't there solidarity with me?"

Another employer strategy tinged by maternalism that nevertheless can help raise a worker's occupational status is to withhold referrals from people who are "bad employers." This category might include employers who make unreasonable cleaning demands or who routinely insult or humiliate their employees. Some employers echoed an interviewee who volunteered, "Honestly, I almost feel like I have to protect the people who work for me from some of the people I know."

"There are times when I will not recommend somebody, a worker who I know and trust and love to a person or colleague who I think would be difficult," stated Ann Evans. "If somebody literally describes to me that they want someone to use the Q-tip to go around the edges of a picture frame and that they're very dissatisfied with the person they have because she doesn't do that . . . I'm not recommending anyone I know to work for that person." She recalled having recently referred her housecleaner, whom she described as an "agreeable, docile, submissive, thorough, undemanding person," to a neighbor who constantly suspected the cleaner of theft.

Although Ann appeared to be concerned about the domestic worker's mistreatment, she also felt personally insulted—the new employer's suspicion reflected a lack of trust in her as the provider of the referral: "I'm outraged at this. I had told them that she was honest, that she had worked for me for a very long time, and they were putting her through such a humiliating experience . . . so I did go to talk to them." Louise Lowinger described with regret two similar experiences. In one case, she said her housecleaner had been "outraged by the implications of that lady. It was a lady I didn't know very well. . . . I would be cautious [in making another referral] because I wouldn't want Lupe to get hurt again."

These responses, though inflected with maternalism, suggest yet another means by which employers can improve the status of the occupation. By deliberately excluding extremely demanding or abusive employers from their network referrals, they reduce their housecleaner's exposure to employment practices perceived as objectionable; at the same time, they protect their own interests, as they enhance the probability of keeping their housecleaner.

This chapter has shown how social relations among employers and among employees undergird and shape economic transactions in paid domestic work. In addition to the vertical employer-employee relationships, horizontal ties among employees and particularly among employers play an important role in private domestic employment. The labor market for paid domestic work in Los Angeles is largely constituted through these social relations, thereby illustrating the sociologist Mark Granovetter's claim that economic activity is embedded in structures of social relations, even in contemporary postindustrial society.[9] An entire school of thought, "economic sociology," has been inspired by this important observation.

Social relations fulfill their obvious, intended purposes: facilitating recruitment, screening, and hiring. Personal referrals exchanged among employers enable new employers to trust Latina nanny/housekeepers and housecleaners with their homes and their children. They also make possible new opportunities for malfeasance, as Granovetter puts it, but these are reined in by socially embedded trust. At the point of hiring, however, the exchanges of information through these employer networks also have unintended consequences, shaping job terms and the going rate of pay. They help explain persistent job patterns—wages, tasks, and the absence of legal benefits—in paid domestic work.

At the same time, there is little exchange of information about *employer* obligations, such as employment taxes or benefits, in part because, as Mary Romero has rightly observed, employers of domestic workers "refuse to see their homes as a place of employment."[10] Hiring practices that rely on informal social networks perpetuate this view. That employers routinely fail to mention what they actually do with respect to taxes and benefits encourages the belief that employers of domestic workers have no such obligations.

As they set pay for housecleaners and nanny/housekeepers, employers do not consult any official guidelines, relying instead primarily on peer information. In a job that is conducted by workers separated in isolated households, and that remains effectively outside the purview of legal regulations, the information exchanged between employers who are friends, neighbors, and co-workers is a powerful—though not omnipotent—force in defining the terms of work. Paid domestic workers, as previous research and some of my interviews indicate, often actively and creatively negotiate over payment and the limits of the job.[11] They may work hard to avoid accepting low-paying jobs, berating their friends and relatives who work in private homes for what they perceive as very low pay; and they may try to discourage employers from passing along information that may downgrade their future jobs. Domestic workers perform their jobs as individuals, but to locate new jobs they must tap into their social relationships. Although often constrained by scarce options and even scarcer resources, they, especially the housecleaners, try to use the employer networks to upgrade their occupations. Yet their successes are a function not only of their own job performance and work culture, but also of the dynamics within networks of employers.

As we have seen, the labor market for private, paid domestic work is largely constituted through informal social networks. At the bottom and top levels of the occupation, however, domestic employment agencies are important players in mediating the needs of employers and employees. The following chapter looks at the inner workings of these agencies.

4

Formalizing the Informal

Domestic Employment Agencies

> I try and tell the people, "They [nanny/housekeepers] may
> be working with your children, but remember it's a job."
>
> Agency owner

Enter the unassuming storefront, and you find a bowling alley–
shaped room, with a row of empty chairs and job applications flank-
ing one wall. Opposite there are office desks, but where one would
normally expect female receptionists sit two white men. Their desks
are cluttered with papers, which on closer inspection turn out to be
job applications with Polaroid snapshots of the applicants attached.
The phones ring constantly. "Yes, Mrs. O'Melveny, she'll be arriving
tomorrow at your home as scheduled," or "No, that job is filled and
Demi Moore hasn't called back."

Next door is another domestic employment agency. Here, a cluster
of Latina job seekers anxiously hover around the desk of a bilingual,
professionally attired Latina, while other Central American and
Mexican women are fanning themselves in a small, crowded waiting
room. These women are among the most desperate job seekers,
and that is why they have come to "Domestic Desperation."[1] They
lack references from prior employers, network contacts, English-
language skills, drivers' licenses, and, often, proper legal papers.

In this chapter, I look at how agencies go about placing Latina
immigrants into full-time nanny/housekeeper jobs. Domestic employment agencies handle primarily live-in jobs, for which the demand is greatest and (because of the typical job conditions) the supply is least adequate.[2] There is a wide range of domestic employment
agencies and practices in Los Angeles. A glance at the local yellow
pages, *L.A. Parent,* or the *Los Angeles Times* Sunday classifieds reveals
an abundance of advertisements for agencies that place nannies,
housekeepers, housecleaners, personal companions, housemen, and
even butlers (figure 1).[3] But not all agencies are alike.

92

Figure 1. Advertisements for domestic employment agencies. As they compete to make a profit by placing nanny/housekeepers in private homes, the agencies' advertisements often evoke images of British nannies and governesses. Many of these agencies place primarily Latina immigrants in these jobs.

White nannies do better than their Latina peers, and racial stratification within domestic work is matched by stratified employment agencies. Some firms are layered into three agencies, each bearing a different business name, serving different tiers of employer clients and job seekers. Employees are funneled into the agency offering high-end, midrange, or low-end jobs by their ascribed characteristics—for example, race, nationality, and age; and by their job qualifications—for example, knowledge of the English language, references, possession of a driver's license, and knowledge of CPR. Race, cultural background, and language are particularly important to this sorting process, and the ability to speak fluent and flawless English serves as a racializing job criterion.

The agencies serving the top echelon generally place American, Australian, Irish, or British "middle-class" white nannies.[4] These women work for wealthy families exclusively as nannies, not housekeepers, and they consistently rely on the agencies to find the choicest jobs, which may be in other states. The next tier consists of agencies that place Latina immigrant women in jobs in which they will have both nanny and housekeeping responsibilities. The Latina women who go through the second-tier agencies tend to be relatively young women who speak English well, have legal papers and perhaps CPR certificates and driver's licenses; equally important, they also have strong references showing their experience in working for well-do-to families. These women earn salaries in the range of $300 to $400 a week. At the bottom are agencies that place Latina immigrants at the very beginning of this occupational ladder, placing women who lack experience, references, English, and papers; and the jobs they secure may pay as little as $125 a week.

In this chapter, I examine how these small businesses mediate a private, informal-sector job. I focus on how the screening process stands in for the personal references exchanged in the employer referral network to assure clients of the trustworthiness of employees, and how screening—which is conducted differently for the white nannies than for the Latina immigrant domestic workers—shapes job terms.

HOW THE AGENCIES WORK

Domestic employment agencies are businesses, many of which operate principally by telephone.[5] Agency owners and staff record what a prospective employer wants; they take applications from job seekers, check references, and then screen and arrange for the client to personally interview the most suitable two or three candidates.[6] The agencies themselves are not the employers of domestic workers, and they bear no responsibility for the employer's obligations (or potential abuses). They are merely the intermediaries.

In exchange for the service that these headhunters provide—checking references and making a successful placement—the employers pay a substantial fee. Fees, which vary across agencies, correspond to the stratum of domestic jobs and employees served.[7] When a client selects an employee, a placement is made. A written contract guarantees the client satisfaction for a certain period—usually ninety days—during which time a replacement employee may be requested, and it specifies the fee to be collected. But this transaction in fact involves not two but three parties: the agency, the job seeker, and the prospective employer (or client).

REFERRALS AND TRUST

First-time employers of live-in nanny/housekeepers may have particular fears and preconceptions that need to be assuaged by the agencies, which must assure them of good, trustworthy, competent domestic employees. Similarly, Latina domestic workers, many made cautious by bitter experience, are wary of finding themselves in exploitative jobs. And because agencies are in business to profit from successful placements, they must be selective about those with whom they choose to work—ideally, fee-paying clients who are not overly picky and employees who are responsible and compliant.

Informal social networks intersect with the agencies, as the agencies thrive primarily on word-of-mouth references and reputation. They advertise to survive in a competitive industry, but agency owners told me that they prefer repeat customers and informal referrals from satisfied customers. Both domestic workers and employers refer their friends to agencies, but both groups also express plenty of animosity toward them. Latina immigrant women complain about agencies that take their application fees (usually $5 to $25) and never call to offer them jobs, and employers recall paying high fees for unsatisfactory placements.

Some of the employers believe that by using agencies they lose control over the type of person they wish to interview. For example, Bonnie Feinstein, a wealthy woman who currently had a small domestic staff at her large home, did not like the selection offered by an agency she had used in the past. Through that agency, she had hired an English nanny, whom she came to perceive as too strict, who cooked with unhealthy ingredients (e.g., gravy, lard) despite her own preference for light, low-fat cuisine, and who dressed the children in embarrassingly formal clothing when they visited their father at the Hollywood movie studio where he worked. She implied that the agency valued race over competence: "She [the nanny] had an English accent, and that's why the agency had her there, and thought they could charge a lot of money for her." On another occasion, the agency had sent, she said, a "girl who was American and very sweet, but so dumb that I was terrified. My kids were not in good hands when they were with her." When I asked Bonnie, who listed her previous year's annual household income as "over $1,000,000," how she would go about hiring if she had to do so tomorrow, she unequivocally declared, "Word of mouth is definitely the way to go. I would never hire anybody from an agency again."

Destitute job seekers who are not well-connected to networks of domestic employees and of employers do sometimes approach domestic employment agencies in search of work. After their application—together with their application fee—is accepted, these women may never be called for an interview. More common (and more successful) candidates are the upper-echelon, experienced employees who are easily placeable. These include Latina job seekers who speak English; who appear to be young, energetic, and attractive; who are without family obligations in Los Angeles (i.e., single and childless); who have the appropriate documents; and, crucially, who have garnered the right references from employers in the right neighborhoods. Increasingly, prospective employers also want someone with a driver's license, a car, and car insurance.

Constraining family ties are a liability for women seeking nanny/housekeeper jobs. For this reason, some agencies advise job candidates to lie about their family situation. Ronalda Saavedra, who had found both live-in and live-out jobs through the agencies, said, "The agencies tell you, 'If you're married, don't say so, and if you have a boyfriend, don't tell them you have one, because you won't get the job.' And you know if they ask, 'Do you have kids?' you need to say, 'No,' or 'They're in El Salvador.' They know if you've got kids here, when the kids get sick, their employee is not going to be reporting for work that day."

For job seekers with the right stuff, the agency personnel report that the agencies offer not only jobs but also a modicum of protection from sexual assault and other abuses. "Let's face it: we're sending women alone into a strange house, and if they got that out of an ad in the *L.A. Times*, I mean, they don't know what they're walking into," said one agency owner. "But if someone [an employer client] calls us, we've got their address and their telephone. If something happens, they know we have all that information." Another agency manager also thought that job seekers felt *respaldadas* (backed-up with support) at an agency. Although many employers and employees have had unfortunate experiences with the agencies, many others are satisfied; there are plenty of prospective employers and job seekers, providing a steady business for the domestic employment agencies in Los Angeles.

Agencies work at building their reputations among prospective employers, and they stress the importance of the client's having contact with only one individual at the firm. Their customers, they say, want personal service. The agency owners themselves answer phones and make placements, but they also use personnel working exclusively on commission to run subsidiary agencies. As one agency owner, Max Rogers, explained, "People want to know they're talking to the owner, or to the person in charge—they're not given someone who's, you know, second choice. It's a service business. . . . I can't take [hire] someone to be at the Rogers Agency because everyone knows me. And they want me or they're gonna use another agency." In this regard the agency resembles a social network, as personal acquaintance builds trust.

The task of the agency is to screen and select job candidates for the employer clients; in particular, they check references, the key credentials for the job seekers. However, a mixture of informal screening and gut-level sizing up occurs before the agency personnel even ask a job seeker for references. At one midlevel agency, I witnessed this informal screening process when I was interviewing the owner. Half a dozen calls came from prospective job applicants, most of them calling to respond to a newly placed *Los Angeles Times* classified ad. After asking them if they spoke English, checking that they had a California driver's license or identification card, and inquiring about references and past experience, the owner referred only one to his assistant for more information. The manager of another agency, Rosalba Flores, said she asked prospective job applicants particular questions about who referred them to the agency, or in what newspaper they saw the ad. "If I see that they're telling lies, I won't ask them to fill out the application form. I'll just say I have no opportunities, and they should return another time."

Phony references provided by job seekers are an ongoing problem. "People lie, people lie," complained one owner. "Out of a hundred people, you only have ten that you end up really seriously working with." Agency personnel ensure the veracity of the references by telephoning the previous employers listed. The agency personnel say that they ask specific questions about the job duties that were performed, the names and ages of the children, and other details. Several agency owners identified Filipinas as the most egregious perpetrators of phony references. At the bottom tier, however, the bar is set much lower. Rosalba Flores, whose low-end agency specialized in $125- to $150-a-week jobs, said that at that price, "the references don't have to be legitimate. I understand they [job seekers] need the opportunity, and it isn't that much money." In these cases, references from the job applicants' friends or relatives were sometimes acceptable.

Latina immigrant women seeking the midrange and higher-paying nanny/housekeeper jobs definitely need good references, and from employers of a particular social class. Most new employers, the agency people say, want to hire someone who previously worked for "someone just like them." The spatial and social location of the employer providing the most important reference helps determine where the agency can place the job candidate. The neighborhood is important because it indicates the previous employer's socioeconomic class. "If you're gonna work in Beverly Hills, you better have a Beverly Hills reference," explained one owner. "But if you're gonna work in the Westside, it has to be a Westside reference," because "they [the clients] want to feel that you've worked in a home similar to what they have . . . nice things, similar to them. And that becomes your salary structure." Spatial and social class location thus serves as a point of both entry and exclusion. "If you come to me with a Long Beach reference, or some area like that, I can't get you a job in Beverly Hills, okay? 'Cause they don't know who they're talking to for a reference." Though areas such as Long Beach or Chino Hills contain affluent neighborhoods, references from the families living in them do not carry the same weight as references from more elite, fashionable, high-status neighborhoods.

Residential distinctions of class may incorporate other nuances. Elizabeth Mapplethorpe, a socialite, the wife of a local industrialist, and a resident of toney Hancock Park, claimed that she refused to consider employees who had previously worked for Hollywood celebrities. Although she managed to let drop on both occasions when we met that she was born and raised in Beverly Hills, she not only refused to live there but wouldn't even hire someone who had worked there. According to her, the *nouveau riche* entertainment industry people and "rich Arabians" (i.e., Iranians) who now live in Beverly Hills lack decorum and proper experience in handling their domestic employees, so someone coming from such an employer would not suit her requirement for more formal behavior and duties (e.g., wearing uniforms, serving meals).

When she described how the agency had wanted to send a job candidate who had previously worked for the actress Kim Basinger, Elizabeth Mapplethorpe momentarily crossed her eyes, which she did frequently to display her frustration. "Heavens, I certainly don't need that." Another had previously overseen an entire staff for an Iranian family. Here, naming the street where the Iranian family lived, she implied that the address made the candidate inappropriate. Even though she had used an agency to find several domestic employees, she often knew the former employer who provided the telephone reference, or shared some personal acquaintance with the referring employer. For a job seeker, length of employment in a prior job is less important than the previous employer.

Together with the job application, most agencies ask to see and copy a number of documents: a California identification card or driver's license, a Social Security card, and reference letters. Small agencies, or perhaps those suffering an extreme shortage of job candidates, may be more relaxed in this respect. One day when I sat with a desperate, temporarily unemployed job seeker while she worked through various job listings in the newspaper, she was told by many of the agencies she telephoned that she would be unacceptable because she lacked a driver's license and legal papers, did not speak English, and was unavailable for live-in work. Yet other agencies assured her that these deficiencies were not a problem, that the only documents required "are whatever ones you have." Latina nanny/housekeepers who succeed in securing some of the higher-paying jobs through the agencies, however, have all the requisite papers and have filled their portfolios with the reference letters, addresses, and phone numbers of previous employers.

Requiring legal documents that show legal authorization to perform domestic work appears to be a relatively new phenomenon. One Latina nanny/housekeeper recalled her arrival in California: "Back then [1988], they didn't ask to see documents of any sort [at domestic employment agencies], and in factories, they did." Logically, she sought a domestic rather than a factory job. Her recollections were shared by Beatrice Galvan, who also began looking for jobs in the late 1980s. "They didn't charge application fees, they didn't ask for anything. Now, all the agencies say, 'Bring your green card, bring your Social Security card.'" This shift reflects not changes in the law—though in 1986 legislation imposed sanctions on employers who do not check the status of their workers—but rather employer paranoia, prompted by the public unraveling of Zoë Baird's political nomination over her hiring of undocumented immigrants and the anti-immigrant hysteria accompanying the Proposition 187 campaign in the mid-1990s.

In recent years, sensationalizing television news programs have regularly presented film footage, shot by hidden cameras, that shows nannies beating and mistreating small children. In response to parents' heightened anxieties about nanny/housekeepers, agencies have introduced new steps into the screening process and new industries have developed.[8] These added security measures have proved to be of only limited efficacy.

RACIAL PREFERENCES

As we have seen, employers may have distinct racial preferences. Some believe that they will accrue more status, or caregivers who speak better English, if they employ a white, fair-haired nanny, who may hail from Iowa or Australia; others prefer the distinction (and lower costs) provided by an indigenous-looking Guatemalan nanny, whose darker complexion, different phenotype, and small stature readily mark her as subordinate and provide a contrast with their own family. They may instruct the agencies accordingly. One woman, currently the employer of a live-out nanny/housekeeper, told me that she had a quiet agreement with an agency to not send her black job candidates to interview. Few African American candidates approached the agencies looking for jobs, but Afro-Belizean, Afro-Brazilian, and Afro-Honduran job seekers did.

Most employers who wish to hire only white employees simply go to the upper-tier agencies that specialize in English-fluent and literate nannies. Linguistic criteria can thus be used to "de-racialize" hiring selections. I also discovered that Latina job applicants—who are, of course, not starting from the same position of strength as their prospective employers—may also specify that they will not work for members of particular racial-ethnic groups. In Los Angeles, as we saw in chapter 2, some domestic workers try to avoid immigrant and minority employers. They identify Iranian and Jewish employers, and especially Israeli Jews, as among the most abusive. One agency manager reported that many job applicants flatly blurt out, "I don't want to work with Jews." Another owner, whose agency was located near the Hassidic area of mid-Wilshire, mimicked the heavily accented English of a hypothetical Latina job seeker by screaming, "No Yooeesh! No Yooeesh!" When I asked this agency owner, who happened to be Jewish himself, if he screened out Jewish employer clients, he replied, with some irony, "Yeah, of course. If I like the girl, and I want her to get a job, I'm not gonna send her someplace where she's not going to get hired. . . . You know if they're Jews by their names. Thank God, Jews have Jewish names." In the agencies, the profit motive enables racial preferences and discrimination for both employers and employees, but it is the Latina domestic workers who are more adversely affected.

MEDIATING UP AND DOWN

Agencies that deal with the higher-end jobs, which generally place white nannies, impose more restrictions and screening devices on the prospective employers than do the lower-tier agencies. Few white nannies are willing to take live-in jobs, despite the high salaries they can earn (perhaps $500 a week), and their employers are willing to pay high agency fees (perhaps over $2,000); this scarcity of employees combined with greater opportunities for profit encourages the agencies to be particularly vigilant in assessing the top-level employers.

Agencies need to verify that clients can pay their high fees. Burton Smiland, the manager of the exclusive "Maid in America" nanny agency, which advertises nationally in such publications as the Sunday edition of the *New York Times* and *Town and Country* magazine, screened prospective clients most rigorously. Sometimes he received inquiries from clients in midwestern or northwestern cities, and to verify their financial resources he would call real estate agents in their area to check on average home prices.

At this high-end agency, the manager also advised all employers to use a written contract when hiring a nanny, and prospective employers were required to fill out an application for the agency. He explained, "Normally I send out, which is a little different than what they [i.e., the lower-tier agencies] do, I send out what's called the family application. I have them fill out the family application for me and it goes into, most importantly, it goes into the duties. I want it spelled out and [I] have them signing what kind of schedule the nanny's going to be working, what kind of baby-sitting extras [are] going to be required, how many loads of laundry will need to be done." He would then share the employer's application with the job candidate. This procedure institutionalized the nanny's daily activities as job duties. By putting the hours and duties on paper, the employer verified that this was a job with definite limits. Presumably, if a nanny was later asked to do extra evening or weekend baby-sitting, she could point to the written document to demonstrate that the new tasks were not part of the original agreement. Such specification of duties rarely occurred in the placement of Latina immigrant nanny/housekeepers.

When it comes to salary, the elite, "white middle-class" nannies are better equipped to bargain on their own. Cost is no object for the wealthy families who hire these women, and the shortage of desirable applicants—white, English-speaking, experienced, and willing to work as live-in nannies—gives the job seekers an advantage.

Moreover, even as subordinates they enter their interviews sharing similarities of race, language, and perhaps citizenship with their prospective employer. In her study of white, educated nannies who are culturally similar to the employers for whom they work, Julia Wrigley goes so far as to refer to them as "class peers."[9]

The hierarchical and racialized distinctions between white U.S.-born, so-called middle-class American nannies (who may be neither middle class nor American) and Latina immigrant nanny/housekeepers were stressed by the agencies' method of preparing employers for their upscale nannies. Burton Smiland explained that he had the greatest need to educate clients who were what he called "tweeners": employers making the switch from a Latina to a white American nanny. "Most of the educating I get is with parents who maybe had a Latin nanny and are going into an American," he reflected. "Mainly I'm educating on what kind of money they're after." He also admonished these employers not to treat their white nannies with the same disregard they had shown their Latina nanny/housekeepers: "They have to know going in that this is no longer a nanny/housekeeper, this is a child care provider and you're gonna have to tone down the housekeeping part of the job and bring somebody else in [to do it]." At his elite level of domestic employment, monitoring the employers was most important; from a business point of view, he explained, "you become a more effective agency if you do a heavier job screening your clients than you do your nanny." In this racial hierarchy, only employers of white nannies require any monitoring.

AGENCIES AND LATINA NANNY/HOUSEKEEPERS

The screening of the clients of midrange and lower-range agencies, where Latina immigrant women are likely to go to seek nanny/housekeeper jobs, is less thorough, and the standards to which prospective employers are held are lower. At the bottom tier, agencies want a high volume of clients, and they want to ensure that those clients will pay their agency's placement fees. "They just gotta pay their bill," said one agency owner. "This is a business. ... You're gonna pay me a fee, I'll work you [as a client], even if you go through people [employees], you know? That's how I make my living."

Lower-tier agencies do not screen out employer clients who request six-day-a-week jobs. The agency operators say they do not list the numbers of hours of work required for the live-in jobs; the assumption is that the live-in is on call at all hours. And Latina job applicants know better than to ask about the hours. "A new employee is never going to say to the *señora,* 'I'll work as live-in, but only eight hours a day,'" observed one nanny/housekeeper. "That's the whole point of having a live-in, so they work you from morning to night!" These agencies know that their job applicants are desperate for work. As one agency owner said, "When they need a job, they need it yesterday." Consequently, the agencies have no incentive to set high job standards.

Of primary concern to these agencies is ascertaining that the wages offered by prospective employers are roughly congruent with the going rates. "If they tell me that they have between $80 and $120 a week and they want someone who speaks English, it's just not gonna happen," said one agency owner. "I say, 'It's $100 a week when you take your children to a licensed day care provider in your neighborhood and she's watching five other kids so her gross is $500 a week.'" Another manager of an agency exclaimed, "They want English-speaking for $130 [a week]. Impossible! . . . I can give them that when they pay a minimum of $200, so I have to tell them that." At the lower-end agencies, agency owners educate their clients about what it costs to employ a non-English-speaking or English-speaking nanny/housekeeper, but give no guidance on hours or specific tasks.

The midtier agencies, which generally place English-speaking Latina immigrants who have experience and strong references, do insist on some basic job standards. According to the owner of one such agency, an early warning sign of a potentially problematic client is that he or she requests a six-day-a-week live-in. "We try to stay away from people that are patently abusive. Um, oftentimes you can pick up on it right away. . . . You know, people that want someone to work six days a week. I mean, think about that, especially if it's a live-in job. Living in someone's house and being a captive for six days? I mean five days is bad, but six days?" His agency refused such requests and raised client fees to further discourage troublemaking employers. "The more abusive client . . . they don't pay the employee anything and they don't want to pay a decent agency fee. The great majority of the problems that we have are with the low-paying jobs, so we've kind of upgraded ourselves. And we got away from those low-priced placements where you're dealing with families that can be really, really troublesome or they don't view a person as a person." Driven primarily by the desire for a good fee-paying, non-problematic client, the midlevel agencies also informally screen the prospective employers. They like the reliability of repeat clients; as one owner explained, given competing job orders, "You're going to take your client that you've known for years." With new clients, "One of the ways that they're sort of screened is how long did they keep their previous employees, you know? I want to know that and I'll tell the candidate that as well."

When agency owners sense that someone will become a difficult client, they may fill out the job order and just leave it to languish. I observed the beginning of this process during my interview with one agency owner. We were interrupted by many phone calls, including a fifteen- or twenty-minute call from a homemaker searching for an English-speaking, professional live-in nanny to care for her two-year-old twins and infant for $300 a week. The agency owner told her that her price was too low, and as he argued in a reasoned manner he silently rolled his eyes and threw up his hands in exasperation. Snippets from his part of the conversation included, "Remember, this is a job for someone," and then, as if making a concession, "No, it doesn't mean they are just in it for the money." Later, he told me that the woman kept reiterating, "We are a *nice* family, we're very hip."

The agency owner eventually passed the call on to his assistant, who also expressed astonishment at the request. What will happen with this particular job order, I wondered aloud. "Well, probably nothing," he said. "Probably nothing because she wants a live-in and they're gonna laugh at this. She wants someone who's educated, speaks English, you know, someone that comes from a middle-class background. And, um, but she, she doesn't want to pay for it. She said, 'My God they're making $300 a week clear' and they have a place to stay and they don't even have a telephone to pay for. That's all very true, you know, but if someone else is offering $400 for the same job?" He finally sighed, "They all think they have a nice family."

Other agency owners confirmed that when agencies are called by clients they know from experience to be "absolutely impossible," they just let the requests sit. "On the phone, you can talk to someone and you can sense in the way they say things, describe their job," said Max Rogers. "If they're sitting there telling me, 'I want them up with the baby and I want them to do the housekeeping and I want this and I want that,' I'm not gonna work a job like that because that person is nothing but a problem."

"So what would you do with a person like that?"

"Oh, I take the job order and you know, that's that. I have no one for them. . . . If I've got one live-in person, that person is obviously going to the job I feel will be best, so that no problem arises."

This informal screening is designed to help the agency collect its fee while avoiding the extra work of providing a replacement worker. It also protects workers from the most abusive and problematic employers, though only at the mid- and high-range agencies. Yet such screening, motivated purely by business interest, also has the effect of making the higher echelons of nanny and nanny/housekeeper jobs into higher-quality occupations. When the agencies must find a substitute because the first nanny/housekeeper didn't work out, they lose money: "The worse part of this business is having to replace these people because it's hard to come up with one person, much less two or three, and not collect another fee."

It is in the agencies' interest to place nanny/housekeepers in jobs with high salaries, as they collect substantial fees for these placements. Soraya Sanchez, a Mexican nanny/housekeeper who spoke English very well and had strong references from households located in wealthy Westside neighborhoods, regularly went through agencies to locate her jobs. She told me that on one occasion the agency owner had revealed to her private information about the *señora* who would be interviewing her. "He told me, 'That woman will pay you whatever you ask for because she doesn't like being with her children.' . . . Well, she was offering $350 [a week], so I said I wanted $450. I got it, but I never imagined that she would expect sixteen-hour days!" In this case, the agency provided information that helped her earn higher pay but did not prepare her for the long work hours, children who were difficult to manage, and an abusive employer. She left the job within a few months. In this instance, the agency was obligated to find a replacement employee without collecting another fee.

For this reason, the agency's profit motives *do* encourage the upgrading of nanny/housekeeper jobs. "One of the biggest challenges," declared the owner of another midtier agency, "[is] educating families. . . . A big part of our job here is to not be an order taker but to educate the family as to what they can realistically expect someone to do. And what sort of hours that they can work. We try to do it in as helpful a way as possible, but we're always battling with that." Alternatively, instead of persuading employer clients to make fewer demands of more experienced employees, the agency may persuade them to lower their expectations of what kind of employees are acceptable.

EXPECTATIONS AT THE BOTTOM

Domestic employment agencies are basically involved in sales, and to succeed they must make sure that the buyers' criteria fit the product available. "I have to educate both groups about what's usual and customary and what's reasonable because often the American client, her expectations are way out of line and often the Hispanic domestic will sort of, well, a lot of her information may be rumor and really not just accurate. And bringing those two together," said Dolores Castro, "feels sometimes like a marriage and if I can do it, then everybody's happy."

Persuading and preparing the employees is part of how the agency upgrades or downgrades jobs. Job applicants may be subtly pressured to take positions that are less than desirable. At one of the three-tier agencies, I observed an agency representative giving a Latina job candidate what sounded like a pitch for a used car, emphatically telling the young woman, "This job is a *very, very* nice job, and it is going to go fast." The agencies must ensure that their job seekers' expectations match the available jobs, so they may readjust and lower the employee's expectations for pay.

In so doing, agencies may persuade a job applicant to take a job that she might view as less than desirable. At the same time, they must ensure that the applicants they place understand what the job entails so that they will do satisfactory work, giving the client no reason to complain and request a replacement. Dolores Castro reported that "there is a tremendous amount of misinformation in the Hispanic community" regarding employee legal rights. She mimicked a Latina immigrant who states, erroneously, what she believes to be her rights as an employee: " 'They have to pay me for federal holidays. It's the law. I have to have time off and I have to be paid.' Untrue. Um, 'They have to give me vacation time.' Untrue. 'They have to pay me sick days.' Untrue. . . . In the world that they travel, there's a lot of misinformation because it's all coming from, it's almost like wives' tales . . . like the way that slaves sort of communicated in the old South. Like there's a little beeline and half of it is true and half of it's not true." Dolores Castro's comparison of contemporary domestic workers to slaves of the old South is telling. Her job is not that of the slave trade, but she earns a living by making these low-wage job placements. To do so effectively, she seeks to align the expectations of both job seeker and employer. "I recommend all my clients [provide] at least a week's paid vacation after a year's worth of service. This is not the law. This would be a typical thing that Hispanics think . . . *Pues tienen que darme mi mis vacaciónes* [They have to give me my paid vacation]. Well, that's not true. The U.S. government only forces employers to pay for actual time worked. . . . I tell my clients, you want to find somebody good and you want to keep them . . . [so then] treat them nicely and fairly."

While Dolores said that she recommends clients pay domestic workers for "the five or six major holidays," overtime, and one week's paid vacation per year of work, there are no regulations governing these practices. In fact, the lack of paid holidays, paid overtime, and paid vacation is virtually institutionalized in the occupation. Misunderstandings about paid holidays are so rampant that several agencies reported to me that the Tuesday and Wednesday following a three-day holiday weekend, such as Memorial Day or Labor Day, were among their busiest days, because so many domestic workers fail to report to work and are fired.

Agencies may also encourage the nanny/housekeepers to remain in bad jobs. Rosalba Flores said that she advised her low-end placements to stay out of concern for their own future. "I tell them, 'You have to build your own references. If you've lasted one or two years in a job where I placed you, then on your next job search, we can put that you've already worked with this agency, and lasted so long with this person, and that helps you raise your salary." Her advice worked to her own benefit as well: when Latina nanny/housekeepers stay in jobs for a minimum period, agencies are spared the trouble and expense of finding replacements.

GROOMING THE JOB APPLICANTS:
"If I Put a Pretty Girl Next to Another One,
They Always Choose the Pretty One"

References are the key job credential, but the agencies also cultivate and depend on image. Matching employee with employer may entail taking photographs and literally grooming the job candidate for the interview, advising her how to dress, how to smile, or how to shake hands.[10] All of the agency staff who work with Latina immigrant job candidates mentioned that the women often have to be advised on self-presentation before they interview. Much has been written in the domestic work literature on the satisfaction and feeling of superiority that employers have traditionally derived from domestic workers' humble mode of dress.[11] The comments of the agency personnel suggest that employers' preference for such attire, which clashes with many Latinas' penchant for eye-catching dress, is alive and well. But there seems to be another tendency at work, since those Latina employees who are young, physically attractive, and relatively light-skinned—more mestiza than indigenous—seem to win some of the best jobs and command the highest salaries.

I began to think about this apparent contradiction while conducting face-to-face interviews with Latina immigrant women who work as nanny/housekeepers and as housecleaners. Many of the Latina nanny/housekeepers who are now earning salaries at the high end of the scale—say, $325–450 a week—are relatively young (in their late twenties or early thirties), conventionally attractive with well-groomed nails and hair, and physically fit. Soraya Sanchez, a Mexicana with a sixth-grade education, was one of these women. She had located her relatively upscale nanny/housekeeper jobs through agencies, and she maintained that her *buena presentación* (good appearance) had something to do with her job successes. She favorably compared her own appearance to that of other women she saw applying for jobs in the agencies, women who were overweight and who wore loud clothes and chipped nail polish in bright colors. I described women such as Soraya to one agency owner, and he chuckled, his eye lighting up with thoughts more of profit than of lechery, "Send them right over. Cash into them."

White nannies apparently also fared better if they were young, slim, and conventionally attractive. Burton Smiland, who ran the exclusive "Maid in America" agency, claimed that "The prejudices in this business aren't just limited to the ethnic background, it's definitely with the physical appearance." He felt that this worked against otherwise well-qualified candidates: "It's very sad, but there happen to be a great percentage of [white] American nannies that are extremely overweight, obese. They happen to be very gifted with kids. . . . [They are] homebodies and they make the perfect live-in placement for a family, but a lot of families won't hire them, obviously because of their appearance." Parents fear that older and overweight nannies will not be able to keep up with their children, but employer preferences are also formed by a culture that systematically devalues older and overweight women.

The physically attractive job candidate, whatever the occupation, is almost universally preferred—particularly when the prospective employee is female, and especially in an image- and body-conscious city such as Los Angeles. Issues of sexual appeal and sexual harassment often intertwine, yet it is typically female employers who are selecting the domestic workers.[12] Most do not wish to have alluring young women living in their homes, potentially catching the eye of their husband, and agency owners reported that female employers frequently specify that they don't want a nanny who looks too sexy. These requests went up, the agency owners said, after the comedian Robin Williams's widely reported relationship with and subsequent marriage to his child's nanny.[13] Still, paradoxically a general preference for the young, physically fit, and attractive nanny/housekeeper persists, and these young women often command higher earnings than their older and less attractive peers. From the employer's perspective, the slenderness, skin color, and youth of a nanny/housekeeper may both confer status and symbolize job competency.

Women who work in the domestic employment agencies intervene more directly in grooming the job candidates than do the men. "Do not wear your party dress to the interview," Dolores Castro instructs Latina job seekers. "Do not wear a lot of hanging, noisy jewelry. Wear sensible, more tailored, calm clothes. I had one woman, who—she had huge breasts—and she used to come with these big, low-cut sweat suits. I said to her, 'Esperanza, you're a great employee. Kids love you . . . but I can't get you a job because you have your boobs hanging all over. Rethink this.'" Another woman who operated a low-end agency advised, "Very little makeup . . . no

plunging necklines . . . pants should not cling tightly to the body. . . .
[They should wear] loose blouses or dresses. They should smile, and
look decent, that's what I tell them. Their bra and bra straps should
not be showing, and they should look clean." Another agency owner
told me he had recommended to job candidates that they remove
facial hair and wear less perfume. The advice is clear: the domestic
job seeker must be clean, neat, and feminine—but above all, suffi-
ciently desexualized.

At one meeting of the Domestic Workers' Association, Dolores
Castro was a featured guest speaker, dispensing job-seeking advice
to the members. After her speech, a finely attired Guatemalan
woman with a short, chic haircut told of once going to a job interview
dressed in clothing similar to what she was then wearing—a dress,
bright pink blazer, stockings, and heels. She didn't get the job, and
the agency later told her that the client said, "Oh, that woman probably doesn't even know how to sweep." In short, clipped phrases,
Dolores Castro instructed the domestic workers to dress down for
the interviews: "No heels. Keep it simple. Wear flat shoes. Clean
tennis shoes are best." She then went around the room, pointing out
who was appropriately dressed for an interview, and who was inappropriately dressed. The elegantly attired woman who had raised
the issue—no. A woman wearing a T-shirt with crinkled velvet
pants—no. Another woman—who in fact was at that moment on the
job with two blond preschoolers in tow, having just come from an
animal fair—was told that her dress was too loose and her tennis
shoes were too dirty. "We just came from the park," she protested.
But Dolores said that for an interview, her clothes were inappropriate. The exemplary person she picked was a middle-aged woman
who wore a jogging suit with embroidery around the collar. Her
clothing was informal and allowed for physical movement, but it
was clearly marked as feminine. Later, in her interview with me,
Dolores Castro stated that white tennis shoes, big white T-shirts, and
"fun white leggings" constituted ideal attire. The emphasis on whiteness simultaneously invokes Western images of cleanliness, the uniforms of maids and nurses, and markers of colonial subordination
in the tropics. In this respect, the Latina domestic workers are instructed to wear attire that simultaneously desexualizes them and
reinscribes subordinate racial identity.

Because an employee's personality may be as important in this occupation as her job performance, job applicants preparing for interviews sometimes also receive advice on "grooming" their personality. Both strong, assertive personalities and overly deferential mannerisms might be perceived as liabilities. Several agency owners emphasized how important it was for Latina nanny/housekeepers to, as one of them put it, "look at their employer at eye level." Their advice on behavior is intended to prevent cultural misunderstandings. "I really try to suggest, always, to look them [prospective employers] in the eye when you meet them. I know in certain countries it's respectful to sort of bow your eyes a bit. But the American woman, when you do that, she thinks you're lying to her." Dolores Castro also advised job candidates to avoid giving a particular type of handshake, which she demonstrated for me: the hand dropped down, with fist clenched, so that the other person must grab the offered wrist. In rural parts of Latin America, those who clench their fist instead of extending their hand with open palm may be showing humility, respect, and deference, as if to suggest that their hand is wet or dirty. But American clients are likely to say, as Dolores pointed out, "Well, she didn't even give me her hand," and to take this reluctance as a sign of being untrustworthy.

At the same time, agency owners caution the job candidates not to come on too strong or show too much familiarity. One young Latina women, with excellent references and fluent English, reported that when she approached an agency, she had been told that her personality was too strong. She was advised to be less assertive or leave the occupation. One agency owner said he advised nanny/housekeepers to not tell their employers much about their personal lives and problems. Young nannies who "pour their heart out to their employers," he said, "sometimes get fired for it." He told them to be less forthcoming: "This is your employer, you don't want them to know everything."

Domestic employment agencies constitute part of the formal sector of the economy, but their business is to procure job placements for an important segment of the informal economy. In the process, they shape, though they do not determine, employment practices.

Agencies vary in the degree to which they intervene to form employer's and employee's expectations of job terms. The agencies that place the white nannies do the most to educate their employer clients about the parameters of the job: they select their clients through careful screening, they place restrictions on the job tasks and hours, and they urge employers to use written contracts that formalize the job. Agencies actively raise the standards in these jobs. Here, race confers privilege to the job seekers. The midtier agencies, which place English-speaking Latina nanny/housekeepers with strong references and past job experience, also inform their clients of some (though fewer) job standards, trying to ensure that their expectations of the tasks and hours are realistic. The agencies may attempt to lower job applicants' expectations of earnings to fit them into available job slots, but in other instances they may work to raise the employees' pay, as they then collect higher fees. Like the white nannies, the English-speaking, Latina nanny/housekeepers with strong references can and do find satisfactory jobs through the agencies.

At the bottom tier, where employers who pay less meet destitute job seekers, the circumstances are worse. The agencies view these employers and employees as requiring the most extensive adjustment of expectations, if the placement is to be successful (and thus profitable). These agency transactions, like the exchange of information in the social networks of employers and employees, ultimately inform the terms of domestic work. When the job conditions worsen, employer-employee conflicts may explode in anger and resentment. These vituperative blowups, the subject of the next chapter, lead to job termination.

5

Blowups and Other
Unhappy Endings

"Get out of here! Grab your things! You're fired!"
"You can't fire me because I quit!"

Domestic employees who are in frequent daily contact with their employers often have at least one story of a blowup—a screaming match that terminates employment. It usually begins with conflict over a minor issue, which quickly flares into an explosive verbal confrontation. The blowup reveals what often lies just below the surface of seemingly civil, if occasionally tense, employer-employee relations. The eruption magnifies, like a photographic enlargement, the otherwise invisible fissures in these arrangements.

In this chapter, I examine the various ways in which domestic jobs end—not just blowups but also less dramatic job terminations—from both the employers' and employees' perspectives.[1] Many employees and employers prefer to rely on white lies and excuses to end jobs. Looking at these various methods of ending a job enables us to better understand hiring practices and the organization of the occupation in general. Job terminations provide yet another telling indicator of the extent to which paid domestic work is not recognized or treated as a "real job."

BLOWUPS

Soraya Sanchez had worked as a live-in at the Brooks family's three-story home for only two months, caring for three young children; but she had already experienced many problems, including over-extended hours, the demand that she sleep with the children when the parents stayed out late, a lack of the fresh fruit and vegetables that she liked to eat, and conflicts with both the *señora* and the seven-year-old child, whom she believed was manipulative and disobedient. Although she had never worked on major holidays in her previous jobs, which were relatively upscale nanny/housekeeper positions, Soraya's employer had coaxed her into accompanying the entire family to a relative's home in Seattle for Thanksgiving. At the relative's house, things went from bad to worse, as the *señora* humiliated Soraya in front of the relatives.

After the catered Thanksgiving dinner, the seven-year-old daughter reported to her mother that Soraya had screamed at her to keep quiet while the baby went to sleep. "The *señora* had been drinking a bit too much at the Thanksgiving dinner," Soraya explained, as she reconstructed the scene. "I can't find another explanation, because she came into the baby's room, opened the door, and she started yelling at me, but in a really loud way, telling me, 'How dare you speak that way to my child!' She was yelling so exaggeratedly loud that I had to be quiet. . . . She was yelling, 'I don't know who you think you are, I've been going out of my way for you.' And I said," she continued, switching to her impeccable English, " 'Justine, you don't go out of the way for nobody, not even your mother!' 'Cause she didn't. 'You don't go out of the way for nobody but yourself!' "

Soraya's narration of the incident was dramatically rendered. Although our interview was conducted in Spanish, she switched effortlessly to English to emphasize exactly how she had stood up to the *señora*. Below, I reproduce first the original transcription, to give a better idea of her syntax and the fluid code switching; the English translation follows.

Cuando vino a gritarme la primera vez, me dice she is firing me, y le digo, "You know what? You don't have to fire me, I won't work for you! Not for a million dollars! I'm quitting!" . . . Le dije, "Sabes qué? Yo ahora ya no soy tu empleada, ni tú eres mi patrona, y tú y yo estamos al mismo nivel. Ahora tú me vas a oír lo que yo te voy a decir! Le dije, yo no trabajo para ti . . . tú eres la madre y ni tú te quieres ocupar de tus propios hijos, se porque tengo que preocuparme yo? Ojala," le digo, "que tú encuentres una persona que realmente entienda a tus hijos, porque ni siquiera tú los sabes entender. . . . I quit, I'm quitting, I'm quitting!" y me salí de la puerta y me empezé a empacar mis cosas. I was in Seattle!

When she came to yell at me that first time, she tells me she is firing me, and I said to her, "You know what? You don't have to fire me, I won't work for you! Not for a million dollars! I'm quitting!" . . . I said to her, "You know what? Now I'm no longer your maid, and you're no longer my boss, and you and I are equals! Now you are going to hear what I am going to say to you!" I said to her, "I don't work for you. . . . You're the mother and not even you want to take care of your own children. Why I should have to worry? I hope," I said, "that you find a person who really understands your children, because not even you know how to understand them . . . I quit, I'm quitting, I'm quitting!" and I went out the door and I started packing my things. I was in Seattle!

Soraya took a taxi to the airport and waited there for a morning flight to Los Angeles. The image here of a Latina nanny engaging in an explosive verbal fighting match with her employer goes against the grain of how women subordinated by race, citizenship, and class are supposed to act. But in private domestic work, such incidents are not unusual.

Blowups are emotionally stinging and traumatizing moments, and as the women recount them, they sometimes switch languages to convey the truth of the moment. In telling her story, Soraya used English to demonstrate the force with which she told off the employer. She regularly used *le dije,* or "I said to her," to underline her own agency in confronting the employer and terminating the job.

Such confrontations also occur when employers and employees have long-standing relationships, often as the culmination of a series of conflicts that may have been brewing beneath the surface for years. The workweek began as usual for Elvira Areola, as she arrived early Monday morning at the Johnston family's suburban home with its white picket fence. She had worked for the Johnstons for eleven years, initially cleaning their house once or twice a week while she held a job in a plant nursery. When Dr. Johnston and his wife adopted their first child, they had persuaded Elvira to work for them full-time. During the previous four years, she had worked for them as a live-out nanny/housekeeper, putting in ten-hour days, four days a week, on Monday, Wednesday, Friday, and Saturday.

Elvira cared for the four-year-old boy, who now attended nursery school two mornings a week, and she was in charge of the upkeep of the sprawling house, which included five bathrooms and delicate antiques. Recently, the family had adopted a new baby, and that eventful Monday morning, Elvira had taken the baby for a walk, as instructed, and had visited, as she often did, with a nanny who worked in another home in the neighborhood. As Elvira tells it, the *señora* came looking for her and, raising her voice, said that she had been frantically telephoning to search for her and her baby. She accused Elvira of not having brought enough food for the baby, and immediately took the baby home herself. The silent treatment followed, but lack of conversation wasn't all that unusual. According to Elvira, although they were the only two adults in the house during the day, they rarely spoke. Often, the *señora* stayed in her bedroom, alone, until two o'clock in the afternoon. This seemingly innocuous incident, however, ignited an ugly fight that culminated with a blowup on Friday.

While Elvira bristled most at the employer's insinuation that she might not be trusted with the baby, the explosion was sparked by the increased workload that accompanied the new baby. Monday mornings, when the boy was in preschool, had previously been Elvira's time for major housecleaning, but her new responsibilities made it impossible for her to spend that time on cleaning alone. She knew from her friends who worked in neighboring large homes that in some households, the nanny/housekeeper's work is supplemented by a weekly or biweekly housecleaner. We can imagine that the employer, ignoring the difference made by caring for the baby, saw only an idle employee, neglecting her housecleaning duties and perhaps even the baby's diet and well-being as she socialized with another Latina nanny. As Elvira recalled, the employer had said that she was being paid to take care of the house and children, not visit with nearby nannies.

When Elvira returned to the job on Wednesday, the two delayed greeting one another, but again that in itself was not unusual. The *señora* eventually took her aside, accused her of having left the house for five hours, and told her that she must become more responsible. The *señora* also said to Elvira, "You're just like one of our family"; and when Elvira had responded that no, in fact, she had her own family, and that one doesn't treat one's own family members this way, the *señora* had retorted, "Remember, you're just a maid." Later, after the *señora* had returned from an errand, she tauntingly said, "See, I trust you." When the husband drove Elvira home that evening, he attempted to mediate the dispute, asking Elvira to apologize to his wife. Elvira passed a restless night at home, wondering if she should quit or remain. She decided to remain, and act civilly, but she vowed never to apologize, as she didn't see that she'd done anything wrong.

On Friday, Mrs. Johnston instructed Elvira to take the boy to the library for story time and then to meet her at McDonald's, where she would hand over the baby so that Elvira might walk home with the children. Elvira waited at McDonald's for several hours, but the *señora* never arrived. "This was her revenge," she said. "It was her revenge to have me waiting at McDonald's, three, four hours in the cold." Later that afternoon, she told the *señora* that she was quitting. "Rethink this. You can't quit," said the employer; and when Elvira held steadfast, the *señora* asked her to put it in writing, knowing well that Elvira could not write in English. The trading of insults ensued. The *señora*, a large woman by Elvira's account, attempted to block her passage through the doorway, but eventually Elvira departed. Downstairs, the husband, apparently oblivious to the blowup, asked, "Elvira, can you please take out the garbage before you leave?" She complied, gathered her purse and sweater, and then walked out of the house for the last time, leaving her employers of eleven years and the four-year-old boy whom she had helped raise since infancy.

Elvira had expected to feel sad and remorseful, but recalled feeling only joy and relief after the dramatic confrontation. "I thought maybe I wouldn't even feel like searching for a new job, that I'd be depressed. But, no! I felt really great! It was my mother's birthday, and I called her [in Mexico]." While Elvira's spirits soared, her mother expressed concern. Elvira, after all, was a single mother, and her four children depended entirely on her earnings. Elvira was confident that she had made the right move, but she did long to see the little boy she had cared for; and while she thought about telephoning him or visiting him, she knew this might be construed as an attempt at kidnapping or some other malicious act. She never once looked back at the job.

In the two cases related above, the employer's perception of employee insubordination and the employee's perception of the employer's behavior as controlling and abusive both contributed to the blowup. Strong emotions, including the pride and self-righteousness of both parties, fueled the flames. The issues that spark blowups— issues of distrust, disrespect, surveillance, betrayal, and perceived insubordination—are least likely to create tension in weekly house-cleaning arrangements. They become most contentious in live-in and in live-out daily jobs, in which employers and nanny/housekeepers regularly interact. When the job involves the care of children, the employment relationship takes on more complex dimensions and the potential for conflict increases dramatically.

Nannies and housekeepers who work each day in the same household, and especially live-in workers, are most likely to experience at least one blowup during their careers. Many employees told me about their past blowups, but—perhaps because these incidents tend to reflect badly on the employers—only one employer did. In these stories, the participants are cast in fairly predictable dramatic roles. From the nanny/housekeeper's perspective, the female employer is demonized as the principal adversary, as an irrational, hysterical woman; the male employer, or husband, is exonerated of all responsibility and may even be cast as a benevolent, benign member of the household; and emotional ties with the children complicate the picture, as the blowup severs that relationship, whose end adds feelings of ambivalence and loss.

The only employer that I interviewed who described a blowup was Candace Ross, a cheerful, thirty-six-year-old wife of a CEO and the mother of three young children. She had recently quit her job as a midlevel manager in order to spend more time with the family. When I asked what problems she had encountered in the past and in the present with several different live-in nanny/housekeepers, she had initially said there were no major problems, just some excessive telephone use. Then, she tentatively offered the following about her Salvadoran live-in nanny/housekeeper.

"I had a couple of little blowups, you know, and I think that's probably pretty normal."

"What was that about?" I inquired.

"Well, let's see. . . . This is so dumb, you know how these things are, but I wanted her to tell the gardeners to plant these plants for me, and then she didn't do it because she thought they looked like they were too busy, and it just really made me mad. . . . The last one was after I was already not working anymore and really, to be honest with you, Carmen's life got a lot easier once I was home, because I am very neat and tidy and I do a lot," she said. From Candace's standpoint, the employee's job "now was watching the baby for me when I go out. . . . So I felt that her life got a lot easier." She was therefore stunned when Carmen chose this time to ask for a raise. After consulting with her husband, Candace decided they would agree, on the condition that Carmen's workdays switched to

Tuesday through Saturday, and the new job duties included regular Friday and Saturday night baby-sitting. Carmen initially consented but then objected, as the new schedule did not allow her to attend ESL classes on Saturday mornings. We can imagine that Carmen also realized that the pay "raise" would be tied to extra evening hours of work. She asked for a pay raise, but she got a raise in work.

"We kind of had a blowup and then, um, she started acting really inconsiderate about her position, in my opinion," recalled Candace Ross. "She said, 'Well, you've never given me a bonus.' And I thought, a bonus! I worked all my work years and I never got a bonus from any employer at all. I don't know where she even got that idea! I just felt real bad, and I said, 'Gosh, you know, it's apparent that you don't appreciate what you have here. I try to have a nice house for you to live in, and um, I said I never ask you to do something that I wouldn't do myself.' You know, again, it goes back to this thing of spoiling these people. But you know, she probably didn't appreciate it or something. So I made some points. I said, 'You know, you say that I didn't give you a bonus, well, why don't you take back all those Christmas presents I gave you and cash them in? There's your bonus!' You know, that kind of thing. I said, you know, 'Is money just really all that's important to you?'"

This last statement starkly reveals a basic contradiction in paid domestic work. Parents hire nanny/housekeepers to do work involving intimate care, yet may fundamentally resist the idea that these services require monetary compensation. What seemed to bother Candace Ross more than the potential ingratitude implied by the request for a raise was the suggestion that her employee was doing the job for money. The question "Is money all that's important to you?" assumes that "labors of love" do not really constitute employment. Parents like Candace want a care worker who will truly love and cherish their children. "I was really hurt," she said, "and I probably said some things to her that I wish I could take back."

Among the statements she now regretted, according to Candace, was the declaration that she no longer needed a nanny/housekeeper five days a week, that she was only keeping Carmen out of pity. "I said, 'So if you want to, go ahead and just leave, go ahead and I'll just try to find somebody to come in two or three days a week.' So it was kind of a blowup, but she came to me later." Ultimately, relations were mended and a new arrangement began, with the nanny/housekeeper working and living in for three days a week, and for two other days cleaning houses in the same exclusive residential neighborhood. Although Carmen still continues as a live-in, which enables her to save on rent and send money to her own children in El Salvador, she now has several employers and is no longer dependent solely on what she earns in the Ross household.

That this blowup occurred shortly after the employer left her job as a manager and began staying at home is hardly coincidental. While nothing about Candace Ross suggests that she is anything but "very neat and tidy," her own exit from out-of-the-home employment and reentry into the domestic arena necessarily affected the nanny/housekeeper's job duties, her autonomy, the rhythms of the daily job schedule, and undoubtedly her interactions with the children. Most domestic employees, as we have seen, prefer to work alone, without employer supervision, surveillance, and moment-to-moment requests. Given the choice, nanny/housekeepers prefer working in the homes of women who are employed out of the home. Those who take care of other people's young children complain that the children are much more apt to be disobedient when their parents are around the house. These changes very likely prompted Carmen to ask for a raise, an act that directly precipitated the blowup. The nanny/housekeeper's request for a raise and then bonus pay caught Candace by surprise—after all, from her perspective, the nanny/housekeeper's "life had got a lot easier." To her, asking for a raise signaled a complete lack of gratitude and deference on the part of her employee.

Although the employees are not wholly blameless in these blowups, the primary responsibility seems to rest with the employers, who don't like feeling that they've lost the upper hand in their relationship with their nanny/housekeepers. When employees ask for raises but refuse to assume new job duties or work schedules, or when employees exercise autonomy in disciplining and caring for the children, they may unwittingly spark a blowup; even the act of giving notice may signal that the employer has lost control.

Some employers react with a quiet rage that can be even more damaging than histrionics. Margarita Gutiérrez, a young woman from Mexico City, once told her employers, with a professionalism rare among nanny/housekeepers, that she would be quitting her live-in job in two weeks. On the night before what was to have been her last day of employment, the couple knocked on her bedroom door and told her, "Here's your money, you can go now." Even though this incident had occurred several years earlier, she still cried as she recalled the indignity of being forced to leave her live-in job and abode unexpectedly, at night. After telephoning her sister, she had waited outside in the dark driveway of a canyon home for her sister to take her to the home of her sister's live-in employer. As she related this incident, she seemed to be reliving it all over again.

THE BLOWUP AS EPIPHANIC MOMENT

For many nanny/housekeepers, the blowup heralds an epiphany of sorts, as they swear to themselves that they will never again allow themselves to be humiliated and degraded as an employee in someone's home. They are overcome by the revelation that they can choose not to endure all the indignities and unfairness of live-in work if they seek a different job arrangement. Rather than blaming themselves as individuals or focusing on personalities (as their employers seem to do), these nanny/housekeepers come to see the job itself as the problem. Although they find fault with their individual employers, they devise solutions that consist of changing the work they do, not simply the people they work for.

Yet though the epiphanic moment often prompts women to seek different kinds of jobs, to stop working in private homes altogether, new job options are scarce and hard to come by, as the cases below suggest. One woman who had resolved to get out of the job after such an incident was Celestina Vigil. After working for a family for two years as a Monday-through-Friday live-out nanny/housekeeper, Celestina was fired on the spot and given one week's severance pay when she denied her employers' request to begin working as a live-in nanny/housekeeper. "They didn't even give me time to say, 'Well, let me think about it,' or to find another job! They let me go that same day," she recalled. "I told them I couldn't stay as a live-in because I was studying [at evening adult school] and already living with Geraldo" (her boyfriend).

"How did you feel?" I asked.

"I felt despair, because to so *suddenly* be told that there is no job on Monday—well, it's awful." For Celestina, the emotional trauma was compounded by having to part abruptly from the two-year-old toddler for whom she had cared since his birth, and whom she had grown to love. Her live-out position had been Celestina's first job in the United States, and nothing in her life as a middle-class woman in El Salvador had prepared her for this incident. She responded to the entire experience with the kind of vows commonly recited by nanny/housekeepers who undergo a blowup or are, in quieter voices as she was, abruptly fired. "I said to myself, 'I'll never work in a house again, and I'll never take care of a child again.'" As Celestina put it, "You get to feeling a lot of attachment for these children. It really hurt me that they took me out like that, so suddenly. So I said, 'No, I'll never take care of a house or children again.'"

Like many promises made in the heat of the moment, Celestina's was hard to keep, especially since she had few job options other than domestic work. Immediately after her firing she found work in a catering truck, preparing and selling lunches to Latino factory workers. While laid off from the catering truck, she received a phone call from a woman searching for a live-out nanny/housekeeper, and she wound up returning to the occupation. She told me with some pride, however, that when she accepted the new nanny/housekeeper job, she drew some new protective boundaries. "From the beginning, I told her, 'You know what? If you decide to get rid of me someday, tell me three months ahead of time. Don't tell me one day to the next. . . . And I'll do the same, I'll give you plenty of time to find a replacement person.' But to this day [six years later], I still work with her."

"I'll never love again," says the refrain of a popular song, and after job blowups, nanny/housekeepers make similar self-protective promises to themselves. "I'll never work in a house again" or "I'll never let myself love someone else's child again" are common refrains. These sentiments are repeated on the buses or at the parks where nannies gather. After a blowup all illusions of job security and harmony evaporate, and nanny/housekeepers then focus on what they must do to avoid suffering such a trauma a second time. They swear off different things. Some vow never again to work as a live-in. Those who have been particularly hurt by the abrupt, forced separations from children of whom they had grown very fond may vow never to care for other people's children again. Other women learn to limit their affections for the children in their care, so that they can avoid future heartbreaks when the job ends. As one woman said, "Now I stop myself from becoming too close. Before, when my own children weren't here [in the United States], I gave all my love to the children I cared for. . . . When the job ended, I hurt so much. I can't let that happen again." Still others may swear off domestic work with only one employer, reasoning that they can make themselves least vulnerable by maintaining multiple employers. Some say they wish to work in less emotionally volatile jobs and look for positions as housecleaners rather than as nanny/housekeepers. Others go even further, proclaiming that they will never work in a private household again. Although some women expect these vows to signal their exit from the occupation, more often than not they instead mark a transition point from one type of domestic job to another.

Elvira Areola, the single mother whose blowup was described at the beginning of this chapter, immediately began looking for work, including weekly housecleaning jobs, after abruptly quitting her job of eleven years; she needed to support her four children. "I haven't rested one day, there's not been one day when I haven't gone out searching for work," she told me several weeks after the incident. She left crudely drawn, handprinted "cards" advertising her housecleaning services on doorsteps in a middle-class neighborhood, but I was the only person who called—inquiring about an interview for my study, not a job. Without job references, she had difficulty finding work. Daily, she walked the streets of Pasadena and other cities in the San Gabriel Valley, stopping to ask about jobs at plant nurseries, motels, hospitals, convalescent homes, and retail stores. "I've got my hands," she proudly stated, raising them in the air, "no one can say to me that I don't know how to work!"

Finally, after weeks of searching, Elvira was ready to begin a new job as a member of a hospital cleaning crew on the night shift, and she was still hoping to pick up a few houses to clean during the week. As a live-out nanny/housekeeper she had earned at the upper end of the occupation's wage scale, approximately $8 an hour; at her new job she would earn only the minimum wage, then $4.25. She was ashamed of the low pay and odd hours she would now be working, but she was also optimistic about her earning potential in the local job market and unshaken in her belief that salvaging her dignity on the job was more important than a wage. "What matters to me most is feeling good, seeing that they [employers or supervisors] like my work. Money is important for material things. I know that without money you've got nothing, but I can't expect to earn the same as I was before." In her case, her determination, persistence in job seeking, and willingness to take a job at sharply reduced pay enabled her to began working again within a few weeks.

Ronalda Saavedra, a young Salvadoran nanny/housekeeper, had experienced several blowups in her upscale Westside jobs. One employer, after accusing her of torturing and killing the family's pet cat while the family was vacationing, had fired her (Ronalda claimed that the cat had wandered into a nearby canyon and had probably been eaten by a coyote). A previous employer in Beverly Hills, in a fit of rage, had fired Ronalda and three other domestic workers en masse. When I interviewed Ronalda, she was working in another multiemployee household; she was one of two live-out nanny/housekeepers. Several months after I had interviewed her, she telephoned me late one Saturday night, sobbing. The *señora* had confronted her with a litany of complaints about Ronalda's driving, indulgent child-rearing practices, general lack of servility, inattentiveness, and other transgressions and had abruptly fired her. The employer had apparently not expressed her strong dissatisfaction with Ronalda's job performance until that moment.

By the time Ronalda phoned me, she had already resolved to leave nanny/housekeeper work forever and to seek instead jobs as a weekly housecleaner. With the help of her aunt, she gradually broke into housecleaning; within a year, helped by her relative youth and physical stamina, her car, and her budding English-language skills, she had established a viable route of different houses to clean. Like others, she never looked back. Although weekly housecleaning is hard on the body, she preferred it to risking more emotional trauma in the less physically arduous work of being a nanny/housekeeper.

THE CAUSES OF BLOWUPS

Why do some employers seemingly go berserk, and why do some employees act so haughty and assume little responsibility for these interactions? As we have seen, live-in and live-out domestic work is often fraught with emotion. Even if there is a minimum of verbal interaction between employer and employee, the employee may construe the absence of conversation as demonstrating a lack of respect and consideration from the employer, while to the employer it may signify the employee's inferiority and social and linguistic incompetence. Both the attorneys and the domestic employment agency owners that I interviewed had a good deal of experience mediating blowups, or trying to remedy their consequences. Their experiences gave them invaluable insights into these imbroglios.

Attorneys who specialize in labor law with paid domestic workers told me that the most common complaint they heard from domestic workers who sought legal counsel was that they had been unjustly terminated, usually in a dramatic blowup such as those already described. "What motivates people to get rid of their domestic workers a lot of times," explained the attorney Sarah Cohen, "is something that they may perceive as disloyalty or a personal affront, and I think it comes from this idea that the domestic worker is their chattel and they belong to them. They paid for them, they're getting a life— you're paying for somebody's life on some level. When the domestic worker shows that she has her own life, and her own problems and her own health to attend to and her own kids to attend to, it's threatening—that they've got some concerns that are more important than taking care of some employer's house or kids." One of Cohen's recent legal cases had involved a Guatemalan live-in nanny/housekeeper who worked in a home that included a stay-at-home mother and school-age children. When the live-in became ill over the weekend, she called in sick. According to Cohen, "The wife became incensed and commanded her to come immediately, and she refused and she was fired." The employers immediately stopped payment on the employer's last paycheck.

As noted in chapter 4, many live-in nanny/housekeepers erroneously believe that they are legally entitled to national holidays such as Memorial Day or Labor Day, and many of them are summarily fired when they return to their jobs after taking the day off. For this reason, the domestic employment agencies are crowded with new job seekers after holiday weekends. Conflicts over pay and requests for raises also spark abrupt firings. Sarah Cohen's recent clients with this problem included a woman who had worked as a live-in at one home for seven years earning $130 a week, well below minimum wage. When the employer had added the care of a sick stray dog to the list of regular job duties, which had already included caring for several animals, the employee had said something to the effect of "give me a raise or you can say good-bye to me." The employer chose the latter.

At one of the high-volume domestic employment agencies, where I had conducted a series of interviews on different days, a phone call came in at closing time on a Friday. An established client was calling to complain about her nanny/housekeeper's transgressions while the agency owner murmured, "Uh-huh, uh-huh, yeah." When he got off the phone, he said to me, "You see, that's a perfect example. She's a trust fund baby, never had to work a day in her life, and she's a high-strung movie producer. This girl [nanny/housekeeper] has been with her for three years, and all of a sudden, she's got to go." His partner at the agency then rolled his eyes and chimed in, "Yeah, right, but she was fine for three years?" He offered his own explanation for the blowups, and for the abrupt changes in how employers perceive their domestic employees: "It's the pills, the drugs, that make them like this. On Monday, everything will be fine again." It is certainly plausible that widespread use of recreational drugs and alcohol, whose excessive consumption is most likely in the home, sometimes plays a role in blowups.

LABOR LAW AND THE BLOWUPS

Two of the attorneys whom I interviewed, Sarah Cohen and Nancy Cervantes, concurred that paid domestic workers who complain at the employment law clinics about being summarily fired expect that they have some legal redress. "They lose their job and they think there's something wrong when that happens," said Cohen. "A lot of domestic workers come in complaining about having been wrong-fully terminated. That seems to be a concept that's really popular and I haven't studied other countries' legal systems, but it appears to me that in other countries the laws around being terminated from a job and your right to a vacation are a lot more progressive than here."

Her impressions are indeed correct. According to the sociologist Alejandro Portes, "Many Third World nations have implemented la-bor regulations that, on paper at least, have little to envy those of the most advanced countries. In Colombia, Peru and Mexico it is more difficult to fire a worker with some minimum tenure on the job than in the United States."[2] In the United States, by contrast, the legal concept of "employment at will" dominates. Employers can fire or hire whomever they wish, so long as they do not employ discrim-inatory criteria. It is perfectly legal in the United States, according to Cohen, to "work some place for seven years and then the employer comes up to you and fires you and doesn't give you a reason, doesn't give you notice." Cervantes pointed out that employment at will also gives employees the legal authority to quit without giving notice. But given the obvious imbalance of power, employers and employees are hardly on a level playing field. Although in recent decades a body of U.S. laws dealing with "wrongful termination" has developed, it is telling that these usually apply only to rich executives able to demonstrate the implied breach of a written contract (think of former Disney studio chief Jeffrey Katzenberg, widely reported to have won $250 million from Disney).[3]

When paid domestic workers approach attorneys after their firing, they believe that they will be either reinstated or financially compensated with severance pay. The attorneys and their staff often discover that though their termination was legal, the former employees—especially the live-ins—had illegal deductions taken out of their pay or were underpaid for hours worked. For this reason, a domestic worker who initially seeks legal help for a wrongful termination frequently winds up pursuing a claim for back wages (discussed in chapter 8).

QUITTING QUIETLY:
EXCUSES AND WHITE LIES

Weekly housecleaners and their employers rarely experience blowups, in part because they see each other only once a week, twice a month, or perhaps not at all. Their meetings typically are momentary, so they find it relatively easy to remain cordial. Since the housecleaners' job duties do not include child care, employer-employee relations are less complex and less volatile. When problems do arise, both housecleaners and their employers prefer to end the arrangement with discretion. Though quieter than blowups, these job endings are often equally irregular, for they rarely involve the advance notice standard in most workplaces.

Many housecleaners find it expedient to just stop going to a problematic job. After finishing their cleaning on a Tuesday afternoon, they may quietly—or at least unbeknownst to the employer—decide to never return. Teresa Portillo used this method to leave a bad job. She made the mistake of taking too much initiative at one house when she did the laundry in addition to the thorough weekly cleaning. Thereafter, the employer anticipated she would complete the laundry each time, and although Teresa explained that their original agreement did not stipulate her waiting until the dryer finished its cycle, the employer left a note saying that she would deduct $5 from Teresa's pay every time she left clothes in the dryer. Teresa Portillo solved the problem: she simply stopped going to that job. Similarly, Lupe Vélez, who had a full route of houses, told me what she did when she was accused by her employer of scratching an old, well-used stove. "I finished cleaning that house, but my eyes were swollen [from crying] for that stove that I hadn't scratched. I went home and I didn't return." For her it was a point of honor to finish the job that she had come to do that day. Still, she never told the employer that she would not be returning.

Other housecleaners leave particular jobs by calling in sick a few times, or by relying on that favorite, time-tested excuse: "My mother is sick and I must immediately return to Guatemala." The identities of the country and the sick person vary, but the pretext is used so often that some Latina domestic workers joke about it, occasionally recalling with laughter the dramatic embellishments that accompany these exits.

Housecleaners are not the only ones who rely on lies and excuses. Live-out and live-in nanny/housekeepers do the same, though they are more likely to invent a story about leaving to care for a sick relative than to just disappear. Gladys Vargas reflected on this practice, and concluded that it was the safest, simplest route out of a job. "About a year ago a friend of mine, who was working as a housekeeper for a bachelor, says to me, 'Look, I'm going to Miami. But I have to tell the *señor* that I'm going back to Honduras . . . because what if something is missing? And then another thing, and then he calls the police?' That would make her life impossible, so it's just easier to say that she's going to Honduras to be with her sick children even though she's going to Miami for a better job."

At first, it might seem that nothing prevents these women from simply explaining that they are quitting, and perhaps giving as a reason their dissatisfaction with the job. But they are subordinates in a relationship marked by asymmetries of race, nationality, citizenship, language, and class, unaccustomed to expressing face-to-face criticism to a superior. In fact, they fear retribution for doing so. A domestic employee who bluntly tells her employer that she is leaving

because she has a better job prospect, or because she disliked something about the current job, may be seen as disloyal and betraying
her employer. Like Gladys's friend, she risks being accused of theft,
justly or unjustly. She may fear that the former employer will retal-
iate by calling the immigration authorities, landing her in jail. Or she
may hesitate to ignite the unpleasant verbal encounter that might
follow if she gave notice. For the most part, Latina domestic workers
want both to avoid future problems with former employers and to
spare themselves the awkwardness and discomfort of confrontations
over the truth. Evasions seem to spare everyone, both the *señora* and
the housecleaner, disgrace and discomfort.

Employers often know that these reasons for quitting are lies. Several of them laughingly recalled seeing their former housekeepers,
women who supposedly had to suddenly leave to visit sick or dying
relatives in their countries of origin, just days or weeks later, waiting
at bus stops in the neighborhood. When a housecleaner calls in sick
for a few days, and then just disappears, the employer may interpret
her action as demonstrating typical behavior of a lazy, unmotivated,
Latina immigrant, not as revealing a disgruntled employee who is
unhappy (perhaps with good reason) with the particular job. As Julia
Wrigley notes, "AWOL workers are sending their employers a message, but it is not a message employers always choose to understand."[4]

Employers do not show much more honesty when they fire domestic workers. With the exception of the furious dismissals after
blowups, employers also prefer to invent some reason why "We
won't be needing you any longer." They might say that they are
going on an extended trip, that their house is going to be remodeled,
or that their former employee is returning. Sometimes these stories
are true, sometimes not. Many employers find it very difficult to
actually fire someone, or to constructively communicate job deficiencies in ways that might allow the employee to improve.

"Unless you're a sadist," remarked the matronly Elizabeth Mapplethorpe, "you don't like deliberately hurting somebody." Elizabeth
Mapplethorpe told me she had fired her last "maid," a young Latina
woman, because she couldn't properly cook and serve a formal dinner for six. Yet she never gave that same information to the employee.
In spite of this employer's years of experience with domestic employees, her ample social graces, and her seemingly unflappable con-

fidence as a superior communicating directives, she wasn't quite sure how to handle the situation. She sought advice from the domestic employment agency that had initially made the placement, which suggested that she tell the woman that the former housekeeper was returning. And that is how she fired her.

Bonnie Feinstein, who employed a round-the-clock rotating group of cleaners, housekeepers, and nanny/baby-sitters in her home, was extremely dissatisfied with two of the women in her small crew— particularly the weekly housecleaner, Sarita. "She started to come to iron and she didn't have any other work, and so then I let her start cleaning," she explained apologetically. "She's not a very good cleaner, and she's not a very good ironer, but I just haven't been able to fire her," she chuckled. "So I just haven't fired her.... I'd just rather stick with someone like Sarita who is not perfect, rather than make a change." Later in our interview, she added, "I'd like to have the strength to fire Sarita."

"Do you think you will?" I asked.

"Yeah, I think I will. We're gonna go away next month, and I've told her, you know, that I'm thinking about changing things around, and we're waiting to hear about this thing my husband is doing in France," she replied. "I'll use that as an excuse. I've told her that that's a possibility."

"Have you ever told her that her cleaning is not up to par?" I inquired.

"No," she laughed. "No, I know I should, but I just haven't." In fact, Sarita's cleaning was so substandard that even the other household employees had complained about it to their employer. Bonnie, at a loss for how to effectively approach the problem, told them to handle it among themselves. Her neighbor across the street, Julie Thompson-Ahib, also employed Sarita, but she acted with less ambivalence. One day she had returned home to find Sarita in her house, cleaning on a day when she was not scheduled to do so. She expressed her anger, but Sarita remained unflustered. "At that point," recalled Julie Thompson-Ahib, "I said, 'You know, I really have to think about this, and I'll let you know when I want you to come back." She did her own housecleaning for eight months, and then, just before hosting a party at her home, she called Sarita. Sarita, she reported, returned to clean and acted as though nothing had ever happened between them.

While not all employers are as diffident about communicating their displeasure and dissatisfaction to domestic employees as was Bonnie Feinstein, and while few would reemploy someone after dismissing her because of a transgression, most employers strongly prefer staying with an imperfect housecleaner who is a known quantity to confronting an unsatisfactory worker or going through the hassle of searching for a replacement. When they do decide to fire someone, the termination is rarely done straightforwardly.

THE CONSEQUENCES OF BLOWUPS, EXCUSES, AND OTHER METHODS OF EXITING THE JOB

When a domestic worker leaves a job because of a blowup, or when she exits with a transparent excuse or simply disappears without notice, she is left without a reference to her immediate past job performance. That absence is especially significant in an occupation in which the recommendation is the single most important credential for future employment and referrals are the most common method of finding a new job. Those who leave jobs without references often suffer downward mobility within the occupation.

Not only the women doing domestic work but also lawyers and owners of domestic employment agencies routinely encounter problems caused by blowups. One owner of a domestic employment agency found these job exits to occur so regularly, and to be so damaging to workers' future job prospects, that she now advised employees to request an annual letter of reference from their current employer. She reasoned that if a blowup occurred in, say, July, the dismissed employee would still have a good letter of reference written in January. On one occasion, I observed her counsel a group of domestic workers, and this was one of her main employment tips. When I described this preventative remedy to another agency owner, he quickly dismissed it. "So here you have a letter and what if the [new employer] family calls? She [the prospective new hire] left in a horrible way, and that puts a seed of doubt into the new family. Don't forget, this person's gonna turn around and pay me a fee. Why should they pay a fee for this seed of doubt?" Another agency owner, the only one who tied the blowups to conditions of employment, took a structural approach to the problem. He wrote a newsletter advising employer clients that they would enhance their chances of keeping their nannies by providing raises and paid vacations. All of the agency owners recognized that these abrupt job endings cause difficulties.

The tendency to end jobs in blowups or white lies has serious implications for the occupation. Under these circumstances, a domestic worker never tells her employer exactly what was bad about the job, and the employer—whether she graciously makes up a story to get rid of an unsatisfactory employee or fires the woman in a screaming match—denies the employee the opportunity to discover what she might have done to improve her job performance, and perhaps save her job. To be sure, some employers and employees would not listen to one another; but others, despite the differences in power between these two groups, would heed honest words. Seen from this angle, the job exits are openings to occupational reform—chances missed when jobs end in the ways discussed in this chapter.

Many years ago, the development economist Albert O. Hirschman observed that consumers express dissatisfaction with company products either by exiting the relationship (i.e., buying their goods elsewhere) or by voicing complaints.[5] The former is a good deal easier than the latter. Exiting an economic relationship requires no verbal skills and no negotiating savvy, and it almost ensures that everyone concerned will be spared messy, complex, and unpleasant interactions.

In paid domestic work, the highly asymmetrical positions of employers and employees encourage the painless exit. It is difficult and risky for employees to voice their concerns; many Latina domestic workers fear that in retaliation for their legitimate complaints about the job, they will be unjustly accused of theft, breakage, or other offenses they did not commit. For their part, most middle-class and upper-middle-class Americans remain profoundly uncomfortable with conflict: quiet dismissals and fabricated excuses seem neater, more manageable, and less offensive than heated arguments. The choices on both sides are understandable, but the avoidance of honest discussion makes it more difficult to reform and upgrade paid domestic work.

The reliance on blowups and excuses to terminate jobs also demonstrates yet again that this occupation is set outside the realm of usual employment practices. The lack of generally accepted standards in the jobs performed makes both employers and employees even more reluctant to communicate their dissatisfactions directly. Blowups and the use of white lies are entangled with ambivalence about control of domestic labor and personal relations between employers and employees, the themes addressed in the next two chapters.

PART THREE

INSIDE THE JOB

Contemporary employers of domestic workers are neither despotic nor maternalistic, but this does not mean that all is well in private paid domestic work. The chapters in this section highlight issues related to control of labor, the quality of relationships between employers and employees, and, finally, efforts to upgrade paid domestic work.

Chapter 6 looks at labor control, how employers go about getting Latina domestic workers to perform the desired tasks, and the ways in which Latina housecleaners and nanny/housekeepers, in turn, comply, resist, and negotiate. A central tension is created by employers' reluctance to give specific instructions. The Latina women who do the work say they want to hear clearly stated directives, though they also cherish autonomy in accomplishing the jobs requested. Employers' expectations (often unstated) and employees' understanding of what is to be done (and how) frequently clash.

Many contemporary employers would rather not, and often do not, engage in personal relationships with their Latina nanny/housekeepers and housecleaners. At the same time, Latina domestic workers say they want consideración *(understanding): they want employers to understand who they are, and to see them not as disposable cogs or servants on call, but as individuals with their own needs. In chapter 7, I explain these divergent preferences by examining the employers' and employees' social locations, their identities as women in contemporary society, the occupational tasks involved in domestic work, and the different job arrangements. I also address prior scholarship on paid domestic work in drawing some distinctions between personalism and maternalism. In chapter 8, I advocate that the occupation of paid domestic work be upgraded and recognized as employment, focusing mainly on three approaches to achieving fairer domestic job standards: formalizing employment through compliance with standard employment regulations, filing claims for back wages, and encouraging collective organizing.*

6

Tell Me What to Do,
But Don't Tell Me How

When Elvira Areola, still feeling wounded by the quarrel that had ended her long-standing job, described her ideal employer, she emphasized that a good employer uses plain directives, together with positive feedback. "If she's happy with her employee, she speaks clearly to her so that everything will go well, she communicates more, says, 'I don't like this, but I do like this,' or 'I want you to do this, but I don't want you to do that.'" Directives and clear communication, in her view, were essential. "That way," Elvira continued, "you don't waste time killing yourself doing something they don't even want you do to." Other housecleaners and nanny/housekeepers echoed these preferences.

But today's employers in Los Angeles tend to shy away from defining the tasks they want performed. When I asked employers to describe their ideal nannies and housekeepers, many of them told me they preferred being spared such explanations. "The ideal person in my life," offered Jenna Proust, who had ample experience employing housecleaners and nanny/housekeepers, "would be someone who anticipates what needs to be done and barely needs to be told. That would be wonderful." Similarly, when I asked a homemaker what she liked best about her live-in nanny/housekeeper of seven years, she replied without hesitation, "She takes initiative. She doesn't really need me to tell her stuff." Another woman who had hired many weekly housecleaners said, "My assumption was that they know how to do the job."

This chapter focuses on labor control, the ability of employers to obtain the work behavior that they desire from their domestics; it also examines the ways in which the housecleaners and nanny/housekeepers comply with, resist, and negotiate over such control. On assembly lines, in office bureaucracies, or at fast-food outlets, labor control is embedded in the organization of work itself.[1]

This is not the case in contemporary domestic jobs. Moreover, the absence of written job contracts, fixed products, and the profit motive suggests that modes of labor control in paid domestic work will be very different from those found in, say, a General Motors plant or a McDonald's. While there is broad agreement about the scope of the job, the tasks are diffuse and there is no standardization of the services that will be performed or of how they will be executed.

Even the specific job requirements are ambiguous. For instance, what exactly is meant by "light housekeeping" or "care for three school-age children"? These phrases are open to multiple interpretations, and employers and employees may have conflicting interests in defining them. Employers—who can hire and fire at will—have more power than their employees; and as we have seen, relations in the domestic occupation in Los Angeles are particularly asymmetrical, as the Latina employees are subordinated not only by race and socioeconomic class but also by nationality and immigration status. Still, it is a rare employer who straightforwardly explains all the daily job responsibilities at the outset of employment. Moreover, job tasks and the way they are carried out differ from one job to the next. Because employers and job sites vary widely, one nanny/housekeeper job will not be identical to another next door; cleaning obligations may be very different at each house on the route.

To further complicate matters, job requirements often change over time. Many employers increase their demands, while others may reluctantly decide to settle for less. Some employers, for instance, decide to overlook a nanny/housekeeper's poor housecleaning because of her superlative care of the children. Nanny/housekeepers are frequently asked to assume more responsibilities without commensurate increases in pay. "Nos aumentan el trabajo, sin aumentar el pago," or "They raise our workload without raising our pay," is a common refrain among Latina domestic workers in Los Angeles.

The variability is, to some extent, understandable: caring for households and young children entails a multitude of activities. Many tasks—mopping floors, cooking, scrubbing bathrooms, changing diapers, doing laundry, and so forth—must be done over and over again, and few are performed in a standardized way or on a strict time schedule. Yet there is an even simpler explanation for the diverse, ill-defined forms of labor control that we see in this job. Employers don't see themselves as employers, and they do not view their homes as work sites.

Many employers, for various reasons, initially feel too awkward to make explicit what they want when they hire a domestic worker. Others refrain from doing so because they are at first uncertain about the services they want performed. Though they unequivocally prefer domestic workers who will take initiative, the direction taken by that initiative may not be the one the employers had in mind. Like the student who works hard to complete a vague assignment only to be told by the teacher, "This is not what I had in mind," so too many domestic workers are criticized and told what they should have done only after their work is performed. At that point, the directives may take the form of harshly phrased commands and angry ultimatums.

Eventually, many employers learn to use different strategies to get the services they want. They exert control through time management, surveillance, evaluation of output, maternalistic gestures, and, more rarely, written or verbal instructions (figure 2). The tension between their desire to get their "money's worth" from their nannies or housecleaners and their reluctance to see themselves as employers, combined with their ineffectualness in communicating job requirements when employment first begins, often creates conflict. Maternalistic gestures of the kind so widely documented in other studies are not common in Los Angeles today. Whenever domestic employees related their experiences with despotic employers, they almost always involved immigrant employers.[2]

For their part, the Latina employees use diverse strategies as they seek to efficiently deliver services while retaining some degree of control over the work process. The approaches of nanny/housekeepers and housecleaners, like their jobs, often differ. Yet members of both groups wish to receive from their employers some directions about *what* to do, while maintaining autonomy in *how* they do it. Conflicts that arise between employers and employees can often be traced not just to a lack of clear directives but also to issues of *time.* To improve the quality of their jobs, nanny/housekeepers seek to limit the hours that they work and housecleaners attempt to win flexibility in their hours.

Figure 2. Advertisements in *L.A. Parent Magazine*, July 1996. New industries arise to help parents exert control over the nanny's care of their children and, especially, to allay their fears about any harm befalling their children. Some parents are ready to send the nanny to school to learn how to handle a health emergency. Others want to conduct video surveillance while they themselves are off at work, even though it is parents and relatives who are most often guilty of physical abuse against children.

NANNY/HOUSEKEEPERS

Many of today's employers of nanny/housekeepers do not want to direct the work or organize and monitor the household tasks that need to be done. While such reluctance to become involved has always been common among male employers, it is now found among female employers as well. When they hire a full-time employee in their home, they prefer someone who will take full charge of most of the household tasks, freeing them of the responsibility not just of doing this work but also of thinking about it. These employers may provide verbal cues or reprimands only if the work isn't done. After all, they are hiring a substitute to deal with their own domestic labor; they don't want to invest time in managing that labor. Employers who work full-time outside the home are more likely to abnegate control, but their expectations of the quality and quantity of work performed may remain just as high. The employee is often left to intuitively figure out what needs to be done. Millie Chu, a pediatric nurse and single mother of two young children, explained that from her perspective, an ideal nanny/housekeeper is "Somebody who can know what you need before you have to ask—like just know you that well."

When I spoke with her, Millie was very satisfied with Marisol, her live-in nanny/housekeeper, precisely because Marisol was attuned to the rhythms of her personal moods and household needs. "Like sometimes when I'm trying to get dinner ready and I'm stressing because I'm looking at the clock, she'll know. She'll ask me what am I making and she's seen me make it so much, she'll just jump in and start cutting the vegetables or cutting the meat or washing the rice, without me saying, 'Marisol, do you think you can help me wash the rice?'" Although Millie also asked Marisol to do special tasks, she preferred to just have her "jump in" to do the work without being prompted. After four years of working in the household, Marisol had become adept at reading subtle cues from this harried, hardworking single parent. "She can totally sense my moods," confirmed Millie Chu. "If I've had a hard day at work and I come home, she can look at me and say, 'Okay kids, hang out with me. Give mom a half hour to unwind.' I'd had another one prior to her who was eighteen years old and the minute I walked in it was like—boom!

She went in her room and shut the door and we never saw her again."

Many employers see the ideal nanny/housekeeper as one who can deftly read these signals and then respond to their needs. Such an employee is able to quickly interpret the employer's emotional moods and needs and is willing to actively step in and respond, even when the clock is ticking well beyond official job hours. A common complaint among nanny/housekeepers in Los Angeles, especially those who live with their employers, is that they must make themselves available round-the-clock. Many are required to sleep in the children's bedroom and find themselves literally on call throughout the night; even those who have their own room often must remain on duty with the children when the employers are home. When I interviewed Marisol, she did not express disgruntlement about overextended work hours, but many other nanny/housekeepers did. The retreat to her room of Millie Chu's former employee signaled one nanny/housekeeper's refusal to extend her hours.

Nanny/housekeepers regularly express frustration with employers who expect them to know what to do without telling them. Several employers acknowledged that it was neither fair nor realistic to expect nanny/housekeepers to telepathically sense what needs to be done. One employer admitted that she herself had been at fault: "You know, I probably get mad without giving them a chance," she said. "Like Sarita, I probably should have told her at an earlier point, you know, 'Do this, do that,' and then if she didn't, gotten rid of her. But I never did, and now I am [getting rid of her]."

Employers who were out of the labor force and at home for a good portion of the day were more likely to give directives. "It's very important that they know what you expect because it's not fair," stated Beverly Voss, a homemaker who employed a live-in nanny/housekeeper in her large, rambling canyon house. "I can't expect Marta to figure out what I want. I need to tell her what I want." Unlike most of the other respondents, Beverly also acknowledged her own obligations in delegating responsibility. When the refrigerator needed to be cleaned out, she asked her live-in employee to do it; but she left it to Marta's discretion as to when and how the task would be performed. Still, even Beverly reported that she would prefer being able to rely on an employee's intuitions. "An ideal housekeeper," she sighed longingly, "would always keep your house perfectly, and would have an eye for things."

These "ideal housekeepers" are scarce, and many employers are at a loss at how to proceed without them. Employers who are new to the world of paid domestic workers may consult with more experienced friends. Carolyn Astor, who had married into a family of much higher social status than her own, went so far as to have a matron who was a friend of her husband's family come to her home on the day that the new nanny/housekeeper began the job. The older woman taught Carolyn how to instruct the new employee on her duties. She translated from English to Spanish, advised Carolyn to drop by the home unexpectedly during the day to check on the work, and helped her devise and explain a daily checklist on which the employee would record routine events, such as "what time the baby went to sleep, what time he woke up, how many peepees, how many poopoos, how many ounces of the bottle." With the list, Carolyn explained, "I came home and looked right on the tablet and I knew how much he ate, how much he slept . . ." The list, which harks back to the era of scientific management, allowed her to monitor what had occurred with her baby while she was out, and it also allowed her to monitor the nanny/housekeeper's activities. She eventually dispensed with the list and the unannounced visits home, as the baby grew into a toddler and as she grew to trust the nanny/housekeeper.

Information exchanged in the employer networks provides important guidelines. Marsha Fama, a wealthy homemaker and mother of a toddler who employed two live-out nanny/housekeepers, reported that her friends marveled at the facility with which she asked her employees to do particular tasks not in the daily or weekly routine, such as cleaning out the closets or scrubbing walls. In fact, she now advised her friends on how to give directives to their domestic employees. "A lot of my friends, you know, see how good Liliana is, and they say, 'How do you tell her?' Because they feel like they can't always express their needs and wants. And I said, it's not so much what you say to them, but it's just *how* you say it." She explained what she meant. "Like they know that I appreciate them. I tell them. I physically show them. I hug them when they do something really good, or um, if I'm sick and they take care of me, I say, 'Well, thank you very much.'" While her approach smacks of something straight out of the positive reinforcement section of a manual on motivating employees, the several hours I spent with Marsha convinced me that it was a genuine outgrowth of her effusive, sugary personality. Unlike many other employers, she relies on a method reminiscent of the maternalistic style, whose reign in an earlier era is documented in a large body of literature.[3]

Many Latina domestic workers in Los Angeles do want some verbal appreciation and recognition of their work from their employer. But they also want clear instructions, with lines of communication kept open in both directions. Patricia Paredes, who worked as a live-in and spoke very good English, had worked her way up toward the top of the occupation. She stated this preference most bluntly. "I tell them, 'If I don't like something you do, I will come to you and I won't hesitate in telling you. So I expect you to do the same thing with me. You know, you sit down with me, whenever, and you tell me in a nice way. You don't come to me and yell, because we're not going to get anywhere with that.'" While few Latina nannies are as forthright as Patricia, another nanny/housekeeper commented that the need to speak up in these jobs had helped her become more assertive. "I learned in my first job," she said, "to lose my shyness." Another woman, who had recently switched from working as a nanny/housekeeper to a cleaner, added, "I like it when they tell me what's okay, and what's bad, and I like to tell them what is okay and what is not."

Yet while employers want employees with initiative, they do not always appreciate assertiveness; and when domestic employees hear negative feedback, they find it hard to take, especially when it is constant. Ronalda Saavedra complained that her employer, Jenna Proust, issued not directives but humiliating reprimands. The underlying dynamic of this arrangement involved Jenna's attempt to make her employee more like a servant, on call at all times, and Ronalda's resistance to such servitude and the loss of all autonomy in her job. "The people I have around me on a daily basis have to be able to help do what I ask them to do," explained Jenna. "It may be embarrassing," she admitted, "to ask someone to quickly come and clean a spill," as she had done at the beginning of our interview when she spilled coffee on a white sofa, "but that is what they're here for, so I can do other things." Indeed, she had become annoyed when her call for help was ignored—though it seemed unlikely that anyone in a different room in her 6,000-square-foot home could have heard her.

Jenna Proust believed she was purchasing the right to have her nanny/housekeeper perform whatever tasks she stipulated; Ronalda Saavedra expected to follow her employer's directives, but she resented having to constantly seek out her employer to ask how she might be of service. This version of servanthood bothered Ronalda, who was required to regularly enter Jenna's home office or sitting room to see if she had any requests. "Sometimes I go and I ask if she needs anything, and she says, 'No.' This *señora* is so illogical! It's like I must report," she exclaimed. "Why can't she come tell me?" Ronalda experienced Jenna's requirement that she submit to occasional requests, rather than be left to complete her instructed tasks or routine job obligations, as a symbol of servitude and a humiliating affront to her dignity.

LONG DAY'S JOURNEY INTO NIGHT: LIVE-IN JOBS

Domestic employees, especially live-ins, wish to establish firm boundaries around their work hours, which employers desire to remain more elastic. As the owner of an agency that specializes in placements of nanny/housekeepers explained, "The truth of the matter is they want a live-in to have somebody at their beck and call. And so, yes, they might give you [the employee] a three-hour break during the day, but they want you to baby-sit at night. That's why they want a live-in. They want the flexibility, the spontaneity, they want to be able to have a life and a relationship with their husband, or date or whatever." Employer flexibility here clearly depends on round-the-clock domestic service.

The employer's schedules and needs may mandate that the services provided by live-in domestic labor begin very early and end very late. It is not unusual for a nanny/housekeeper to be on the job twelve hours a day, or even longer. Some of the Latina nanny/housekeepers, as we have seen, must sleep in the children's bedrooms. Given such arrangements, limiting the workday to twelve hours may be a major achievement, gained only after deliberate negotiations. Many Latina women who held live-in jobs complained to me, "I had to hold the baby in my arms, even when I brushed my teeth!" After several months in such a job, one woman who cared for the baby of entertainment industry executives negotiated new work hours, which included some break time in the afternoon but still spanned eleven and a half hours, from 8:30 A.M. until 7 P.M. For her, this was a vast improvement.

As Julia Wrigley has pointed out in *Other People's Children* (1995), nannies provide a very different service than day care centers, which mandate that parents must pick up children by a certain hour. "When already paid-for labor is available," notes Wrigley, "it takes a strong-minded parent to keep shouldering the work."[4] Many nanny/housekeepers complained about employers who do not engage with their children when they return from work. The nanny/housekeepers generally prefer to care for the children without interference: children, they explained, tend to misbehave more when their parents are around. But parents' interaction with the children every day is crucial to enhancing their job satisfaction. "All of those people who have money," proclaimed one live-in nanny, "don't spend time with their kids, not because they're busy, but because they are tired, they come home, they think that only ten minutes is enough. It is not, you know, but some parents don't see their kids all day and it can be a week, and they don't see them and they don't care." Another nanny told me, "They come home from work, fix themselves a drink, lie down to watch TV in their room, and shut the door." Another alleged her employers came home to smoke pot in their room, while she was stuck with the children. Live-in nanny/housekeepers bitterly criticized such behavior, not just because it reflected employers' unwillingness to recognize limits on their hours of work but also because it branded their employers as irresponsible parents who didn't want to be with their children. In their view, these were simply bad mothers, bad parents, and bad employers.

The parents, however, do feel exhausted when they come home from work, and as employers, they want their money's worth. If their children spend the day at school and return at three o'clock, they sometimes suspect that their nanny/housekeeper enjoys too much idle time during the day. They wonder, "Is she just sitting around watching *telenovelas* or chatting on the phone?" If the nanny takes young children to the park daily, the employers may believe that she is neglecting the housework in order to socialize with other nannies. Employers may assuage their fears by various means of surveillance. The highly publicized monitoring via hidden video camera lodged in a teddy bear is less common than audio surveillance (listening through the intercom system, or eavesdropping from the hallway) or simply surprise visits. Parents sometimes drop by their home unannounced or arrive unexpectedly at the park to make sure that the caregiver is indeed on the job, playing with the children and not just conversing with other nannies. A few of the nanny/housekeepers complained about this, but most agree that looking after young children is a big responsibility, and that parents are entitled to check on how they are caring for the children. Surprisingly, I found that the nanny/housekeepers were much more disturbed by poorly defined job hours than by surveillance.

Enforced isolation is another means of controlling live-in domestic workers. Some employers forbid their employees to regularly meet with other nanny/housekeepers. The nannies may be told not to take the children to the park, because the employers fear that they will network, learn about going pay rates and better jobs, and then ask for raises or shorter hours. Several employers that I interviewed blamed what they perceived to be unfair requests for raises on the informational exchanges among Latina nannies and housekeepers who chat at bus stops and parks.

TIME ON TASK VERSUS TIME ON THE JOB

Much of domestic work is invisible. When a nanny/housekeeper is in the home five or six days a week, she may devise routines that relegate laundry to Monday, vacuuming to Tuesday, and so forth, perhaps leaving time for her own rest when the children are napping, or before they return home from school in the afternoon. When the employers are homemakers, they may actually observe this rest time—as Beverly Voss had recently done. Her youngest daughter had just begun attending school, thereby relieving Marta, the live-in nanny/housekeeper, of some child care duties. To counter what she perceived as long periods of idleness, Beverly was trying, without much success, to find new tasks that might occupy Marta. Marta kept the 5,600-square-foot home looking perfect, and Beverly and her husband had already made Friday and Saturday night babysitting part of Marta's weekly job duties. Grocery shopping and meal preparation were possibilities, but Beverly did not want to relinquish control over selecting what food came into the home ("you can't know what's fresh and looks good until you're there"); and though she wished she could ask Marta to do the nightly cooking, she felt that the request would be inappropriate, because it was a large addition to the initial duties and they had not started off this way. Moreover, as the homemaker wife and mother who had been largely relieved of cleaning and child-rearing duties, she felt it her responsibility to prepare evening family meals. After all, buying food and planning and preparing meals are, as the sociologist Marjorie De-Vault has shown in *Feeding the Family* (1991), central arenas through which women construct the family. Still, she continued to ponder other new tasks to assign Marta.

Beverly Voss held back on these impulses, but many other employers do not. Thus the Latina nanny/housekeepers often complain of "aumento de trabajo, sin aumento de sueldo"—"raises in work duties without raises in pay." Because most households no longer have multiple servants handling different jobs, the one employee tends to be given all available tasks; and when the employees learn to manage their time so efficiently that they create some free time, employers think that they have a right to add more responsibilities.

Racial inequality increases the likelihood that employers will require the same employee both to care for children *and* to take full charge of the housekeeping. While white "American" nannies are generally not expected to do housecleaning work, Latinas regularly are. As Wrigley found in her study, parents with sufficient means often make the transition from employing a lower-wage Latina nanny/housekeeper, when their children are young, to a higher-priced English-speaking British or American nanny as their children grow older and begin to talk.[5] As noted in chapter 4, a headhunter I interviewed saw these employers—the "tweeners" moving from one kind of job arrangement to another—as among the most challenging. An American nanny, he maintained, is very different from a Latina nanny/housekeeper, and he must instruct employers that they cannot expect white American nannies to clean and so must bring in someone else to do the housekeeping.

Some of the employers bore out his observations. Ellen Maxson, who had recently hired a young white woman from the South to work as a part-time live-out nanny/housekeeper, said that her family members had counseled her against hiring a white woman. "My mom," she reported sheepishly, "said, 'Well, you know, if you hire the Hispanics,' or 'if you hire the Mexicans, I guess you can order them around a little bit more.' And I was thinking through that because my spouse also said something to the same effect, like 'Don't you really want a Mexican woman that you can order around or something?'" She went against their advice; and as her family members had predicted, the young white woman refused or was unable to do much in the way of housecleaning. For various reasons—her husband was away on an extended business trip, the children had chicken pox, and she desperately needed continuity—Ellen found herself in a relatively weak position to negotiate, so she settled for less. She had experienced a similar problem, however, with a Guatemalan woman who had previously been hired to care for her young children and do "light housekeeping": the immigrant employee, not the employer, had prevailed in defining the latter job. Perhaps the Guatemalan nanny's relatively high socioeconomic status (she was a homeowner, while Ellen was not) provided some leverage. Class, but more frequently race, nationality, and immigration status, can strongly influence negotiations to redefine the job, more readily enabling employees with relative privilege in one or more of these areas to circumscribe their job tasks.

Latina nanny/housekeepers did not respond uniformly to the demand that they take on more work. Some of them went out of their way to take initiative and find new chores that needed to be done in the households where they worked. Others remained more guarded. In informal settings, I observed Latinas cautioning one another on many occasions against volunteering to do extra household cleaning tasks. "If you start doing them, then they think it's your responsibility," offered one woman. "The more you do," complained Gladys Villeda, "the more they want, see?"

USING EMOTION TO LEVERAGE PRIORITIES: CLEANING OR CARING?

Some nanny/housekeepers develop very strong ties of affection with the children they care for. It is not unusual for nanny/housekeepers to be alone with their charges during the workweek, and for long stretches they have no one else with whom to talk or interact. During the day they are not only vacuuming, scrubbing, and washing dishes but also cuddling, teasing, giggling, and clowning with the children.

Not surprisingly, many nanny/housekeepers and young children grow genuinely fond of each other. These emotional attachments do not remain "outside" the labor process, but are often used by both employers and employees to get what they want. They thus become critical elements in the labor process of these care providers.[6]

Nearly all the employers who hire Latinas for live-in and live-out positions and have children at home stated that caring for the children should be the most important priority. Objects in the home are replaceable, they emphasized, while their children are not. Most maintained that "light housekeeping," or "whatever she can get done" was all they required. Yet many Latina nanny/housekeepers told me a different story, frustrated by their employers' expectations that they keep the house spotless *and* simultaneously look after rambunctious children or needy babies. They worried that their cleaning responsibilities would cause them to neglect the children, who might then have an accident for which they would be blamed. They are hired to do, in essence, two jobs—caring and cleaning—and employers and employees do not always agree on which comes first.

Both parents and care providers may exploit the emotional bond between the nanny/housekeeper and the children for their own benefit. Parents are deeply concerned about the quality of care their children receive, and over time, some came to expect less cleaning from their nannies. These parents viewed it as folly to lose a trusted, loving nanny because she did not meet their original requirements for a housekeeper. One employer, who complained that at one point "you could carve your initials in the dust" and that she herself was mopping the floor, resolved the problem by hiring biweekly cleaners to come in on Saturday morning, when the nanny/housekeeper was not there. "It annoys me," Karla Steinheimer said of this arrangement, "but I just tell myself that I don't have to worry that the baby is safe. I don't worry that the baby is well loved and feels happy and comfortable, and that's what I'm hiring Filomina for. Look, I could make lists and have her do that, but I don't want to have that kind of relationship. The baby is the focus and that's what matters." In this instance, by providing superior care the nanny won lighter cleaning responsibilities, effectively redefining her job tasks.

Some nanny/housekeepers used concerns about the children's safety as leverage to strengthen their position. Maura de la Covarrubia, a young Peruvian woman who not incidentally had previously worked as an attorney, relied not on her emotional bond with the children but on concern for the children's safety and social development to redefine her job so that her "nanny" duties outweighed "housekeeping" chores. "When it's a question of taking care of children, it's a lot of responsibility, and if something happens to them, they'll put me in jail. In one second," she said, snapping her fingers to illustrate the haste with which employers might act, "they can do whatever." She reported that she had used this reasoning to tell her employers that cleaning would have to come second to the children. A young Mexican nanny/housekeeper was waiting a few months before asking for a raise, but she felt confident that the employers would approve her request, as she knew they wanted their child to experience the stability of having only one care provider over a period of time.

Employers want good, loving care for their children, but they don't want to lose their children's affection or feel displaced as parents. Experienced nanny/housekeepers know that they must not antagonize the parents, especially the mothers, by garnering too many overt demonstrations of affection from the children. The *Americanas*, they have noted, tend to become jealous when they see their children running more eagerly to the nanny than to the mommy, or hear them cooing "I'm Concha's baby." If a nanny/housekeeper watches a one-year-old take his first steps, she may try to stage it again, out of consideration for the mother, who can then think she is seeing that breakthrough moment. And clearly, there are limits on appropriate displays of affection. Still, nanny/housekeepers know that parents want someone who will genuinely "care for" and "care about" their children; and because of that desire, parents may sometimes accept the trade-off of superior child care for less cleaning.

When employers hire Latina immigrant women to work in their homes on a daily basis, they usually expect both cleaning and care work to be done. Some of the employers interviewed created job task lists, but these methods of formalizing the cleaning chores were not always successful. One employer complained, "I have my little list posted inside one of the cupboards that says these are my priorities. When the child is asleep, do this, this, this. Even though they haven't been done, I'll find her reading a book, just doing her own thing." But she was reluctant to push: "I really don't want any conflicts, so I'm just not saying anything." Another employer added, "It's just kind of a trade-off. Is it worth confronting the person? In general, it's not." A third recalled, "When I told her [to clean], she became exceedingly defensive and upset, and then do I want somebody who is upset looking after my kids?" To explain such behavior, Wrigley notes that in the United States members of the middle class generally avoid face-to-face confrontations; instead, "They routinely refer disputes to specialists, including police, lawyers, and public officials."[7] While this cultural proclivity certainly contributes to the decisions of employers who settle for higher-quality care in lieu of cleaning, we should also note that these employers are acting as parents who desire high-caliber, stable care for their young children. When that wish is fulfilled, and when their children are flourishing, some employers are willing to choose superior caregiving over thorough cleaning.

The leveraging goes both ways, as the emotional bonds between care providers and the children may anchor nanny/housekeepers to less-than-desirable jobs. Margarita Gutiérrez, for example, stayed at a live-in job in which she remained on call at all hours and for which she was poorly paid; she had passed up better job offers because she felt pity for the little "abandoned" boy whose parents were always gone. If she left her job, "What would happen to him?" she wondered. Another woman, Eloida Ruíz, felt the same way. "I must do everything that she [the employer] indicates she would like me to do, because," explained Eloida, "it is her house and she is paying me. And I feel so sorry for the little boy, *pobrecito!*"

Latina nanny/housekeepers who had their own children "back home" in their countries of origin also became emotionally anchored to their jobs. For nanny/housekeepers who are transnational mothers, the loving daily care that they cannot give their own children is sometimes transferred to their employers' children. Still, experienced nanny/housekeepers know they can lose their jobs when employers unexpectedly move or put their children in day care centers, or when blowups occur. Some nanny/housekeepers told me that painful experiences with jobs that ended abruptly had taught them to moderate the love they feel for the children of their employers. Several women reported that they now remained very measured in their relationships and guarded emotionally, so that they could protect themselves against the moment when connections might suddenly be severed. As one woman said emphatically, "I love them, but not like they were my own children because they are not! They are not my kids! Because if I get to love them, and then I go, then I'm going to suffer like I did the last time. I don't want that."

AUTONOMY AND AUTHORITY IN CHILD REARING:
WHO KNOWS BEST?

Taking care of young children encompasses a multitude of tasks that require making many detailed decisions. Mundane daily events, such as eating meals and snacks, involve so many choices that even employers who do communicate to the nanny/housekeepers what the children should be fed will find themselves at a loss to cover everything. How the food is prepared, what constitutes a nutritious snack, and what passes for table manners are some of the minutiae that require attention. Similarly, rules about child discipline, television viewing, or methods of quieting and comforting a crying baby may not be clearly set out. Even when instructions are plainly given, they may include many matters about which the employers (usually the mothers) and the nanny/housekeepers disagree. Are nanny/housekeepers hired to follow parents' orders, or are they hired as professionals who "know best"?

Hierarchies of race, nationality, immigration status, class, and, to a lesser extent, age persist among nannies. Wrigley argues that employers who choose private nannies "similar" to themselves with respect to race, language, culture, and so on not only pay them higher salaries but are also most likely to concede authority to these "expert" care workers.[8] Conversely, employers who hire, say, Latina immigrants who speak little English, are poor, are dark-skinned, and have little cultural capital are more likely to call the shots. Still, there is variation even within this group.

Latina nanny/housekeepers themselves have divergent views on the permissive child-rearing methods that they often witness and are sometimes asked to follow. Some women openly admire American middle-class parents for setting limits on television viewing, or for punishing their children with "time-outs" rather than spanking, and are eager to learn these child-rearing strategies. Other Latina nanny/housekeepers criticize what they see as American parents' indulgence and coddling of children. Some of these critics try to follow their employers' example because it is their job to do so, while others attempt to establish their own authority as professional care providers, instructing parents on how to properly raise children. All the Latina care workers agree, however, that their biggest problems include neglectful parents and parents who openly undermine their authority.

Many nanny/housekeepers were given no instructions by the parents on how to care for the children. Often it was up to them to figure it out on their own, sometimes with the help of those in their social networks. Some of the Latina nanny/housekeepers who admired the child-rearing strategies of their employers reported that they consciously modeled their discipline strategies by observing and imitating the parents. "You have to do is do what the mother does," explained Celestina Vigil. "So for example, when he was a baby and he would hit faces, she would grab his little hand and say, 'No, you don't do that.' She would speak very loudly, so then I would say to myself, 'Well, that's what I have to do.' The child wasn't even a year old, and she was already giving him a time-out." Maura de la Covarrubia, who had worked her way up from being one family's nanny/housekeeper to specializing as a once- or twice-weekly nanny/baby-sitter who brought along special crafts materials and did minimal housecleaning or laundry, said that the best part of her job had been learning about different ways of child rearing. "In our countries, children are educated with repression and punishment," she reflected, "but since that's not allowed here, you need to develop other types of activities. I like working with children, and I've learned a lot. It's a very gratifying experience." Both Celestina, who had been a university student in El Salvador, and Maura, formerly an attorney fighting for social justice in Peru, had urban, middle-class backgrounds, which may have predisposed them to American middle-class child-rearing methods. Yet even they, who were so eager to follow this approach, had to take the initiative to learn and then modify this kind of child rearing. Directions and how-to hints are scarce.

All the Latina nanny/housekeepers want jobs in which the employers will allow them the authority to discipline the children. Most of them are happy or at least willing to follow the discipline method that the parents prefer, but they are profoundly disturbed when the parents interfere with how they administer it. One woman described what had happened when she had placed a child in a time-out for striking another child. The mother walked by, asked the child what had happened, and then affectionately embraced him; after telling him not to do it again, she released him from his time-out. The similar experience of another nanny/housekeeper led to a serious confrontation. Soraya Sanchez recalled an obstinate child who refused to get out of the bathtub; since the parents had told her to get the children in bed by 8 P.M., she had drained the bathtub and threatened to rinse the child off with cold water. When he began to scream, the mother walked in, sided with him, and shouted at her. Soraya told me that later, she had taken the mother aside and said, " 'Don't yell at me again in front of the children, because I'm trying to get them to listen to me and respect me; and if you come in and yell at me, I won't be able to control them.' " Apparently her warning had little effect, because the same pattern continued for the remainder of that job. When parents routinely undermine their authority over the children, Latina nanny/housekeepers are apt to quit.

The paid caregivers and the parents also disagreed on matters such as what children should eat, how warmly they should dress, and how best to deal with crying babies who refused to nap. In these struggles, nanny/housekeepers sometimes secretly subverted their employers' wishes. Eloida Ruíz, a Mexican woman who worked in a live-out job caring for a toddler, expressed deep frustration with the *señora*, who instructed her to feed the child only peanut-butter-and-jelly sandwiches, macaroni and cheese, and jars of baby food. "Many times," she recited, as though it were an incantation, "I pray, Lord, today I brought yogurt with me, and a little salad or soup. And I say, if they don't see it, I'll switch it for what they have left. And I give it to the little boy, because I want him to eat yogurt and fruit, because it's good for him." In a dramatic, histrionic style, inspired by her Evangelical background, Eloida raised her hands high in the air to condemn peanut butter and jelly. "That's not food! Lord, help me and allow her to one day set me free in the kitchen!"

In this instance, the real issue was not the food or workload but autonomy. Eloida Ruíz did not directly confront her employers, but quietly supplied fresh foods in place of processed foods when they were off at work. Another Latina nanny/housekeeper believed that her employer was too rigid in demanding that a seven-year-old boy, who had been diagnosed as hyperactive, never shout in the pool and always eat with utensils. She reported that the mother shielded herself with earplugs and that at dinner, in an ill-fated effort to get the child to use a fork, the mother had once tied one of his hands to the chair. Under these circumstances, the nanny/housekeepers did not directly challenge the employers' authority or attempt to change the rules—but neither did they enforce the rules with conviction. On the contrary, they attempted to quietly subvert those rules of which they disapproved. Most employers want, as one of them said, "someone who will do it my way"; but though nanny/housekeepers will accept and even welcome directives, they want a modicum of authority and autonomy in carrying them out.

Other employers shy away from giving directions even about something as basic as their child's diet, and some nanny/housekeepers do give the children inappropriate foods. Alice McCoy-Fishman, who worked full-time as a physician, recalled her and her husband's distress when they discovered their live-in nanny/housekeeper's penchant for handing out Tums antacid tablets as candy for the children. Yet neither wanted to speak to her about it. "I remember talking to him about things like that. 'You tell her.' 'No, you tell her.'" They were both dissatisfied with their employee's actions, but they did not want to risk conflict over a relatively minor issue (i.e., too much calcium in the children's diet). The employers' abnegation of responsibility here afforded the nanny/housekeeper autonomy—and numerous opportunities for placating the children with Tums.

HOUSECLEANERS

Housecleaners are involved with different issues of labor control than nanny/housekeepers for a number of reasons. First, as we have already noted, cleaning other people's household objects is a job less complex and less fraught with emotional baggage—and therefore less apt to spur contention—than caring for other people's children. Second, the face-to-face interactions between the housecleaners and their employers are usually rare and fleeting. Many cleaners enter the home with their own key, clean the house in solitude, and pick up their payment, seeing the home's occupants only briefly or not at all. Other cleaners work while some members of the employer's family are present, but even then they meet only weekly or twice a month, not daily. Finally, unlike their peers who work in live-in and live-out arrangements, housecleaners have several different employers, cleaning one or two different houses on different days and perhaps maintaining other part-time jobs. Thus a well-established cleaner with multiple jobs runs little risk if she drops one that has become particularly problematic. Far fewer conflicts over labor control issues emerge in housecleaning than in live-in and live-out nanny/housekeeper arrangements.

The sociologist Mary Romero, who has studied Chicanas who clean houses in Denver, uses the term "job work" to refer to these arrangements because the workers are paid not by the hour but rather by the job, performing agreed-on tasks at their own pace and using their own methods. Under this system, Romero argues, domestic workers are able to position themselves as professionals who sell their services in much the same way that a vendor sells a product to various customers.[9] The housecleaners can set their own hours and work schedules, and can avoid the personalistic entanglements that live-in and live-out nanny/housekeepers often experience.

Housecleaners deal with great variety in their work. Those who are successful in building up a full route of houses must become accustomed to different job sites, different cleaning products, and different items to clean, as well as various types of employer relations. Housecleaners must be flexible. At one job, they may feel encouraged to exhibit great deference; at another, the employer may dislike deferential gestures. Cleaning the oven may be included as part of the job at one house, but not at another. In Los Angeles, standard cleaning routines include vacuuming and mopping floors, dusting and polishing furniture, and thoroughly cleaning bathrooms and kitchens. Other, sometimes contested, duties include doing laundry, ironing, changing bed linens, and cleaning ovens and refrigerators. Most housecleaners do not see it as part of their job to bathe and groom animals; clean out garages, basement playrooms, and boxes of cat litter; clean patios and patio furniture; and wash cars. Doing windows, the cleaning cliché, is rarely requested but sometimes performed. More than in the cleaning itself, the cleaners must exercise creativity in responding to the employers.

"It takes a long time to understand them [employers], to understand their ways," observed one, "because the truth is, they're all different." The cleaners prefer to work alone, and the vast majority of their employers prefer to be out of the house while the cleaning occurs. Happily, on this point housecleaners and most of their employers concur. "Don't think I prefer working alone because I'm going to do bad things when they're not around," explained Celestina Vigil. "It's just that the job takes longer when they're there. When I go into the kitchen to mop, there they are, in the middle of the kitchen, so then you lose time." Other cleaners said that they became nervous and dropped fragile items when the employers were watching, and a few mentioned that the chatty employers set them behind in their work. But most employers make a point of not being present when the cleaning occurs. Still, conflicts over job issues sometimes do arise.

"NOS EXPRIMEN: THEY ARE WRINGING US OUT"

Most Latina housecleaners in Los Angeles resist taking jobs in which their time is strictly monitored. They may welcome cleaning guidelines and some initial directives, but they want to arrive at the households, do their cleaning unencumbered by surveillance or added tasks, control their own pace and cleaning methods, and move on to the next job or return home when they finish. They resist efforts to control their labor by time restrictions and monitoring because they know that unscrupulous employers try to use these means to get more work out of them without compensation. Erlinda Castro, a Guatemalan woman who had recently secured a full route of housecleaning jobs, described the least desirable employer this way:

> The bad one for us is the one who's there *craneando* [using her cranium], as we say, trying to devise new work to make the exact eight hours. "Clean the patio around the pool! Wash the patio chairs! Clean the garage! Go sweep outside!" That's the bad one, the one who wants a full eight hours. It's inconsiderate, and among ourselves we say, "They are wringing us out!" They are wringing us out for forty or fifty dollars.

As she spoke, she grimaced and pantomimed the wringing out of a washcloth to emphasize how some employers try to squeeze out every last drop of effort from their workers in the allotted period of time. But when I asked her to define her ideal employer, her enthusiasm became palpable:

> One who tells you what they want done, and who doesn't follow you around, supervising every instant. One who supervises after the

work is done, but one who isn't behind you, behind you, behind you, behind you! See, because you feel pressured that way, and no one works well that way. When one is alone, one works very nicely. It feels really beautiful! It's tranquil and you might even sing. And if I leave the house very pretty, one stands there, looks at the mirrors here, looks over there, and sees everything clean and shiny. That's the ideal, that the woman isn't home!

Notice that she does not object to the supervisory role of the employer but rather to any infringement of her ability to work independently. The pride and satisfaction in doing a job well that this housecleaner and many others describe are linked to autonomy on the job, and to the visible outcome of their efforts. Unlike nanny/housekeepers, who may watch their work immediately unravel when a child tracks mud onto a newly mopped floor, housecleaners who work alone and according to their own pace—and then can see the results—express satisfaction with their jobs. Conception, execution, and brief visual appropriation of the job are unified. The last step, even if it is merely a backward glance at the job completed, may be an important moment in exerting control over their work. Another woman told me, "I really like cleaning the bathrooms and then going back to see them, because whenever I do things well, I say to myself, 'The work is laughing with me.' " Unlike a worker standing next to a conveyor belt that moves the product down the assembly line, the housecleaner can, if she wishes, give a second to the work already completed and pause to appreciate her mastery and the finished job. This moment of satisfaction can occur only when cleaners control the pace of their work.

In some housecleaning jobs, the control of time remains a point of contention. While most of the employers I interviewed pay by the job, some of them noted that they felt cheated when the cleaner left earlier than anticipated. One employer, a retired teacher, recalled having been rushed to the hospital; when her husband returned to their home to pack her bags, he discovered that the housecleaner had left early. The housecleaner later said she had had a family emergency, but the employer didn't believe this. She felt that her trust was betrayed, even though her house had been cleaned. Employers with this attitude toward the job may try different strategies to get their full six or eight hours' worth of work.

Among the most forthright in describing these tactics was Julie

Thompson-Ahib, a former surgeon who had given up her practice to stay home with her two children, both in elementary school. She complained that housecleaners in Los Angeles were not as pliant and willing to work as those she had employed elsewhere. She was particularly offended that they would respond to her requests for extra chores, such as cleaning the pool cabana, by requesting an extra $10. In other words, she resented the loss of control that the switch from time to task signified.

> Some don't really want to work for their money, some want more money for anything extra. Maybe I was spoiled, because for the first ten years [in San Diego and Vancouver] it was like, "Okay, I'll pay you money and in exchange for the money I get *x* number of hours," so if today I tell you "I don't want you to clean the house, but I'd prefer to have the chandeliers washed or I want you to sweep outside," I thought that was part of the deal. But here, I find a lot of resistance to being able to make suggestions as to what I would like them to do in *my* house as opposed to what they want to do in *my* house.

Julie blamed the housecleaners themselves, as well as very wealthy employers (whom she assumed paid too well) and employers who live in apartments (which she assumed required only light cleaning), for this sorry state of affairs. "Here, I feel like they're doing me a favor for showing up!" she exclaimed. Whenever her cleaner was about to leave, Julie would try to stall her and make her work longer. "If there's something that I know she hasn't done, I'll usually say, 'Well, why don't you clean the top of the fridge, and I'll get your check.'"

Few Latina housecleaners that I interviewed had tried to charge more when extra tasks were requested. Many of them accepted the need for a certain flexibility in approaching their jobs, noting that particular tasks might be required in one house but not in another. When presented with unfair requests for extra chores, some cleaners relented and did them, a few negotiated, but many others quietly resisted. They may say "Yes," when asked if they would scrub stubborn, permanent stains out of carpet or bathe the dog, but then, recognizing these tasks as properly under the purview of a professional carpet cleaner or dog groomer, ignore them. If they are lucky, these tactics will enable them both to avoid confrontation and to placate the employer, at least momentarily. Bonnie Thornton Dill found such chicanery and cajolery to be common among African American domestic workers who worked on the East Coast during the mid–twentieth century.[10]

Homemakers have more time to dedicate to household activities than do women who work outside the home. Although current versions of domesticity tend to be more child-centered than hygiene- and home-centered, and no longer rely on nineteenth-century notions of household supervision and scientific management, homemakers' identities are still closely tied to the appearance of their home. For these reasons, they may keep close tabs on their housecleaners' work.

Employed women often take a more laissez-faire approach to managing their housecleaners. For example, Nora Powers, a theater critic and drama coach, and Alice McCoy-Fishman, a physician and mother of two school-age children, both had complaints about the ways their houses were cleaned but hesitated to make their concerns known. They were kept quiet by a mixture of absorption in their busy work lives and liberal guilt. Moreover, when it came to housecleaning, they preferred known imperfection to the hassle of seeking out and getting used to a new housecleaner.

Nora Powers, who had employed numerous housecleaners over a span of thirty years, complained that cleaners would over time begin to neglect the heavier tasks (vacuuming, mopping, and waxing hardwood floors) in favor of lighter work (such as dusting books). That bothered her, yet she sometimes held back from complaining. When I asked her why she wouldn't say something to those cleaners, she said, "They kind of take control, and I just—I'm embarrassed. I don't like to be critical and I don't like to play the boss. I'll hint something like, 'Hmm, the floors look a little weird.' But I don't want to think about it. I'm not on top of everything all the time. And then things slide."

Nora was clearly uncomfortable with delivering commands, directives, or even guidelines. As a Jewish woman who still identified deeply with the civil rights movement and progressive politics, she had a liberal social conscience that militated against being

"the boss" to women of a lower social class and subordinate racial-
ethnic groups. Several times she mentioned that fear of retribution
prevented her from giving orders: "It's like I'm afraid they're gonna
yell at me or afraid that they're gonna say, 'Well, you are the boss,
you know, and you're a hypocrite because you don't believe in
bosses and yet here you are, you know, I'm poor and you're able
to afford. I have so little and you have a beautiful house and you
can afford to rent help and I'm a human being.'" While no one had
ever actually *said* anything like this to her, the mere possibility of
such sentiments being voiced kept her from asking for what she
wanted.

Her striking admission that she is "not on top of everything" in
this part of her life also strongly suggests that she did not say anything about cleaning because she thought about it only infrequently.
She was often immersed in theater productions, and she traveled
internationally with her husband. Vigilantly monitoring the cleanliness of her home was a relatively low priority for her. Similarly,
Alice McCoy-Fishman had in the past held back her criticism of a
cleaner who was rough on the appliances and furniture, and who
would inappropriately use suds on the hardwood floors. "She would
destroy vacuum cleaners," Alice chortled. "It was like having the
L.A. Rams come in! You couldn't buy a mop with an orange post
because you'd have little orange spots all over the walls!" When I
asked why she didn't instruct the cleaner not to do these things, she
replied, "I just couldn't. She was strong willed and she just wanted
this to be clean, you know." While Alice may have felt too intimi-
dated to confront this cleaner, whom she described as "just such an
imposing figure of a person," she mainly wanted to avoid the trouble
of finding someone new. "Rather than go through a search like you
do for employees at work," she said, "it was just good enough. It
was fine."

Of course, employers who are themselves in the labor force can
provide instructions or ask for particular services, such as to wipe
down the cobwebs or vacuum under the beds. They can—and some
do—leave written notes, perhaps consulting a Spanish dictionary, or
they can arrange to be home when the cleaner arrives and ask that
specific tasks be done. Some purchase standardized Spanish-English
checklists that allow them to simply mark off what cleaning they
want performed. None of the women I interviewed had used this

last method, but at the time these checklists were widely available in Southern California. Employed employers can customize their cleaning and attempt to control how it is done; but most of them—with, as we will see, significant exceptions—are not inclined to do so.

Of those employers who are not working, only a few reported that they cleaned alongside and watched the cleaners. Most of them, as already mentioned, arranged to be out of the way. Some scheduled appointments, had lunch dates, or ran errands on the days when the cleaners arrive, and others retreated to the home office or den. Regardless of what they did, nearly all of them reported feeling uncomfortable in the presence of someone else cleaning their home. They either felt guilty about a less privileged woman cleaning their house, feared that they were in the way of the cleaners, or felt that the cleaners intruded on their privacy. Some found the sounds of vacuum cleaners and the banging of other implements annoying, and left the house entirely. "If I'm going to pay for cleaning," crowed one woman, "I'm going to enjoy it." Many of them said they prepared for the "cleaning lady's day" by decluttering countertops, maybe checking the stock of cleaning products, and then making themselves scarce.

Those women who do like to clean alongside and supervise the cleaners are, for the most part, homemakers, and they tend to be older than the baby boomers. One such woman, the wife of an attorney, said, "I could never sit and read a book, and I can't now either when I have a cleaning woman. So, if I'm home, I'll be on the other side making the bed, or I'll grab the towels and be washing them when she's in the bathroom." She performs the activity not to ensure that the work is done properly or quickly, but to prevent the appearance of idleness. A homemaker's job involves, among other things, domesticity as display. "I feel guilt not doing anything while she is there, so I do have to pretend to do something."

Several women, among both the homemakers and the employed, reported that their husbands were particularly concerned about the possibility of theft. In some cases, a husband would allow a cleaner in the house only if his wife agreed to be present. Here, surveillance was used not to manipulate the cleaners to work harder or longer, but to guard against theft. For their part, many housecleaners fear that they will be unfairly accused of stealing from their employers.

CLEANING SERVICES:
RATIONALIZING THE IRRATIONAL?

Cleaning firms are small businesses that take many different forms. There are national franchises as well as small, independently operated businesses, typically owned by one person who books the jobs and who may drive a van transporting several employees to the different work sites. The sociologist Jennifer Bickham Mendez has studied both types of businesses, and she finds that workers in firms often are exploited more than those in private cleaning arrangements. Contrary to many researchers who have argued that informal, personalistic relations are the source of exploitation in paid domestic work, Mendez finds that in a bureaucratic, rationalized organization, the cleaners lack autonomy, lose control over the work process, and receive lower wages, since the firm must extract a profit.[11]

A USC college student whom I interviewed, a young white woman, had taken a summer job with a cleaning service in Southern California. She complained that the firm, which operated on a shoe-string out of a woman's home, had misled her into believing that she would be earning $8 an hour; in fact, her pay hovered closer to minimum wage. On the job, standardized cleaning checklists served as her nightmarish supervisor.

> The kitchen had twelve things. I had to wipe down all the counters, wipe down all the appliances, get the cobwebs out of everywhere, take everything off the refrigerator, and wipe down the top and the sides of the refrigerator. On the stove you have to take off all the knobs and soak them, take out the burners and soak that and then wrap them in aluminum foil, sweep and mop, oh, and clean the top of the broilers, which I never did because it was just too time-consuming, and if I did it I would be getting paid like $3 an hour.

Cleaning the bathroom involved twenty-two steps. At her firm, both the clients and cleaners were instructed to check off items and sign the checklist, but few participated in this mode of labor control.

Only two of the employers I interviewed were currently having their homes cleaned by a cleaning service (in fact, both used the same agency, which consisted of three men), but several others had in the past. Some of them said that they liked the cleaning agencies precisely because it allowed them to remove themselves from the supervisory role. If they were unhappy with the result, they would simply call the agency and ask for someone new next time, thus sparing themselves the potentially messy and unpleasant task of directly communicating their displeasure with someone's work. They lacked any expectation that they would ever have to act as employers. This distancing, Mendez points out, also spares them from investing time in forming face-to-face, personalistic relations with the cleaners.

Most employers prefer the private, informal housecleaning arrangements. They are generally less expensive than the agencies—which have to support their overhead—and afford employers flexible, customized cleaning. One woman referred to the cleaning firms as "the McDonald's" of paid housecleaning. "You know what you're gonna get," she said, presumably referring to a product that is fast, predictable, uniform, and perhaps of mediocre quality. Several employers who had very large homes noted that several rooms scarcely saw any human traffic. Their weekly housecleaner might always clean the kitchen and bathrooms, but clean the other rooms or floors only every other week. Finally, some employers did not like the sensation of having individuals they didn't know cleaning their home. "I had a weird feeling," recalled Margaret Hamilton of the people from the cleaning service. "It was like having strangers in the house. I guess because I didn't get to know them, it was like having your house broken into."

The contractual, rationalized checklists used by the cleaning agencies sometimes seep over into the culture of private cleaning. In an attempt to gain some control over the work performed and get their money's worth, a few inexperienced employers had created long lists of household duties, which they duly presented to their cleaners. One young homemaker recalled her first experience hiring a cleaner: "I really didn't know what to expect. I had never at all been involved in managing the gal who cleans my stepmother's home. So I wrote down this huge, long list of what cleaning substances I used on each piece of furniture, and then now of course, I've thrown all caution to the wind!" Several others had initially made lists and then dispensed with them.

Of all the employers I interviewed, none had drawn up so ambitious a list as Lena Jenkins. She included not only what should be cleaned but precisely how it should be cleaned—specifying which products and tools should be used, and how often the cleaning should occur. "That way," she explained, "I knew I wasn't getting ripped off and I knew that they had something to reference." She recalled one cleaner who liked having the list, but she admitted that "most probably thought it was condescending of me." When I asked to see the list, this very well-organized woman readily retrieved it, even though she had not used it in three years:

LIVING ROOM, DINING ROOM:

Dust all furniture, use only cloths supplied, vacuum carpet and upholstered furniture and lamp shades, dust lamps, clock, china closet with feather duster;

Note: Upholstered furniture need only be vacuumed once a month. Use rubbing alcohol on mirrors. Mirrors need to be cleaned monthly.

KITCHEN:

Mop floor and shake rug, wash counter tops with Soft Scrub, wash behind all items on counter, wipe items on counter with damp cloth, wipe all appliances with damp cloth, use Dust Wax on kitchen table, wash kitchen window above sink inside and outside;

Note: Grout should be cleaned monthly. Use special solution and scrub brush. Cupboards should be cleaned inside quarterly, outside monthly with Old English polish.

FAMILY ROOM:

Vacuum carpet and upholstered furniture and lamp shades, dust furniture, clean glass tables with rubbing alcohol, feather dust clocks, pictures, etc.

BATHROOMS:

Scour shower and tub and sinks, scour toilet bowls, clean mirrors, vacuum guest bathroom floor and mop and wax master bathroom floor. Wipe off lid, back in base of toilets, outside of cupboards, towel bars, toilet paper holders and light fixture above mirrors. Feather dust mini blind.

ENTRY WAY:

In the front entry way mop floor, vacuum runner rug, wipe off
baseboard, dust antique sewing machine, feather dust lamp and
picture frames.

BACK ENTRY WAY:

Mop floor, wipe off washer and dryer with damp cloth including
inside of washer lid.

BEDROOMS:

Vacuum and dust all bedrooms. Clean all mirrors (don't forget the
wall mirror in master bedroom), feather dust toy shelves in Tif-
fany's room, wash shelves on changing table, clean pad of table
with rubbing alcohol, change bedding.

Note: Vacuum lamp shades monthly.

GAME ROOM:

Vacuum carpet and upholstered furniture, dust furniture, use alcohol on pinball machine rather than dust cloth, wipe off leather
sofa and brown chair with clean damp cloth. Dust or wipe with
damp cloth on window sills. Use rubbing alcohol on the glass
bookcases.

MUSIC ROOM:

Vacuum carpet, dust furniture, clean mirror.

MISCELLANEOUS:

Weekly: Ensure all baseboards are dusted. Ensure all wall items
are feather dusted or wiped with damp cloth or alcohol.
Monthly: Check all brass and silver for possible polishing, wipe off
all glass shelves and china cabinet, wash windows if necessary.

Lena Jenkins had begun by having her home cleaned by an
agency; as she gradually switched to private cleaners, she initially attempted to control their time and direct their labor through an elaborately customized—though, I suspect, a much more demanding

—version of the agency's cleaning checklist. Eventually she found a steady housecleaner, a Mexican woman, and she stopped relying on the checklist. Still, she kept it in a file for possible future use.

HISTORICAL CONTINUITIES
AND DISJUNCTIONS

In the late nineteenth century, white middle-class women emulated the capitalist factory system and applied scientific management principles to their homes and to their servants.[12] They instituted work speedups; downgraded the domestic jobs by depersonalizing, deskilling, and standardizing various household tasks; and took seriously their own roles as supervisors. "Domestics," writes Mary Romero, "were reduced to unskilled labor and subjected to constant supervision."[13]

The historian Faye Dudden refers to this process as the change in labor control from "task" to "time." Rather than "having a certain amount of work to do, as help had, domestics were expected to work constantly unless explicitly 'off.'"[14] The employers, in this case middle- and upper-class housewives, would then devote themselves to enriching family life, managing the household by devising lists of commands and by monitoring the quality of the manual labor performed. Romero refers to the expectation that domestics would work constantly as the shift from the hiring of "labor services" to "labor power," and she understands contemporary housecleaners' occupational struggles as an attempt to recapture professional expertise and to resist the extraction of pure labor power.[15] Today, the scientific management of domestic workers' labor finds its fullest expression not in private housecleaning or nanny/housekeeper arrangements, but in cleaning service agencies and in the hyperregulation of domestic labor overseas; in Hong Kong, for example, private agencies, employers, and governments impose strict job rules, Tayloristic timetables, and "codes of discipline" to control Filipina domestics.[16]

In the twenty-first century we find many variants of white middle-class womanhood in the United States, but none of them are so squarely centered on the cult of domesticity as their historical predecessors were. The entrance of many white middle- and upper-middle-class women into the paid labor force not only has prompted greater demand for paid domestic work services but also has profoundly changed the quality of labor control and directives in the domestic occupations. As many *patronas* have themselves gone off to work, they have ended their constant and direct supervision of domestic job sites. Some homemakers who employ daily live-in or live-out nanny/housekeepers are better able to monitor the work that occurs in their households; and though they may attempt to maintain the domestic job's definition as constant labor over a set time, even they are sometimes reticent about identifying just what it is that they want. In fact, as Wrigley suggests in her study of parents who hire private nannies, they may be at a loss when it comes to wielding "the skills of command."[17] Other employers ask their domestic employees for what they want and don't get it. Today we see multiple forms of labor control and multiple forms of resistance and compliance at work.

As has been clear throughout this chapter, domestic workers now want jobs that offer clear directives and rules, but their employers often fail to define the tasks they want performed. At first glance, it may seem paradoxical that paid domestic workers should desire rules, directives, and precise job definitions of the sort that many industrial workers have struggled against. When paid domestic work and factory work are compared historically, however, the puzzle disappears. Factory workers, after all, organized into unions not only over bread-and-butter issues of wages and hours but also to regain the control they had enjoyed as craft workers; paid domestic work, in contrast, has evolved from arrangements more characteristic of slavery, feudalism, and despotic control.[18] In this sense, the efforts and desires of Latina domestic workers to obtain clear job directives are parallel to those of contemporary industrial and service-sector workers whose unions negotiate collective contracts that carefully delineate their job tasks. Their demands for clear job parameters are modest ones.

Paid domestic work is an occupation that takes many forms. We see clear distinctions in labor control between nanny/housekeeper jobs, which typically involve day-to-day child care, and weekly housecleaner jobs. Nanny/housekeepers struggle to impose and maintain finite hours of work—especially live-in employees, who may be expected by their employers to be on call twenty-four hours a day. Nanny/housekeepers provide extensive care for young children, and intense emotional bonds often tie the children and their care worker. As we have seen, both nanny/housekeepers and their employers may deploy these bonds as leverage in their struggles and negotiations to control the employee's labor. But in housecleaning jobs, the employees want, as Romero's research has indicated, flexible schedules and standardized tasks.[19] They also resist, as we have seen, the imposition of extra work without extra pay. Both nanny/ housekeepers and housecleaners want clear instructions, but they remain adamant about the importance of having autonomy on the job.

The ability of nanny/housekeepers and housecleaners to control both the pace of their work and the methods by which it is performed depends on their employers. Employers who work away from home, who are thus absent from the work site and who do not always bother to keenly observe the minute details of their households, are less able and less likely to interfere with a domestic worker's autonomy on the job; homemakers are better positioned to monitor work and interpose themselves. Yet both groups of employers prefer domestic workers who will take initiative and spare them from delineating the job requirements.

Throughout contemporary Los Angeles, paid domestic workers and their employers have created a myriad of strategies to get the work done. The process need not involve conflicts, but those that do arise can often be traced to one of two problems: undercontrol or overcontrol of labor (sometimes the latter following an attempt to correct the former). Across the board, the employees prefer employers who give clear, fair directives, and who then get out of the way. Nanny/housekeepers resist servanthood by trying to establish firm boundaries around their job hours, and housecleaners take control over their labor and their lives beyond work by establishing flexible times for starting and stopping their jobs.

7

Go Away ... But Stay Close Enough

What should be the relationship between employers and employees? So much popular discussion today focuses on workplace relations— the pleasures and dangers of office romances, the challenges to bureaucratic hierarchies posed by Silicon Valley computer firms, and the flux and brevity that now characterize interactions, caused by a growing reliance on temporary workers, subcontractors, and consultants. Clearly, social relationships in today's workplace look very different from those in the mid–twentieth century. But what of employer-employee relations in paid domestic work? Tellingly, popular discussions of work and workplace relations rarely touch on this area.

Scholarly research on U.S. paid domestic work in the late nineteenth and throughout the twentieth century has generally seen close, personal relations between employer and employee as a key mechanism of oppression and labor control.[1] According to this line of thinking, the employer's maternalism mandates the employee's rituals of deference, which reinforce inequality and hierarchy. For example, maternalism often imposes heavy quid pro quo obligations on paid domestic workers, blurring the distinction between paid work and unpaid favors. Employers may require from their employees deference, gratitude, and perhaps extra hours on duty. In the process, they gain not only unpaid services but also a sense of superiority and enhanced racial, class, and gender status.[2] Moreover, employers may hold the domestic workers' personalities to be as important as, and sometimes more important than, their competence at the job itself.[3]

Other observers have argued that close employer-employee relations can help empower domestic workers.[4] As the sociologist Bonnie Thornton Dill notes, "The intimacy which can develop between an employer and employee, along with the lack of job standardization may increase the employee's leverage in the relationship and give her some latitude within which to negotiate a work plan that meets her own interests and desires."[5] Accordingly, close personal relationships with their employers may make it possible for some paid domestic workers to win more favorable job terms.

In contemporary Los Angeles, domestic employer-employee relations do not follow any one pattern. Many of the Latina immigrants doing domestic work are relatively new to the occupation, as are a number of their employers. But a couple of trends are clear: maternalism among employers has declined, and most Latina employees say they prefer employers who interact more personally with them. In this chapter, I try to make sense of these preferences by distinguishing between *maternalism*—which I see as a unilateral positioning of the employer as a benefactor who receives personal thanks, recognition, and validation of self from the domestic worker—and *personalism*, a bilateral relationship that involves two individuals recognizing each other not solely in terms of their role or office (such as clerk or cleaner) but rather as persons embedded in a unique set of social relations, and with particular aspirations.[6] Many Latina domestic workers today want more closeness and consideration of their personhood from their employers, who, for various reasons, are reluctant to engage in these exchanges.

These desires by both parties seem to contradict the conclusions of researchers who have concentrated on domestic work in previous eras: they are new social patterns that demand sociological explanations. Such explanations lie in the employers' and employees' social locations, their identities as women in contemporary society, the domestic job tasks involved, and the ways in which paid domestic work is organized. I begin by discussing those who have greater power in determining the quality of the relationship, the women who are employers.[7]

EMPLOYERS AND PERSONALISM

EMPLOYED EMPLOYERS AND THE TIME BIND: "MY TIME, OR HER TIME?"

Karla Steinheimer, a talkative, fast-thinking thirty-six-year-old, drank a lot of coffee and worked in a fast-track office. Her quick-mindedness and determination had helped her land a job as a manager in a film production company, a job with considerable responsibility and always-looming deadlines; her husband Bob was a self-employed accountant. Both had extremely demanding schedules, and each worked at least fifty or fifty-five hours a week. Neither one had taken any time off from work since immediately after the birth of their two-year-old son. Consequently, their live-out nanny/housekeeper, Filomina, worked eleven hours a day, Monday through Friday, taking care of the Steinheimers' toddler. She had not taken a vacation since beginning the job two years prior to our interview.

A harried working mother cannot simply turn over her toddler to a nanny/housekeeper; she must spend some of her precious and limited time with her employee, and time was already in short supply for this quintessentially harried working mom. Karla had come to resent the time and emotional energy given to Filomina, but increasingly she saw it as a "necessary evil"—a view shared by many in her circle of busy working women. "I think it's always an issue—everyone I know faces this," she explained. "It's a lonely job, so when we are home Filomina will follow us around and you know, will talk because she's alone in the house all day. But we're usually in a hurry to get out the door or otherwise. So, there's always that issue."

With a previous housekeeper, Karla had found such demands for conversation easier to ignore. Now, she felt obliged to reciprocate with Filomina because of the child. "I think it's very important to spend the time talking to your child care provider because if you don't, you don't know what's going on," she reasoned. "I always have a lot of questions I want to ask Filomina about how the day went. What did he [the baby] have to eat, you know, was he constipated . . . you know, all those issues; but then it always turns into a whole thing about Filomina's cousin's friend's brother who did this and on and on and on."

"So, how do you deal with that when it gets into the cousin's friend's brother?" I asked.

"Just, the best I can. I don't mean to be ungracious or unkind but I try to limit it if I'm running out the door to an appointment or have things that I need to do in the house." To minimize these annoying verbal interruptions to their own work, employers like Karla may shift their schedules, rearrange their furniture, and even momentarily confine themselves to one part of the house—all tactics that Karla herself had tried. Most recently, she had moved her home office into her small bedroom, because "that's an area that I can be shut off from Filomina. The desk was set up in the baby's room, but if I went in there, then she was going in and out all the time. So now if I have to work and make phone calls I go in my bedroom and shut the door and then there's no disturbance." Instead of the domestic worker, as is traditional, being relegated to invisibility and confined to the "backroom" kitchen of a large home, the employer, now in a much smaller house, seeks to establish privacy by sequestering herself in a makeshift bedroom office. Both arrangements reflect the employer's privilege to search for and maintain her own privacy; but in this contemporary example, it is the employer who is spatially confined.

Instrumental personalism, of the type that the sociologist Jennifer Bickham Mendez observed in the cleaning agencies she studied,[8] characterized Karla and Bob Steinheimer's relationship with their nanny/housekeeper. To ensure good care for her son, Karla felt obliged to participate in some personal conversations with Filomina. She contrasted these interactions to the "nonrelationship" she and her husband had maintained with a housecleaner who worked for them for approximately ten years, before the birth of their son. Karla recalled literally fleeing the housecleaner, whom they perceived as overly chatty and needy. "If we were at home by any chance with our cleaning lady, who used to absolutely follow us around, you know, it was impossible to do anything when she was there. When I was in my first trimester of pregnancy and I was feeling so sick, come hell or high water, I was out of that door at eight o'clock because I didn't want to run into her or her incessant questions." The housecleaner often asked for advice on how to deal with credit problems, but Karla and her husband preferred "very little contact." "To be honest," she confided, "we would try to stay out of the house, because you know, she would drive us crazy—talk, talk, talk."

The Steinheimers were dissatisfied with Filomina's cleaning, or, as they put it, the lack of it: "It got to the point where you could swipe your finger and write your name in the dust." But rather than losing a trusted, patient, and loving nanny, they accepted her poor cleaning and had recently hired a Latina housecleaner to come in and clean once every three weeks. When that woman, accompanied by her daughter, arrived on Saturday mornings, the Steinheimers promptly scooped up their son and departed to the corner café for cappuccino and croissants: "We just make it a point to never be home on those Saturday mornings." Once again, the Steinheimers are able to avoid time-consuming and awkward personal interactions. They thus maintain the type of anonymous, contractual relations with the housecleaner that they are prevented from having with their nanny/ housekeeper.

Women engaged in full-time employment just don't have the time to establish personalistic or maternalistic relations with their domestic employees. With demanding careers and work schedules, they are too busy to cultivate such personal relationships. Indeed, as Arlie Hochschild so compellingly argues in *The Time Bind* (1997), today's working mothers and fathers often find it hard to pull back from their jobs to spend the time they think they should devote to their children and spouses; clearly, their domestic employees are a much lower priority. Many of the employers work away from their homes, and when they see their nanny/housekeeper or cleaner they do little more than touch base—perhaps inquiring about her health and family, but mainly focusing on issues strictly related to the domestic job.

These employers may also be less interested than homemakers in establishing close, personalistic relations with their domestic employees. Working women who pay someone to work in their home derive their own identity largely from their jobs and careers, while the lives of homemakers often revolve around school, home, and family activities. Working women are therefore less likely than homemakers to view a domestic employee as a personal assistant or an extension of themselves. As Mary Romero has observed, "A homemaker who has her identity tied up in the home and family cannot simply hire another woman to care for her family's needs without threatening her self-image. Thus, when private household workers are hired to maintain a particular life-style, many homemakers feel obligated to retain control even though they do not actually perform the work."[9] For working women who pay nanny/ housekeepers and cleaners, the organization and rapid pace of their life—what Hochschild calls the "Taylorization of home life"—often lead to their viewing a personalistic relationship with the nanny/ housekeeper not as a means to gain personal satisfaction or a feeling of superiority, but rather as one more time-consuming burden. They wish to minimize or, if possible, avoid altogether such interchanges.

Many women find the pace required to maintain both their career and family life unbearable. Even well-to-do women who can afford private nanny/housekeepers find it hard to keep up, and many women with young children opt out of the rat race entirely. Others, like Ellen Maxson, choose to work part-time. She had earned a J.D. and a Ph.D. in art history from Ivy League universities; but while her children were young, she had decided to work limited hours as a museum and art gallery consultant, enjoying, she said, "the best of both worlds."

When I interviewed her, she reflected on her strained relations with the many nanny/housekeepers who briefly cycled through her home. Ellen attributed these "failed relationships" to her assumption that they could be covered by a "business contract." Indeed, unlike most employers, she had developed a systematic hiring strategy that included a job application form and a typed list detailing the employee's hours and pay, her own expectations for cleaning, and rules for the children's television viewing, meal preparation, and park excursions. While she had recently become slightly less controlling, the change had barely salvaged a sour relationship with her current nanny/housekeeper, a young white woman from Louisiana who tried to quit after ten days on the job. The Guatemalan woman she had employed previously left after two months. Ellen recognized that in order to minimize employee turnover and to establish more satisfactory domestic relations in the future, she would need "to spend more time on, you know, the human dynamic."

Still, she had trouble finding the time required for a more personalistic relationship. "When she [the nanny/housekeeper] comes [to work], I'm ready to get going with my own work. When I'm taking over from her, she's ready to get on with her own life, and so whose time do you spend developing the relationship? My time in the morning when she gets here? Or her time when she's leaving and she's ready to get on with her stuff?" Ellen tried to remedy the situation by scheduling her nanny/housekeeper to work four and a half hours a day, rather than only four hours, thereby buying herself an extra half hour to chat. "I found that I need to be a little bit freer with a few dollars here and there," she confided sheepishly, "for the long-term investment." When I asked if she had approached the relationship with her employee in such a businesslike manner because of her background in law, she said no, instead attributing it partly to her desire to replicate the reserve that her upper-class mother had maintained with household servants and partly to "just being busy and in not wanting to put time into what might feel like an unpredictable friendship." For Ellen Maxson, time was the major consideration. Employed parents who hire a part-time nanny/housekeeper may see developing a satisfactory relationship with the employee as taking too many of the total hours of employment.

Major gender inequities with her husband were also part of Ellen's problem. Her husband, who worked as a museum curator, encouraged her to invest more time cultivating a personalistic relationship with the nanny; yet even though he was sometimes home during the day, he refused to participate in fostering that relationship. "He wasn't going to spend it [time] on getting to know her. He thought this was important and wanted me to do it . . . for maybe a longer child care relationship with her." Both she and her husband rationalized giving her the responsibility by pointing to their different employment statuses: she worked part-time, while her husband worked full-time. But even when both husband and wife work full-time, the wife, as a rule, handles all transactions with the domestic worker. Of the thirty-nine employers I interviewed, thirty-two were married; and in only one instance did the husband take responsibility for hiring, communicating with, and paying the domestic employee.

Working women who employ domestic workers in their home sometimes complained to one another about the burdens of personalism, as Ellen Maxson did with her friends: "A friend of mine up the street," she said, "has someone who worked for her mom and now works for her, and she said, 'Oh, I'm just spending so much energy in this friendship relationship. I wish I could just have a business relationship.'" For these women, employing a nanny/housekeeper solved the problems of how to care for their children and clean a dirty house, but it simultaneously pressured them to take on not just a second but a third shift—the work of building and maintaining a relationship with the women who cared for their children and their homes. The cost of being relieved of household duties involves not only money but time, spent building a personal relationship with the woman who does their domestic work.

Employers who hire live-ins find it easier not only to get more work from their employees but also to establish personalistic relations with them. Live-in nanny/housekeepers, are, after all, on the premises day and night, five or six days a week. One woman with a full-time job who had established very personalistic relations with her live-in nanny/housekeeper was Rosamaria Stranski, a Mexican American midlevel manager with two young children. After describing the extent of her relationship, which included maternalistic involvement (giving used clothes and unsolicited advice on prospective suitors) with two different live-in employees, she summarized her experience: "You tend to become—at least I have—kind of caught up in their lives. . . . I tend to try to assist these people in their situations . . . doing little things."

The assistance certainly went both ways. Rosamaria was herself very dependent on paid domestic help. Unlike Karla Steinheimer and Ellen Maxson, she had hired full-time, live-in nanny/housekeepers to accommodate her demanding schedule. Because she typically departed for her office at 6:30 A.M., she required her live-in nanny/housekeeper, Lupe, to sleep in the children's room. If the children awakened at night, the nanny had to get up with them. When Rosamaria returned home from work, she sat down to eat dinner, prepared by Lupe, together with the children and Lupe; her husband, Ray, who arrived home later, ate alone. Unlike live-out domestic workers, Lupe had no finite hours to her job; there was no rushed transition as the responsibility for child care passed from the employer to the nanny/housekeeper. The time clock was, in effect, not ticking. Indeed, this live-in nanny/housekeeper experienced no separation between work and social life. Rosamaria reported that on weekday evenings, she and the nanny/housekeeper ate together, watched television, played with the children, bathed them, and put them to bed.

Like other employers of nannies, Rosamaria Stranski emphasized the importance of getting to know the child care provider. "These people are watching your children, who are supposed to be the most precious things to you. If that alone is the only common bond that you have with them, you still have to have an interest [in them]. You need to find out what they think about certain things or how they handle things because it does affect how they are going to treat your child." The relatively close quarters of the modest ranch-style house in which the family coexisted with the live-in employee and the informality of their lifestyle also encouraged a more personalistic relationship. Rosamaria imagined that upper-class employers have a different experience: "When we have people who have lived here, they end up becoming part of your family. It's almost like whether you want to or not, they are there," she said. "It's not like we're a San Marino or Beverly Hills family that has specific maids or people that you are detached from." Although she did not describe the relationship as draining and onerous—as had Karla Steinheimer and Ellen Maxson—she concluded that creating personal ties was mandatory, "whether you want to or not."

Employed mothers who hire domestic workers to care for children as well as clean find that they must engage in more personalistic relations than do their peers who hire only housecleaners. Most of them hire a nanny/housekeeper to work five days a week, so they necessarily see their employees far more frequently than do the employers of weekly or biweekly housecleaners. More important, hiring a care giver for their children requires not only a high degree of trust but also regular and fairly intimate communication. Besides daily greetings, they need to engage in regular conversations about the child's daily routines. How long did the child sleep? What did he eat? How high is her fever? Is there homework to be completed? Parents who hire someone to provide child care also want assurances that their model for disciplining, stimulating, and nurturing children will be followed, assurances they can receive only by getting to know the caregiver. Yet all these time-famished employers face the same dilemma: they need to spend time talking with their nanny/housekeepers, but they don't have much time to spare.

Such women may find that putting the children in a child care center and hiring a cleaning service, rather than an individual, to clean the house is one way out of this bind. Jennifer Bickham Mendez found that the cleaning businesses and franchises in northern California are particularly attractive to busy, dual-career employers because they enable people to purchase cleaning services without engaging in close relationships with the cleaners. She explains that "clients often hire a household service agency precisely in order to achieve distance between themselves and housecleaners, thereby avoiding the emotional work involved in the management of domestic workers or personalistic relationships with them."[10] That work is left to middle managers in the cleaning firms, who often deploy "strategic personalism" as way to control workers and combat employee turnover. Those who contract with cleaning services must pay not just for cleaning but also for the agency's managerial costs and investment in personalistic exchanges. When these same employers hire nanny/housekeepers to care for their children as well as their home, however, they must spend their own time on such exchanges.

EMPLOYED EMPLOYERS AND HOUSECLEANERS:
FLEETING GREETINGS

Unlike their peers who hire nannies, employers who hire someone to clean their homes need not invest much time or emotional energy in the employer-employee relationship. Employed women typically maintain fairly distant relations with their weekly or biweekly housecleaners. Since they themselves are generally at their office during the day, their interactions with the housecleaners tend to be brief and businesslike.

Tess Miller, a single professional, had a Salvadoran woman clean her house biweekly. She described her relationship with the cleaner as consisting of a fleeting, twice-monthly greeting, made stilted by the language barrier: "She comes, she says hello, I say hello. I try to remember," she chuckled, "how to say something else [in Spanish]. A lot of times I just say, 'Hello, I'm going to work, good-bye, the money is on the table.'" Although Tess's job as a magazine editor allowed her to work at home a good deal of the time, she intentionally left when the housecleaner arrived—because, she explained, "I like not having to figure out what to do with myself while someone is in the house [cleaning]."

Many employers feel awkward, even guilty, about having a poorer Latina immigrant cleaning around them while they themselves appear to sit idly; Tess was no exception. Part of her job entailed reading popular magazines, but she did not want the cleaner to misinterpret that work as leisure activity. Her modest-sized home—approximately 900 square feet, with no hallways—made it impossible for her to hide away in the study while the housecleaner was there. Regardless of whether employers' work responsibilities or their desire to avoid social awkwardness pulls them out of the home, the upshot is the same: little contact between employer and employee. Other employers who occasionally work at home described similar efforts to minimize social interactions. A writing instructor reported, "I'd call it a kind of touching-base kind of conversation . . . a few health things . . . the mechanics of rearranging the day [for cleaning]. . . . I'm usually out. I don't like to feel like I'm in her way." A business consultant echoed this sentiment: "I don't like being home because I feel like I'm in the way. I think it's easier [for them] to come in and do what they have to do without stepping over me." A busy physician and mother of two school-age children, accustomed to only greeting her weekly housecleaner as she leaves for her office, lamented dryly, "Every time that I'm so sick that I have to stay home, it's always a Tuesday that she's here. It never fails." Employed employers who hire weekly cleaners tend to shun personalistic relations.

HOMEMAKERS AND HOUSECLEANERS: GENERATIONAL DIVIDES AND DISTANCES

Well-to-do homemakers who have weekly cleaners generally have more discretionary time than do employed women. Even if they are busy buying food, chauffeuring children to their various activities and appointments, and volunteering at charities, they are more likely to be home and have the time to casually stop and chat with the housecleaner or the nanny/housekeeper. But the personalism exhibited by today's homemaker employers varies considerably, depending on life stage and generation. Women in their thirties and forties seem to feel the tug of personalistic domestic relations less strongly than do homemakers in their late fifties and sixties. The older women, whose children are now grown, often seek close relations with their housecleaners, although they are not always able to achieve them.

It is not clear whether the younger homemakers' preference for stricter limits on personalism is due to their absorption in their children and family lives, generational differences, or their own prior experience in the workforce. Compared to their harried employed peers, however, they had more time and personal energy to spare in talking with their domestic workers. Tara Mostrianni, who had formerly worked as a stockbroker but was now at home caring for her two preschoolers, clearly exemplifies this pattern. She had hired a Mexican housecleaner to come once a week, and a Guatemalan woman watched the children on Mondays, Wednesdays, and Fridays while she ran errands and did volunteer work at her son's preschool.

"Yeah, we've gotten friendly and that's fine," she commented. "I mean, I don't want to hear if she's having marital problems or whatever. She would never burden me with that." Tara reported discussing topics such as children, neighborhoods, crime, and safety, but she did not wish to delve too deeply into the lives of her domestic workers. She did not know, for example, who cared for the children of her weekly housecleaner or of her three-day-a-week nanny while they were working for her. At the same time, however, she spoke disapprovingly of the very distanced relationship that a career-oriented friend of hers had established with a nanny.

Similarly, Beverly Voss, who had worked for fifteen years as a midlevel manager and was now the stay-at-home mother of two young daughters, reported that she preferred not having a close relationship with the live-in nanny/housekeeper. "It's kind of distant, which is probably better than getting too involved. She kind of has her life and we have ours, and obviously I know about some of what she does on the weekends, but I don't pry very much and she doesn't disclose a lot." Beverly said there was nothing about the relationship she would like to change. "I don't want it any closer than it is. There should be a certain amount of distance, because she is working for us, yet she is part of our family." Unless Beverly's husband, a prominent attorney, was absent, the nanny/housekeeper ate her evening meals apart from the family, and Beverly emphasized that the nanny/housekeeper was an employee, a subordinate: "We're not at home kind of equals. She *is* working for us." Yet at the same time, she insisted on their interdependence, saying, "I think she knows that we're there for her, and she's there for us, like a family." Like other younger baby boomer women, she preferred distance to personalism and intimacy.

MATERNALISTIC DESIRES: DENIAL AND FULFILLMENT

Older homemakers, who were born prior to the end of World War II and who were in their fifties and sixties with their children already grown, generally preferred closer relations with their paid domestic workers. In some ways, they attempted to use their housecleaners to fill their "empty nests." Such was the case with Evelyn Potts, a fifty-eight-year-old who had recently retired from teaching and was now devoting more of her time to making and trying to sell ceramic sculptures. When her housecleaner arrived, she told me, they often sat down to chat. "If it looks like something has happened in either of our families in the last two weeks that we've been apart, we will spend some time before she gets started talking about that. Sometimes I'll insist that she have a cup of coffee and something to eat with me to go over that. . . . Our conversations usually revolve around family, around difficulties that she may be having in making her way in Los Angeles." Family conflicts, medical and financial problems, and immigration issues were common topics. While many employers dwell only on the travails and hardships of the housecleaner, Evelyn reported that they also discussed the housecleaner's children and their successes. "I think she's enormously proud of them," she noted.

The relationship went far beyond conversation; Evelyn Potts watched out for her employee's health by prohibiting the use of certain chemical cleaning products, and she even took the housecleaner, Mrs. Gonzalez, to her own doctor to prevent her from having an unnecessary hysterectomy. When Evelyn's husband asked Mrs. Gonzalez to iron his shirts, she intervened to put that onerous task off-limits. She enjoyed her intimate relationship with the housecleaner; and unlike most employers who have engaged in this sort of maternalistic involvement, she did not call the housecleaner by her first name, preferring a more formal and respectful address. She also expressed surprise at the extent of her involvement: "I did not expect to form a personal attachment with Mrs. Gonzalez. I did not expect I would know her whole family, and I did not expect that I would ultimately sponsor her for her green card, and in fact, the whole family."

Despite their greater power, employers cannot force their employees to accept personalistic relations. Several homemakers fondly recalled relationships they had had with previous domestic workers, and they spoke with some frustration about their inability to foster closer relationships with their current weekly housecleaners. Laura Jaspers, a retired schoolteacher who had worked only after her children started going to school, retained a very strong homemaking sensibility, as the wall of family photos in her suburban family room suggested. She had established very maternalistic relations with her previous housecleaners, who had reciprocated by showing personal interest in aspects of her own life, especially the celebrations surrounding the weddings of her three children. She recalled one woman who had cleaned her house for five years, who would "get excited with all that stuff. She really liked seeing the wedding dresses." The interest went both ways, as Laura inquired into the personal and family matters of the housecleaners. Yet they shared portions of their lives asymmetrically. What Laura remembered most vividly about her previous housecleaners was the voyeuristic pleasure she herself had derived from observing the "soap opera" quality of the housecleaners' lives. "They were always," she told me, "putting everything in my lap."

"What kinds of things would they tell you?"

"Oh, all their problems with their marriages and their husbands getting in jail and their kids getting in trouble, and you know, all those kinds of things. And the gossip about their sisters and their sisters-in-law." She listened to "all of this chaos" not simply because she enjoyed the drama but because she also became quite involved in responding to these personal crises. Perhaps acting as a personal benefactor enabled her to experience herself simultaneously as superior, altruistic, and benevolent; much previous scholarship has emphasized this function of employers' benevolent maternalism. Laura Jaspers sometimes went to considerable effort to help them. She once offered her home as temporary refuge to a housecleaner and her children who were escaping a violent, battering husband and father. Another housecleaner had a chronically ill, disabled child, and she had, on many occasions, driven them around Los Angeles to various medical clinics. In both instances, Laura's husband raised objections to her "getting too involved personally," but she had ignored him.

Although Laura preferred this type of closeness, she had been unable to foster it with her current housecleaner. "She really holds me at arm's length, and I know almost as little about her three years later as I did the first two weeks that I had met her. It's just become more of a business thing than the other ones were." Initially, she was bothered by this and tried to get closer. "I'd be blabbing away and she'd just nod and say yes, no, and you know, that kind of thing." While Laura used to enjoy working alongside the other housecleaners, she now deliberately left the house while the cleaning was performed. She had become more reserved and less intrusive. "When the other gals were here, they were dusting, I'd be putting the books back in the cupboards or jabbering away or something or changing sheets together. Now, I must say, I do try to stay away from her more than the others. It's just a different person." Laura reports that she was "much more comfortable with the ones who I was closer to," but she has adapted. When she drives the current housecleaner down the hill from her canyon home to the bus stop, she has learned to keep conversation to a minimum.

Similarly, Norine Christophe, a fifty-eight-year-old affluent home-maker with three grown children, longed for the type of close, per-sonalistic relationships she had established with several previous housecleaners. In particular, she fondly recalled her chatty relation-ship with Elena, a Mexican woman who had cleaned her house weekly for seven years. When she met her, Elena was single and worked as a live-in for a neighbor. Over time, Elena built up a weekly route of houses, had four children—with three different fathers, as Norine emphasized—married, and ultimately withdrew from em-ployment to raise her children. Yet they continued to stay in touch. Elena remained poor, needy, dependent, and demonstrative with Norine, who responded by giving her advice, used household items, and once even an old car. "She has the need, so I still save my old clothes," she explained. "Last time Elena came it was Easter, and I had box after box. . . . And I'll be darned, they took every one of those boxes!" Elena had always reciprocated with gratitude, affec-tion, and appreciation, and though she no longer worked for Norine Christophe, she still telephoned her and sent holiday cards.

When I interviewed her, Norine was employing Marta, whom she described as a very "self-sufficient" woman who had no need for used items, unsolicited advice, or excessive chitchat. Norine missed the open, loquacious ease with which Elena had discussed her boy-friends, her pregnancies, and other personal matters. Now, when she asked Marta a question—about her mother's health or her daughter's progress in school—"Well, she'll just give me minimal answers and then I assume that she doesn't want to talk." Contrasting the two, she said, "I had a real personal relationship with Elena. Marta is pretty much very businesslike." When I asked which she preferred, she quickly retorted, "Oh, Elena, hands down. Because I know to this day—she cares for me, and I care for her, so it went beyond the employer-employee thing."

At the end of our interview, Norine Christophe asked if I didn't know of a poor, needy family looking for a personal patron such as herself. She told me about how her friend Diane, "who is very, I mean, really very wealthy," had through her church befriended a single black mother and begun helping her. "Diane has almost adopted them," she pouted, "and I'm just so envious! Don't you know of a little family that I could get to know, that I could visit?" She stipulated the type of involvement she imagined, noting that she would act "sort of like I did with Elena":

> Of course, it couldn't be on a regular basis. Since we travel so much, I wouldn't be a good member of anything anyway, but maybe someone that I just care for, and think of in the holidays, and sort of like I did with Elena. If you know of anyone like that, maybe, say, a single mom with some kids and she's struggling . . . just that I could know on a personal basis—I am on a nonscheduled basis, this wouldn't be two o'clock every Tuesday kind of thing, so I could be flexible with my schedule. But I think I could really offer someone some caring and time and love and help and money too . . . so I could have the fun of seeing the kids go through school.

I responded by telling her about Mission Dolores, the activist Catholic parish located in Boyle Heights, in East Los Angeles. I knew they operated, among other programs, a soup kitchen, a shelter for homeless women and children, and classes for gang youth. "Oh," she gasped, "but wouldn't I have to actually go there? Isn't it very dangerous?"

As other observers of paid domestic work have pointed out, maternalistic employers of paid domestic workers may become accustomed to helping the poor without the discomfort of leaving their own safe, affluent neighborhoods.[11] Instead of a benefactor like Norine Christophe transporting used clothing to the ghetto or the barrio, the needy come to her garage. There are other benefits to this maternalistic approach to charity. While employers may offer care and demonstrate affection, they do so on their own time, when they feel like it. The employer may get satisfaction from her intimate view of the private tribulations of a woman whose life is so unlike anything she knows that it might seem to have come from a novel—a woman who is poor, who lives in a crime-ridden neighborhood, who is raising children without the financial support of a husband, who is Latina and perhaps lacks U.S. citizenship or legal papers. Moreover, for her offered guidance and care, the employer receives personal recognition and appreciation.

In this scenario, the maternalistic homemaker employer gets more from her employee than better job performance or loyalty. She derives pleasure both from her voyeurism and from perceiving herself as kind and altruistic. Unlike someone who, say, writes a check to a charity organization, she can directly view the benefits of her contributions and "have the fun of seeing the kids." In fact, she need never see where they live, only what she gives them. Without leaving her affluent neighborhood or following anyone else's schedule, such an employer can construct a sense of herself as generous, altruistic, and kind—key attributes of the ideal bourgeois feminine personality.

Several caveats must be inserted into this discussion of homemaker employers and employed employers. The distinctions between the two groups are not absolute. These are not static characteristics: some woman have shifted from domesticity to full-time employment, and vice versa. After these transitions, their attitude toward personalism with their domestic workers may change. Rita Hamilton, who had been a homemaker when her children were young, later returned to finish college and graduate school; by the time I interviewed her, she had a demanding career as a consultant to large corporations. When she was at home raising five children, she had employed an elderly black couple to clean the home once a week, and she recalled with fondness her relationship with them and their family. But now that she was a career woman, she used a three-person cleaning service; one Anglo owner and two Central American men enter her home and quickly clean it. Though she had enjoyed personalism as a homemaker, the more distant relationship seemed more appropriate to her present life: "I've always felt family with people [who clean]. I'm the most distant from the group I have now because we don't chat. They kind of come in and do their thing, and they're out of here. They are cleaning professionals . . . and I'm not around as much to talk with them either."

Finally, even though employers hold the upper hand, there are always two parties to a relationship. As we have seen, employers cannot unilaterally determine the quality of the relationship with their paid domestic workers. Homemakers are not able to impose close, intimate relations, though they may try; and harried working women who won't make time to talk with their nanny/housekeepers are sometimes forced to do so. Even paying employers can't always get what they want.

CLASS DISTINCTIONS:
UPSTAIRS, DOWNSTAIRS, OR ALL IN THE FAMILY?

Class is a slippery concept in the United States, where nearly everybody, from warehouse loaders to millionaire entrepreneurs, is likely to identify as middle class. Distinctions between the middle class and the upper class, like those between homemakers and employed women, are often blurry. Moreover, even though class reproduces itself with remarkable consistency, some individuals move sharply up or down the social scale. For example, Carolyn Astor, the daughter of a waitress and a used car salesman, had recently married into a prominent, wealthy philanthropic family. When I met her, she was already, without irony, a diligent student of upper-class life, eagerly calling on her mother-in-law and her in-law's family friends to receive guidance on being the employer of a three-day-a-week nanny/housekeeper. Carolyn was openly affectionate with the Oaxacan nanny, who happened to unexpectedly arrive with flowers, hugs, and birthday wishes for her on the morning I interviewed her. Along with picking up pointers on noblesse oblige, Carolyn was learning how to rule with authority. When her nanny/housekeeper had missed work to attend prenatal medical appointments, she had consulted her mother-in-law's friend; thereafter, she began paying the nanny daily instead of biweekly, to ensure, as she put it, "no work, no pay."

In general, very high income employers tend to favor more distant relations with their domestic employees than do middle-class and upper-middle-class employers. They prefer an American version of the "upstairs, downstairs" segregation of master and servant. In part, this physical separation is encouraged by their palatial, mansion-sized homes. Spatial distance appears to facilitate emotional distance between employer and employee. The telephone systems with which these large homes are equipped hint at the physical obstacles to easy conversation. In each room, an office telephone with an elaborate array of push buttons sits on a table. When a call comes in, it can be transferred to any of about a dozen phone extensions located in other rooms throughout the house. Upper-class employers often hire a small staff of domestic workers; they may trade confidences with a primary housekeeper but retain greater distance from the others. Hierarchies of job tasks also affect personalistic relations; like the less-wealthy employers described above, those in the upper class may have closer relationships with employees who care for their young children than with those who do only cleaning. Yet I found that in these homes, there are limits—not always well-defined, but present nonetheless—on how informally and intimately employees may interact with employers.

When I interviewed Jenna Proust, the wife of a Hollywood agent, she was employing four women of color to ensure that her household ran smoothly. One Guatemalan woman performed most of the cleaning Monday through Friday from 8 A.M. until 2 P.M.; on weekdays at noon, a young Salvadoran woman arrived to clean, cook, shop for groceries, drive the children home from elementary school or to appointments, and look after the children until 8 P.M. On Saturday evenings, an African American woman served as the babysitter for the two children; and on Tuesday evenings and Sunday afternoons, a young Chicana—who had previously worked as their live-in—came to work as a nanny. Jenna Proust and her husband paid approximately $4,000 a month for these women to take care of their 6,700-square-foot home and their two children.

As we sat down in her cavernous living room, Jenna propped her feet up on the distressed, antique coffee table and told me, "I think I've gotten to the point where I'm hiring more passive people." She was referring to Latina immigrants, whom she saw as reserved and demure, as opposed to Martha, the U.S.-born Chicana whom she had previously hired as a live-in and now had working only two days a week, or to the European au pairs that she had employed in the past. Although she perceived Ronalda, the young Salvadoran woman who worked from noon until 8 P.M., to be barely competent at her usual tasks and totally at sea in interactions outside the family, such as with the children's orthodontist or with the plumber, she was, for the time, willing to overlook these failings because of Ronalda's quiet, deferential manner. By contrast, she had complete confidence in the abilities and judgment of Martha, a Chicana from the rural area of Oxnard, California. Martha could be counted on to purchase the right kind of coffee filters when she did the shopping, or to know that a child should not have an allergy shot while on antibiotics, but Jenna Proust found her loud, brash, and too familiar.

"For instance," she explained, "I've been trying to lose weight this year and exercising a lot, and Martha has trouble with weight too. I don't want to share that with her but she has taken it upon herself to burst onto the scene, like last night telling me exactly how many pounds she lost, like a child almost, and more like a close friend. This is where I would like a little distance." Martha had not only incorrectly assumed that Jenna would be interested in reciprocal exchanges on dieting successes and struggles, ones that perhaps highlighted the employer's failures, but she had also refused to act submissively. This too bothered Jenna: "She'll say, 'Don't say anything to me or I'll bite your head off, I have PMS!' And that to me is just, well, I just don't like living with someone who's put me on notice, especially someone who works for me and I won't pull the class thing, but excuse me, I'm the one who is paying the bills here." Although Jenna believed that when hiring someone to care for children, it is important "to know who this person is a little bit," she also found herself preferring to keep relations with the domestic workers more distant, "more businesslike than previous relationships. My children are older, and I think I am getting to be less interested in the level of involvement I had because I'm asking the people to be less involved in our family life now." In the past, she had taken several sick live-in nanny/housekeepers to doctors, but she no longer wanted to engage in this sort of maternalistic assistance.

At the same time, she remained ambivalent about these choices. She emphasized to me that as a "child of the sixties," she didn't require the same type of deference, distance, and formality that her mother had. The daughter of a corporate attorney and, as she put it, a "charity ball mother," she recalled growing up in elite enclaves of Los Angeles with a uniformed maid ringing a bell for dinner. "I dislike the bell. I really dislike treating someone like a servant," she murmured in a hushed voice. Jenna Proust did not identify with that kind of formality—she herself dressed in jeans and sneakers—yet she wanted distance and personal privacy from the domestic employees. Martha was her main negative example, and she commented, "She gets a little too close. . . . I really don't want to be on intimate terms with my workers. At the same time, I like being on a very comfortable and causal basis with them. You're raising kids together, how can it not be?"

Bonnie Feinstein, a part-time interior decorator and wife of a Hollywood director, employed three domestic employees at a cost of $3,000 a month to manage her large, rambling home and her three elementary school–age children. A Salvadoran woman worked as the full-time, live-out nanny/housekeeper from Monday through Friday, a Filipina woman worked Saturday morning through Sunday, and another Salvadoran woman cleaned the 5,700-square-foot house two days a week. Both Bonnie and her husband were so bothered by the familiarity exhibited by Sarita, the two-day-a-week cleaner, and by the Filipina nanny that they had discussed firing them.

Bonnie described how Sarita had cheerfully greeted her husband, an Academy Award–winning director, with a teasing, affectionate, "Hello handsome!" Irritated by the lack of deference but, like many husbands, unwilling to speak to the domestic employee himself, he had passed the problem to his wife. Uncertain of what to do, she said nothing to Sarita. More recently, Sarita had offended the husband again by joining the family and the husband's parents at the kitchen table while they were eating lunch. "He was like—ahh! He went out and dove into the pool and came back and said 'Get rid of her. Send her home.'" Bonnie said that she enjoyed listening to the warm, homey banter of her domestic employees gathered around the table for lunch, but Sarita had clearly crossed an invisible boundary by joining the family and the in-laws at the table. "He feels like she doesn't know her place," she explained. Although she shared his view, she didn't know how to establish barriers to this sort of personal interaction. "Me, I might feel that it was improper for her to do that, but I wouldn't really act on it. . . . I think I probably let my help push me around in certain ways, but when it gets too much for me, then I call it quits." In fact, she had plans to fire Sarita, but she did not intend to tell Sarita the real reason why she was being fired.

Elizabeth Mapplethorpe, a mature socialite, mother of three grown children, and self-described "wife of a California cheese magnate," was the only employer respondent who required her housekeeper to dress in uniform. She claimed that Hollywood employers were ruining the labor market for domestic workers because they lacked decorum and experience as employers. "It sounds excessively snobby," she confessed, "but it's basically actuality. Most of them never had help when they were a child, so they do not have an idea of what is expected . . . so you don't have quite the same caliber of help." What bothered her most was that these nouveau riche employers did not know how to demand deference and distance in their employees.

At the Mapplethorpe residence, a rotating staff of five nurses provided round-the-clock care for the Mapplethorpes' disabled daughter, and a recently hired Polish woman arrived in uniform Monday through Friday to clean, cook, and serve dinner. This stylish matron preferred distance and servitude in her domestic employees; and unlike many employers who want distance but find themselves reluctant to impose it, she was not plagued by liberal guilt. *"Housekeeper* is such a euphemism. They're maids," she explained matter-of-factly. While we spoke in her 7,500-square-foot mansion, an elaborately decorated variation on a European chateau where each piece of furniture seemed to have a particular name, I could see the maid fluffing the cushions on the pool patio furniture. When we went outside after the interview, the uniformed maid discreetly entered to take away our empty diet soda cans. No interaction or verbal directives seemed to be required. Even as Elizabeth Mapplethorpe mourned the declining quality of domestic service brought on by the Hollywood industry employers and "rich Arabians," she confessed that her own style fell short of that found among the European aristocracy. Commenting on an acquaintance who had married a German prince, she said, "She rang the bell for him [the servant] to come and put the log on the fire! I mean, this is so much greater than what our level is, so you realize that we're not really at the apex yet!"

Female upper-class employers such as these generally don't work, so they may spend considerable time together with the domestic workers in these large homes. Despite the size of the homes, contact with round-the-clock help is unavoidable, increasing the possibility of misunderstandings and potentially explosive contacts. These employers therefore find it particularly important to hire employees who will gauge and maintain just the right measure of distance.

EMPLOYEES:
"I Want Them to Know Who I Am"

My ideal employer? Someone who would talk with me
about her family, who would ask questions about mine,
about what I did in Mexico before I came here. Someone
who would be considerate of my time.

Marisela Ramírez

As the epigraph suggests, there is a dramatic mismatch in what employers and employees desire from their relationship. Employers
who hire someone to clean and look after their children at home
generally want some distance from the women who do the work.
They are often too pressed for time because of their work and family
schedules; they may feel it is beneath them or a waste of time to
personally interact with subordinates; or they simply feel too awkward about having someone taking care of their home and children
to establish personal bonds. They want some breathing space—but
the women they hire want more intimacy.

The structure of the job, the extent to which care work (and not
just cleaning) is involved, and the organization of the lives of the
domestic workers as newly arrived immigrant women prompt many
Latina domestic workers in Los Angeles to prefer personalistic employer-employee relations. These are women who have left their
homes, jobs, friends, and family members in Mexico, Guatemala, and
El Salvador. Many of them have young children of their own, left
behind in their countries of origin, whom they have not seen for
years. Some had been born into middle-class lives, complete with
social recognition and public status, and perhaps homes with their
own domestic help. Now, they may spend very long days and even
nights on the job, giving intimate care; some hold down second jobs
on weekends or evenings. When they do have time off, it is filled
with their own household chores, with visits to the coin-operated
laundry, or with English classes. Their many personal sacrifices leave
little time for human contact as they try to establish themselves on
secure financial ground. The relative anonymity of their lives, the
quality of their jobs, the larger political context of racialized nativism, and the rushed pace of life in Los Angeles leave many domestic
workers without any sense of belonging and aching for some personal recognition. In addition, they have cultural expectations for

everyday social interactions that clash with what they find on the job. Latin Americans are a good deal more likely to emote, hug, and verbally express affection than are typical Anglo-Americans. This *cultura de cariño*, or culture of affection, also contributes to the mismatched expectations of domestic workers and their employers.

Latina immigrants who do domestic work for pay are not, of course, a homogeneous group. Among the factors distinguishing them is their relative degree of social incorporation in the United States. At one extreme are recently arrived immigrant women, who lack nearby family and close friends and indeed may have only a handful of acquaintances in Los Angeles, who do not speak any English, who do not drive, and who do not know their way around downtown's *el centro*, the swap meets, or other commercial centers. At the other extreme are women with well-established local ties, who navigate easily about the city either on the bus or in their own cars, who have their families and strong social circles surrounding them, and who may participate in church or community organizations. As chapter 2 made clear, the former are more likely to be employed in live-in nanny/housekeeper jobs, and the latter in weekly housecleaning. Not only job arrangements but also the level of social incorporation determine how personalistic they expect relations to be. Recently arrived women working in live-in jobs are generally more eager for personalistic employer-employee relations—and more critical of their employers who deny them this closeness—than are more established women working as housecleaners. Still, both groups of women express a preference for personalism with their employers.

NANNY/HOUSEKEEPERS VERSUS HOUSECLEANERS

Women who strictly do housecleaning expect less personalism than do their nanny/housekeeper peers, in part because of the nature of their work. Those women who care for children on their jobs feel that their employers have a duty to acknowledge the intimate care they provide. Nanny/housekeepers who care for young children feel most poignantly the inherent contradiction between their tasks and their treatment. They work in the midst of a family; and unlike their housecleaning peers, they are paid for activities—nurturing, singing songs and reciting nursery rhymes, coaxing children to bathe, nap, or eat—that are emotional, intimate, and particularly tailored to each child. They often become genuinely attached to the children as they perform these tasks day in and day out. When they are treated coldly or as if they were invisible by their employers, who may be standing right next to them, they find such actions insulting and alienating. As one nanny put it, "Here I am caring for their children, and look at how they treat me!" Some nannies point out that self-interest should persuade employers to change this behavior, observing that employers who treat their employees well can expect those employees to provide better care for the children and remain in the job longer.

In short, because their work engages so intimately with the children, the Latina women who work as nanny/housekeepers want verbal, personalistic recognition from their employers. Deborah Stone, who has examined caring work in institutional contexts, argues that what is produced in caring work is a *relationship* between the giver and recipient of care. Thus to improve poor quality care, we must valorize caregiving as relationship building. The problem in managed elder care, the area on which she focuses, is that caregivers are discouraged from "caring about" or showing favoritism to the recipients.[12] Private nanny/housekeepers appear to have the opposite problem: while these caregivers are expected to care about their charges, the employers do not seem to personally recognize them or find value in building a relationship with them.

While Latina domestic workers do not desire personalistic relations with their employers in lieu of decent pay or fair job terms, many of them prefer an employer who takes personal interest in them to an employer who pays more and treats them disrespectfully and coldly. They want to keep their dignity on the job, and thus they want employers to talk to them and listen when they speak. As Stone observes, talking and listening are key components of caregiving, so it should be no surprise that caregivers want their employers to listen to their own concerns and even aspirations. They don't necessarily want or expect gifts and advice (although many are grateful for these gestures). And they don't, of course, want interference—as we have seen, for a Latina domestic worker, the ideal employer is one who is out of the home for most of the day, not monitoring her and issuing ad hoc orders. But caregivers do want employers who will talk with them in an open and respectful manner—employers who will listen to and respect them as persons.

JOB STRUCTURES

Live-in and live-out nanny/housekeepers find that the spatial and social isolation of the job intensifies their craving for personal contact. Typically they work for only one employer, and spend each day at the home of the same family. With the exception of those hired by very high income families who simultaneously employ several domestic workers, they generally have no co-workers with whom to speak. The job is, as one employer conceded, "a lonesome one." Nanny/housekeepers may be alone for most of the day, or they may spend the entire day with infants. If they are lucky, they may meet up for an hour or two with a group of nannies at a public park, or on arranged play dates.

Nanny/housekeepers with live-in jobs are the most isolated. They work long hours—on average, more than sixty hours a week—leaving the employer's home only on Saturday afternoons, when they retreat to a shared apartment or a rented room until Monday morning. During the rest of the week, they remain confined to their work site. Without anyone to speak with day after day, many of them become emotionally distraught and depressed. It is little wonder that they often seek more personalistic relations with the only adults they see, their employers.

Erlinda Castro, a middle-aged Guatemalan woman and mother of five, had spent three years working as a live-in housekeeper in three different households before finally establishing her route of weekly housecleaning jobs. In the first of her live-in jobs, she worked for a family whom she described as good employers, because they paid her what she had expected to earn and because they did not pile on an unreasonable number of duties. The school-age children were gone for most of the day, and her job tasks seemed fair and physically manageable. The employers did not criticize her work, and they never insulted or yelled at her. Unlike many other live-ins, she had her own room and there was food for her to eat. Yet Erlinda found her employers cold and impersonal, unresponsive to her attempts to engage them in conversation; and she told me that their aloofness drove her out of the job.

"I would greet the *señora*, 'Good morning, *señora* Judy,'" she recalled. "They spoke a little Spanish, but the *señor* never spoke. If I greeted him, maybe in between his teeth he would mutter, 'Heh,' just like that. That's how one is often treated, and it feels cruel. You leave your own home, leaving everything behind only to find hostility. You're useful to them only because you clean, wash, iron, cook—that's the only reason. There is no affection. There is nothing." She expected some warmth and affection, but instead she found a void. Erlinda Castro entered the home of these employers directly after leaving her home and five children in Guatemala. On weekends she visited with her husband, whom she had joined in Los Angeles. It was her first experience with paid domestic work, and although she was not put off by the pay, the job tasks, or the low status of the job, the impersonal treatment became intolerable. "I felt bad, really bad. I couldn't go on with that, with nothing more than, 'Good morning, *señora'* and, 'Good night, *señora.'* Nothing else. They would say nothing, nothing, absolutely nothing to me! They would only speak to me to give me orders." Erlinda stayed on that job for approximately one year, leaving it for another live-in job that a friend had told her about.

Being treated as though one is invisible is a complaint commonly voiced by domestic workers of color working for white employers. As the historian David Katzman has noted in his study of the occupation in the South, "One peculiar and most degrading aspect of domestic service was the requisite of invisibility. The ideal servant . . . would be invisible and silent[,] . . . sensitive to the moods and whims of those around them, but undemanding of family warmth, love or security."[13] In her early 1980s ethnographic research, for which she posed as a housecleaner, Judith Rollins revealed a telling moment: an employer and her teenage son conducted an entire conversation about personal issues in her presence. "This situation was," Rollins wrote in her field notes, "the most peculiar feeling of the day: being there and not being there."[14] At different times, African American, Japanese American, and Chicana domestic workers in the United States have had the same disturbing experience.[15]

Some domestic workers see personalism as the antidote to these indignities and humiliations. Verbal interaction affords them respect and recognition on the job. Elvira Areola, a Mexicana, had worked for eleven years for one family. I interviewed her several days after an acrimonious fight with her employer—a disagreement that became physical—had left her jobless and without an income. As a single mother, she found herself in a frightening position. Still, she expressed no regrets, partly because the almost completely nonverbal relationship that she had maintained for several years with the *patrona* had been so strained. Her female employer had not worked and was physically present in the home, yet they hardly interacted. "I would arrive [in the morning] and sometimes she wouldn't greet me until two in the afternoon. . . . I'd be in the kitchen, and she'd walk in but wouldn't say anything. She would ignore me, as if to say, 'I'm alone in my house and there's no one else here.' Sometimes she wouldn't speak to me the whole day . . . she'd act as if I was a chair, a table, as if her house was supposedly all clean without me being there." Her dissatisfaction with the lack of appreciation and verbal recognition was echoed in the accounts of many other women.

Domestic workers tend to accept much more readily the minimal verbal exchanges they often experience with male employers. Ronalda Saavedra described her male employers' blur of unchanging, monosyllabic greetings: "In the morning they say 'Hi!' and then 'Bye!' Then in the evenings they come around again with that same old 'Hi!' and then 'Bye!'" Similarly, while Maribel Centeno often enjoyed conversing with her female employer, she noted that "the husband is different. He sometimes doesn't greet me, and sometimes I want to think it's just because he is so into his profession." Fears of sexual harassment may help explain the domestic workers' different responses to the same behavior.

DOWNWARD CLASS MOBILITY

Prior class status plays an important role in fueling an expectation for personalism. In contemporary Los Angeles, Latina nanny/housekeepers who in their countries of origin had enjoyed middle-class status and jobs that brought them into contact with the public are acutely sensitive to their employers' failure to recognize them as people. Sometimes they suffer depression and low self-esteem as a result. Twenty-five-year-old Maribel Centeno, a former university student, worked as a live-out nanny/housekeeper. Although she was happier in that job than in her former position as a live-in in her first few years in the United States, she cited as one of its biggest disadvantages the *bloqueo* that it had produced in her—a kind of emotional and communicative wall that had developed because she lacked daily interaction with others. She now found it hard to speak with other people in informal social gatherings. In Guatemala, she had been surrounded by friends, family, co-workers, and student peers. She had attended university, worked part-time as a radio operator and in her parents' general store, and frequently socialized with friends. The daily monotony and loneliness she endured as a nanny/housekeeper provided a stark contrast to her former life. Exaggerating only slightly, she said, "Sometimes I go for days, and then I realize I haven't heard myself talk."

Nanny/housekeepers try to address these problems as best they can. Despite owning a car, Maribel sometimes deliberately took the bus so that she could enjoy the company of other domestic workers on her way to work. Even though she found their discussions rather dull, uninformed, and uncultured, she welcomed the personal contact. She lived with two of her cousins and had a steady boyfriend; but as new Guatemalan immigrants, they too were busy, working long hours and attending ESL classes. Maribel's female employer did not work, so she was usually present when Maribel was cleaning the house and looking after a hyperactive adolescent boy when he arrived home from school. Although their relationship was rife with tensions—over wages, time off, and the employer's underestimation of her—Maribel cited the conversation and personalism she had with her employer as one of the best things about her job. "She always greets me and gives me a kiss, and when I leave, it's the same. She asks after my parents, for my sister, she asks how I'm doing in school. . . . At noon, maybe I'll be upstairs and she'll call out that she's making a turkey sandwich. 'Do you want one?' "

Maribel deliberately initiated conversations with her employer designed to showcase her considerable knowledge and curiosity about politics, music, and history. In fact, she believed that her employer usually showed respect and interest in her precisely because she had proven herself to be well-educated and informed about current events. There was a genuine warmth between the two, which I witnessed when we gathered at a hotel to celebrate Maribel's graduation from a U.S. high school. The employer beamed at Maribel's accomplishments and applauded her goal to move out of domestic work and into cosmetology or teaching. Describing their relationship, Maribel said, "I feel that she's, ah, not really my friend, but there is a certain kind of respect. I think that's because I study, because if it wasn't for that, well I don't know." Yet tensions between the two remained. Maribel also reported that during the day, her employer often ignored her, spending most of her time holed up in the pool cabana smoking, talking on the phone, or paying bills. Moreover, the employer did not always show her respect, and Maribel resented these indignities.

Maribel recounted a number of painful incidents that demonstrated her employer's tendency to objectify and underestimate her. On one occasion the employer, assuming that Maribel had never heard of a submarine sandwich, condescendingly explained how to assemble one out of bread, mayonnaise, and sliced meats. "At first I didn't say anything, I just looked at her. How could she think I didn't know what a submarine is!" Maribel told me that she had then launched into a speech that Guatemalans enjoyed the same modern technology as Americans, and that in fact, Guatemalans had much more, as their Mayan civilization had developed advanced mathematics and the concept of zero years before they were in use in Europe. On another occasion, the employer allowed a friend to drop off children for Maribel to watch—creating extra work without extra pay. The employer assured her friend not to worry: "Maribel knows how to dial 911 and she has attended university." The other woman had exclaimed, "Oh, really?" Maribel mimicked the look of disbelief by raising her eyebrows and added, "and she looked at me like I was an animal in the zoo!"

Such incidents highlighted the employer's (and her friend's) view of Maribel as backward, inferior, and ignorant. For a number of reasons, Maribel saw her job as less than perfect. She wanted higher pay and the assurance that it would continue when the employers vacationed or had the house remodeled, and she disapproved of the employer's liberal child-rearing style. Yet more objectionable than these more material drawbacks was her employer's insinuation that she and other Latinas and Latinos were inferior, which hurt her deeply. "She's even made comments like, 'Did you see the housekeeper across the street? She has seven children! Now, *you* must know how to think. You don't come here just to have children!' Of course, she'll never say, 'Oh, you're all a burden on the state,' but that's what she means." In Maribel Centeno's relationship with her employer, respectful warmth coexisted along with deep antagonism rooted in inequalities of class, citizenship status, and race, and both found daily expression.

Domestic workers who prefer personalistic relations with their employers are looking for some recognition of their humanity. Yet personalistic relations, as Maribel's case illustrates and as previous literature argues, can also emphasize the employees' inferiority and the employers' sense of superiority. Although domestic workers differ on how much of their private lives they wish to share with their employers—and many of them have learned that intimate details are best kept to themselves—all object to being treated as invisible nonpersons or as replaceable cogs. Certainly they want fair pay and decent working conditions, but they also want to be treated as more than just generic employees. Many of them say they prefer personalism because it recognizes their own needs, preferences, and feelings.

While the literature on paid domestic work has stressed how employers deploy personalism as a mechanism of control, contemporary Latina domestic workers in Los Angeles see nonpersonalistic employers as potentially more exploitative. For the most part, these women had no illusions that a personalistic relationship with their employers signified the friendship of equals; but they saw personalism as an avenue through which employers could show respect for them as people. Without it, a domestic worker loses all individual identity. Several of the women used words such as "robot" or "disposable" to describe how employers view them. They assume that employers cannot fully subordinate or manipulate someone seen instead as a person.

Maura de la Covarrubia, who had worked as an attorney in Peru, had an unusual arrangement: she worked as a nanny for several different families, visiting each one day a week, and for another family as a nanny/housekeeper only on the weekends. She had established fairly close relations with most of her female employers, and she used her educational and class background to her advantage. Maura held very clear ideas on what constituted a desirable employer. "An ideal employer," she offered, "is a friendly person, someone who pays well, and above all, who thinks that the person who works for her, whether as a 'housekeeper' or as a 'baby-sitter,' or whatever, is a human being. I think there are some people who don't see us as human beings, but rather we're just, just some *thing* that works there, some *thing* that if you get tired of, you just exchange it for another, for another, and for another! It's as if we're disposable!"

Although Maura claimed most of her employers as confidantes and friends, she also cried inconsolably at the conclusion of our interview when she recalled how she had felt dehumanized by one family, for whom she worked Saturdays and Sundays, when she broke her ankle on the job. First, the employers had not offered to help her receive medical attention, apparently believing that she was faking an injury to extort money from them. Maura tried on her own to get treatment, but she was turned away from several places despite her willingness and ability to pay for medical services. As a middle-class professional in Peru, she had never experienced such blatant discrimination and disregard. Ultimately she was directed to "a mediocre doctor," a phrase she repeated several times to underscore the shock and indignity of being able to receive only second-class medical treatment. Maura remained out of work for two months, recuperating at her brother's home, and the employers at whose house the accident occurred waited six weeks to call and ask how she was doing. For Maura, this incident clearly demonstrated that they viewed her only as a cog necessary to the smooth running of their weekends, not as a person.

Other Latina nanny/housekeepers contrasted their dehumanizing treatment by some employers with recognition as persons by others. Patricia Paredes, a very savvy Mexican live-in nanny/housekeeper whose job required that she live across town from her husband and three young daughters during the week, said, "I like it when people treat you right, when they know you are human and have feelings. I like being treated like a human, not a robot." She went even further, praising her employer for treating her "as family . . . that's how I like to be treated. I'm never humiliated or put down."

Paid domestic workers seek a personalism that goes beyond superficial cordiality to recognition that their health, well-being, and personal circumstances affect their ability to work. They want employers who don't simply ask how they feel but adjust the job to take into account illness or a personal crisis. Gladys Vargas, a heavyset Salvadoran woman who worked as live-out nanny/housekeeper, had painful, swollen knees, which she kept propped up on the sofa during our evening interview. That day, her employer had reacted to her discomfort by telling her that she should watch her diet, and not eat so much guacamole and beef. "I've been sick, but she's never said, 'Look, lie down for a moment. Take an hour to rest.' No, what matters to her is having her house clean. There is no consideration on these jobs." Another Salvadoran woman, Celestina Vigil, who worked three days as a housecleaner and two-day-a-week nanny/housekeeper, had the opposite experience, and she was particularly appreciative of the employer for whom she did child care. On several occasions when Celestina had to leave work early to tend to her partner's illness, the employer had returned home immediately to relieve Celestina of her job duties. Comparing this employer with others for whom she only cleans house, she said, "She is extremely humane, which is a quality difficult to find in someone. I work with other people who even give me the key to their homes—many times I don't even see them. But with her, we can get along. It's already been five years, and she has helped me with everything that she can. I know I can count on her."

HOUSECLEANERS

Unlike live-in and live-out nanny/housekeepers, the housecleaners work in different houses and for various employers, often enjoying a great deal of flexibility in scheduling their jobs. Since they generally don't care for children as part of their job, they develop fewer emotional ties with their employers, whom they generally see briefly or not at all. While they are happy to work without employer supervision, most of them also voice a preference for employers who exhibit some personal interest in them. For example, Marisela Ramírez—a young Mexicana from a rural background, who rented a small suburban bungalow with her husband, toddler, and sister—told me that her favorite employer was a woman who always asked after her and her family. She told me, "She's really sweet, always worried about what's going on with me, how I'm doing, and if she sees me looking sad, she says, 'What's wrong? I'm your friend, you can confide in me. Maybe I can help you with something.'" While the employer also asked Maria questions that might be seen as patronizing, such as whether her husband treated her well or beat her, Maria was not offended. She saw these questions as expressions of genuine caring.

Erlinda Castro had only recently established a steady route of different houses to clean on each day of the week, but she also told me that her favorite employers were not the wealthiest or highest-paying. She was particularly fond of a *chinita* (a Korean woman) who always chatted with her, and treated her with kindness and respect. She was very grateful to this woman because she had gone out of her way to find more houses—especially big, more lucrative, houses—for Erlinda to clean on different days. Erlinda, however, spoke as much about the employer's friendliness as about the concrete material help that she had offered. She also praised an elderly couple who, on her cleaning days with them, always called her to join them for lunch at noon. "We talk a lot. They have some happy moments when I'm there. They speak a little Spanish, and me, a little English, and using bits of those two languages, we laugh a lot."

Because housecleaners maintain several different employers, they are not completely dependent on any one of them for their full earnings. While having multiple employers diffuses the potential for (and lessens the serious consequences of) explosive conflicts, it also means that the housecleaners must gauge the appropriate degree of distance, deference, and personalism at each job and remember these individual requirements from week to week. One important decision faced by housecleaners in the homes where the employer is present concerns mealtime. Should the housecleaner sit at the table to eat with the employer, or should she not? No well-established, well-understood rules cover this question, and employers can hold quite different and sometimes self-contradictory positions that are never made explicit. Recall Bonnie Feinstein's upper-class household; though Bonnie told me that she enjoyed seeing her domestic help gathered around the table for lunch, she was appalled when her housecleaner joined her, her film director husband, and her in-laws at the table. The Feinsteins saw this behavior as reason to fire the housecleaner. Yet an employer who lived just minutes away from the Feinsteins, on the Westside of Los Angeles, complained to me that she had finally "let go" of one housecleaner because she had acted with too much humility. Her subservience made Eleanor Zabrinsky, a retired teacher, feel uncomfortable. "She didn't want to sit at the table for lunch," she explained. "She wanted to stand in the kitchen, and that bothered me." Though housecleaners generally have less personal interaction with their employers than do nanny/housekeepers, they must constantly readjust to different work sites and different employers.

SOCIAL INCORPORATION

Recently arrived women who work as nanny/housekeepers are often bereft of family and community, in a sense out of necessity. Recall that 40 percent of the 153 domestic workers surveyed who were mothers reported that they had left at least one child "back home," in their countries of origin, and that this was much more likely to be true of live-in nanny/housekeepers, least likely of weekly house-cleaners. While some Latina domestic workers in Los Angeles have rich social networks of friends, kin, and community, others are basically on their own.

At one end of continuum might be someone like Lupe Vélez, who is firmly entrenched in her own family and community life. A Mexicana, Lupe entered the United States when her father, a contract laborer who came to California in the bracero era, brought the family in the late 1960s. She had married in the 1970s; and when I interviewed her, she and her husband, a welder, had two cars, owned a house on the east side of Los Angeles, and had five U.S.-born children, including two who were already attending state colleges. Lupe cleaned about nine houses a week, driving to them in her Toyota. She also kept busy with her teenage children and Latina social circles, with *comadres,* sisters-in-law, neighbors, and church life. I spoke with her one hot, summer evening in her tiny, neatly furnished living room, where family photos adorned nearly every available space, a group of teenage boys socialized on the front porch, and the phone rang often. With all the activity surrounding her, Lupe didn't have a great need to receive personalistic treatment from her employers. As a weekly housecleaner, she saw many of them only fleetingly, and she clearly understood her job as a money-earning activity. Yet she too desired employer appreciation, reporting that it felt good when an employer sometimes called her at home to simply thank her for her excellent cleaning. When I asked what she liked best about her job, she said with an easy laugh, "Well, the pay is important—but especially that they treat me well!" But because Lupe Vélez had a full life with family and friends, she was not as concerned about employer personalism as were some Latina immigrants who had arrived more recently.

At the other end of the continuum is Carmen Velasquez, a thirty-nine-year-old Mexican woman. She had worked at live-in jobs for ten years in the United States, and had no complaints about her current job. In fact, when I asked her to describe an ideal employer, she replied, "The ones I have." She currently worked for an attorney and a schoolteacher, caring for their toddler and living in their home. They treated her with respect, paid her on time, acted friendly, and were not too demanding in their expectations. Unlike many other live-in nanny/housekeepers, she ended her workday when the female employer returned home at 5 P.M. Yet her longing for more personalistic, familylike relations with her employers was revealed when I asked her what she might do differently if she herself were to employ a domestic worker. "If I had lived through all of this," she reflected, "I would try to make sure that person felt as though she wasn't a stranger to my family, so that she would feel like part of my family, and that of my children. [I'd make sure] that she could share those moments when I was there—not as a maid or employee, but rather as a friend."

More than any cultural explanation, the social conditions of Carmen's life explain her preference for personalism. Carmen, a single mother, had no family life of her own in Los Angeles. She had left her three children in Mexico ten years earlier, when they were four, five, and seven years old. She sent money to the children and communicated with them and her *comadres*, who cared for the children in Mexico; she had not seen them for a decade. A series of traumatic events had left her completely estranged from the father of the children, her parents, and her siblings. In spite of these familial hardships, Carmen maintained a warm, loving, upbeat personality. Whenever I saw her around young children—the children of other domestic workers, or my own three-year-old—she could scarcely contain her affection, extending her arms to embrace them or give their chubby arms a squeeze.

Although she had been in the United States for ten years, she was still working as a live-in nanny/housekeeper, with no residence of her own. Unlike many live-in employees who share an apartment or at least rent a room to which they can retreat on weekends, Carmen stayed at her employer's house. This enabled her to send a larger portion of her earnings to her children in Mexico, but it also kept her isolated from Latino community life. Her Anglo employer's home was located in a secluded canyon neighborhood, home mostly to Anglos and Armenians. The nearby streets had no sidewalks, no pedestrians, and no commercial life. On weekdays, Carmen sometimes took the toddler to the park, where she met with two other Latina nannies; during the evenings, she attended English classes, joining a small group of Latino students within a largely Armenian student body. In her room she studied English and enjoyed reading self-help books that focus on self-esteem. "I always try to stay positive," she told me. One Sunday afternoon each month, she attended a meeting of the Domestic Workers' Association, but she spent many weekends riding aimlessly around on public buses, just to get out of the employer's house.

DISTINGUISHING MATERNALISM FROM PERSONALISM

In the large and theoretically sophisticated literature on paid domestic work, employer maternalism is roundly, and rightly, condemned as a principal source of exploitation.[16] One alternative, most forcefully advocated by the sociologist Mary Romero, is to maintain businesslike, contractual relations concerned specifically and exclusively with job tasks and schedules. The contractual ideal may be realizable in housecleaning work—which is, not coincidentally, the form of paid domestic work on which Romero's primary research has focused. When care work is involved, however, emotional connection is an integral part of the job and a clear-cut relation between client and customer is far rarer.

More important, as we saw in this chapter, both Latina nanny/housekeepers and housecleaners report that when employer-employee relations remain devoid of personalistic interactions, they feel ignored and disrespected. While it might be tempting to dismiss their statements as exemplifying what Marxists would denounce as false consciousness, we should take seriously what they say about their work and how it makes them feel. To understand why these Latina domestic workers want more affinity and personal connection with their employers, we must distinguish between maternalism and personalism. Employer maternalism is a one-way relationship, defined primarily by the employer's gestures of charity, unsolicited advice, assistance, and gifts. The domestic employee is obligated to respond with extra hours of service, personal loyalty, and job commitment. Maternalism underlines the deep class inequalities between employers and employees. More problematically, because employer maternalism positions the employee as needy, deficient, and childlike, it does not allow the employee any dignity and respect. Personalism, by contrast, is a two-way relationship, albeit still asymmetrical. It involves the employer's recognition of the employee as a particular person—the recognition and *consideración* necessary for dignity and respect to be realized. In the absence of fair wages, reasonable hours, and job autonomy, personalism alone is not enough to upgrade domestic work; but conversely, its absence virtually ensures that the job will be experienced as degrading.

To be sure, employers can use personalistic relations as a strategy to mask low salaries, lack of benefits, and long hours of work without overtime pay, but for the most part, Latina housecleaners and nanny/housekeepers see cold, impersonal employer-employee relations as blatant reminders of the low regard in which society holds them. They experience this on-the-job treatment as continuous with the various anti-immigrant, and particularly anti-Latino, campaigns in California during the 1990s. Racialized nativism sets the stage on which these relationships or nonrelationships acquire meaning.

For their part, many employers would prefer to have more distant, impersonal relationships with their paid domestic workers, not because they wish to rationalize labor practices but because personalism obligates them to care about their employees. As their time becomes increasingly scarce, they resist spending time and emotional energy even on talking with their domestic workers. As we have seen, many contemporary American employers are not quite comfortable with having someone do domestic work in their home. Though they may not voice or even feel class or racial guilt, they are still made profoundly uneasy by the darker, poorer, Spanish-speaking women toiling away in their homes, making them masters and mistresses—an image that doesn't fit their view of themselves, or their sense of the United States as a modern, democratic, classless, and color-blind society. Finally, personalism implicitly limits employers' power and flexibility to control their employees.

Yet despite what they might prefer, and despite their greater power, employers must still negotiate their relationships with their employees; compromises are often necessary on both sides. As we have seen, the social characteristics of employers and employees, as well as the structure of domestic jobs, affect the degree of personalism in employer-employee relations more than individual wishes do.

8

Cleaning Up a Dirty Business

During the period that I was researching this book, I attended fu-
nerals for three children of Latina domestic workers. Two perished
in an apartment blaze with their mother, victims of suspected arson,
and another fell to her death from the balcony of a public housing
project while her mother was at work. To my mind, the deaths of
these three young children were neither accidents of fate nor the
result of parental abuse, but rather tragedies of poverty. If their
mothers, who worked as domestics, had earned higher wages, they
could have afforded safer housing, and these children might still be
alive.

These deaths are among the most glaring costs of the way paid
domestic work is done today in Los Angeles. The more mundane
costs to the domestic workers—the loss of dignity, respect, and self-
esteem; the inability to even live with their children; and the daily
hardships of raising families on poverty-level wages—do not command the same attention, but they are, nevertheless, social prices.
When working people who earn the legal minimum wage cannot
bring home enough money to keep a family of three above official
poverty levels, Latina domestic workers who earn *below* minimum
wage are in big trouble.[1]

As we have seen, the arrangements of paid domestic work give
rise to many problems, largely because paid domestic work is not
treated as bona fide employment and because the women who do
it—in Los Angeles, Latina immigrant women—are among the most
disenfranchised members of society. Yet I believe that many of these
problems are remediable. For this reason, and because domestic employment in the United States will continue (absent a major restruc-
turing of our society) to be not only one of the best sources of employment for many Latina and Caribbean immigrant women but also
a necessity for many of the families who employ them, I advocate
the upgrading, not the abolition, of the occupation.

In this chapter, I explore several pathways to better employment opportunities for domestic workers. I focus on regulating employment, filing for back wage claims through the courts, and collective organizing among *domésticas* as the principal routes to improving the occupation, but I also suggest that important means of reform include educating employers and doing outreach to the social networks used for hiring and recruitment.[2]

THE REGULATIONS ON THE BOOKS

Formalizing the informal employment arrangements in paid domestic work is a necessary first step toward upgrading the occupation. Such "formalizing" entails bringing paid domestic work into conformity with state codes and regulations governing employment. This is a modest but essential reform.

People hiring and paying individuals to clean their homes and care for their children are already obligated by federal law to follow standard employment practices. The federal and state labor regulations that apply to U.S. domestic work have evolved slowly, in the face of much resistance from employers and those representing their interests. In California, for example, when the state issued an executive order requiring employers to carry workers' compensation insurance for domestic workers, elected officials immediately responded with a bill to repeal the new policy.[3] Efforts to force employers of domestic workers to pay a share of Social Security taxes also prompted newspaper editorials that condemned these regulations as too onerous. One such editorial went so far as to suggest that "it might be fairer to relieve the household employer entirely of the Social Security burden and just collect the tax directly from those domestics willing to report their income,"[4] in effect treating all domestic workers as self-employed contractors.

Most people involved in domestic work, employers as well as employees, still do not know that wage and hour regulations cover paid domestic work. The reason for their ignorance is obvious: virtually no attempt has been made by the government or media to educate domestic workers and employers about these laws. If we examine newspaper editorials and reports on regulations concerning paid domestic work, especially those published after the Zoë Baird debacle, we find an overwhelming focus on employment taxes, not wages and hours. Often, through no fault of their own, employers remain unaware of the various laws protecting domestic workers' employment rights. Even those employers who strongly wish to comply with them are likely to find, as I have, that the regulations are complex, badly written, and ambiguous or even seemingly contradictory. Yet these regulations already on the books remain our most effective point of departure for seeking improvements in the job.

WAGES AND HOURS

Among the most basic labor protections are those regarding wages and hours; these are codified in the federal Fair Labor Standards Act (FLSA), which was enacted in the wake of the Great Depression. Based on a model of industrial wage employment, the FLSA initially excluded private household workers; but in 1974, because of the advocacy efforts of the National Committee on Household Employment (discussed later in this chapter) and pressures that had begun with the Great Society initiatives of the 1960s, Congress amended the act to guarantee private domestic workers the right to receive minimum wages and overtime pay.[5] The amendment covered a range of domestic occupations, including the jobs of butlers, cooks, housekeepers, and maids. Accordingly, domestic employees who work more than eight hours in one workweek are entitled to receive the minimum wage. Various legal precedents, including the successful wage claim of Yuni Muliyono, discussed below, have established that undocumented immigrant workers are also covered under the FLSA. It would seem, then, that basic legal protection with respect to wages is already in place.

There are two significant limitations in this federal legislation, however.[6] First, domestic employees who work as personal attendants—for example, baby-sitters, caregivers to young children, or companions of the elderly and infirm—are explicitly *excluded* from the right to earn minimum wage and overtime pay; only those domestic employees who can show that they devote at least 20 percent of their work time to housekeeping duties are covered. Thus, while our society may pay great lip service to the value of caring for people, especially for the young, the elderly, and the ill, those who do private care work are not granted the same legal rights as those who clean and care for material possessions. Indeed, this legislative divide suggests that those responsible for caring for other human beings are not recognized as workers at all. However poorly this exemption reflects on the values of our society, most Latina nannies are technically not affected by it, since they do substantial housecleaning as well as caring for young children.

A second and far more serious weakness of the FLSA is that live-in employees are completely exempt from overtime coverage. Accordingly, domestic workers who reside in the households where they work have no right under federal law to overtime pay. The legislation seems to encode the assumption that live-in domestic work is closer to being "just like one of the family" than to wage employment. This stipulation hurts many Latina live-in nanny/housekeepers: recall that more than 93 percent of the live-in domestics surveyed in west Los Angeles in the mid-1990s worked more than sixty hours a week and that their mean hourly pay was $3.80, well below minimum wage (then $4.25 an hour). California laws, however, to some extent remedy the FLSA, regulating deductions for room and board and mandating overtime pay for some domestic workers.[7]

A third weakness of the statutes already on the books lies outside the law itself: when it comes to paid domestic work, there is effectively no enforcement of these laws, or even encouragement of compliance. When I spoke with a federal labor investigator who had contacted me because of his agency's concern about classified advertisements listing clearly below–minimum wage domestic jobs, he confessed that his unit had only twenty investigators to spread out over five Southern California counties. Twenty agents are charged with the monumental task of investigating and enforcing labor practices among a population of millions. Given their scarcity of resources, labor investigators naturally focus on work sites such as factories or farms that affect more than one employee. Moreover, investigating infractions of wage and hours in a home raises far more sensitive issues of privacy than does searching a factory.

State wage and hours laws complement the federal Fair Standards Labor Act. Some states (usually those with relatively high costs of living) mandate higher hourly wages than does federal law. Others specifically expand the labor rights of paid domestic workers. New York, for example, extends overtime protections to live-in workers. Still other states, among them Alaska, Delaware, Hawaii, Idaho, and

Kansas, exclude domestics from state minimum wage laws and from other protections,[8] leaving them only the inadequate protection of the FLSA. More than half the states also exclude paid domestic workers from the protection of civil rights laws, which are intended to guard against discrimination, and some state laws exempt domestic employers from compliance with occupational safety and health regulations.

In California, as of January 1, 2001, private domestic workers are entitled to earn $6.25 an hour and by 2002 the minimum wage will be $6.75.[9] Live-in domestic workers in California are now entitled to one and a half times their regular hourly rate for overtime, if that work meets certain criteria.[10] Nevertheless, many employers provide compensatory time to employees in lieu of overtime pay, perhaps giving time off on an hour-for-hour basis. This may suit some domestic employees, but others find that time off on weekday afternoons does not begin to compensate them for the loss of cherished moments socializing with family and friends on Saturdays or Sundays. The state's Industrial Welfare Commission Wage Order 15 regulates wages, hours, and working conditions in "household occupations."[11] Practices allowed in domestic work are stipulated in these wage orders, and all employers are required to keep a copy of the orders and to make them available when employees request them; but none of the employers I spoke with knew of their existence. Some of the rules in these wage orders are quite specific, covering, for example, permissible penalties for an employee's breakage of household items, or the use and cost of employee uniforms.[12] Of the various domestic job arrangements, live-in work differs the most from industrial wage work, and it remains, as we have seen, the domestic employment arrangement in which we find the greatest abuse.

Employers, employees, and observers alike often justify and defend the subminimum wages paid to live-in domestic workers by pointing out that live-in jobs include "free room and board." Under "Meals and Lodging" (item 10), the wage order clarifies when this practice is legal and when it is not. Thus "Meals and lodging may not be credited against the minimum wage without a voluntary written agreement between the employer and the employee"; and when employers do credit meals and lodging against the minimum wage, deductions may not exceed a dollar limit. They must also provide food and lodging of adequate standards.[13]

SOCIAL SECURITY AND MEDICARE

The Social Security Act of 1935 established a federal program of old-age, unemployment, and disability insurance, and two years later the Federal Insurance Contributions Act (FICA) was passed, requiring workers to partially finance the system through payroll taxes (then 2 percent). Like the FLSA, Social Security was a Depression-era program; and also like the FLSA, paid domestic workers were not included until much later. In 1951 employers were directed to collect a 3 percent tax from them as well.[14] Today the rate is higher, but the onus still remains on the employer, who currently must collect and remit a 12.4 percent tax to the federal government. This amount is to be split equally by employer and employee; or, if they are willing, the employers may assume the total cost.

Many people believe that Latina immigrants who work as domestics do not want to pay employment taxes, and certainly some (like many Americans in other occupations) prefer tax evasion. But a striking number, despite their low earnings, do pay or want to pay these taxes. In fact, one of the most well-attended sessions of the Domestic Workers' Association in Los Angeles is a question-and-answer forum held each spring that features a tax specialist. A specialist is needed, because the law contains a number of major ambiguities. Perhaps the most important is whether a domestic worker is an employee—for whom employers must pay withholding taxes—or an independent contractor, who is solely responsible for paying her own FICA taxes.[15] If the employer pays the domestic worker more than $1,000 per year, the employer must comply with the federal Social Security Domestic Reform Act of 1994 and pay Medicare and Social Security taxes. Even if a nanny or housecleaner works in a household only a few hours each week, she becomes a "common-law employee" when she earns $1,000 a year—an amount reached by an employer who pays a housecleaner the relatively modest sum of $45 twice a month.

The uproar over Zoë Baird's failure to pay withholding taxes for her household employees led not to reforms to improve working conditions for domestic workers but to legislation to better accommodate employers by lessening some of their tax obligations.[16] The many newspaper and magazine articles that appeared to clarify the procedures that employers should follow in hiring domestic workers paid almost no attention to wage regulations. Even the official Internal Revenue Service pamphlet written for employers of domestic workers in response to the Baird debacle and the new legislation, "Employment Taxes for Household Employers" (Publication 926), does not mention that wage and hour laws apply to domestic workers. This omission suggests that the government is more interested in collecting the tax revenue that can be supplied by domestic workers than in ensuring that housecleaners and nannies are accorded the same rights as employees in other occupations.

Because of the way that the government and media have framed the issue, even those employers who are well informed and intend to follow the letter of the law often find themselves out of compliance when it comes to their nanny/housekeepers' wages and hours. This point was brought home to me after one of my presentations at a conference, when a world-renowned scholar of immigration approached me. The researcher, who was routinely interviewed by the media, confessed to me over lunch, "I didn't want the *New York Times* asking me how many illegal immigrants I employ at home." So when recently hiring a live-in nanny/housekeeper, this individual had not only insisted on hiring a legal permanent resident for the job but had also filed the requisite "I-9" form for the Immigration and Naturalization Service and had paid employment taxes. In other words, this conscientious employer did exactly what the Baird case had taught about legally hiring household employees. Yet this same individual was startled to learn from my presentation that these efforts were not enough: the employer's family was breaking the law, because their live-in employee was in fact earning well below minimum wage.[17]

THE REALM OF INDIGNITIES

"We're trying to do legal work," sighed the attorney Sarah Cohen, "but I think we miss out on a whole other area of abuses that I think is important to look at and to report and to document; but a lot of times, there's nothing you can do about it." I knew exactly what she was talking about, but she put a much better name on it than I or anyone else had offered: "the realm of indignities."

The realm of indignities is an inherently imprecise category, but the job dissatisfactions of the Latina domestic workers center in it. It

includes a gamut of treatment that nanny/housekeepers and housecleaners experience from their employers, ranging from the most
egregious abuse, such as being expected to eat old, moldy food or
to sleep on cots in laundry rooms, to other seemingly less harsh but
no less hurtful acts, such as being offered leftover food when members of the employer family are eating fresh fruit and meat; having
employers eye with immediate suspicion, instead of compassion,
any job-related injury; or simply being ignored all day long while in
the presence of others.

In one of the flyers created and distributed by the Latina women
organized in the Domestic Workers' Association of the Coalition of
Humane Immigrant Rights of Los Angeles (CHIRLA), the members
published their goals. Not surprisingly, dignity and respect top the
list, ranked above a fair salary. Employer compliance with Social
Security, a legal requirement on which so much popular attention
has focused as a defining feature of fair employment for domestics,
appears near the bottom of the list.

WHAT DO WE WANT?

1. Respect for our rights and dignity as a person. We don't want
   to be ignored and humiliated.

2. A fair and dignified salary.

3. Equal rights.

4. An end to sexual harassment.

5. Adequate breaks and work schedules.

6. No leftover food.

7. Sick days.

8. Paid vacation.

9. Medical benefits.

10. Employer paid social security.

11. No more threats and discrimination of workers without papers.

12. To be recognized as professionals by society.

Domestic workers' call to reclaim dignity and respect reflects their
desire—stressed in chapter 7—for employers who will recognize
them as persons and appreciate them as persons. "I want them to

know who I am," a statement that more than one Latina domestic worker shared with me, probably best sums up how many dissatisfied nanny/housekeepers and housecleaners feel about their jobs. Latina domestic workers don't expect or necessarily want maternalistic employers to care *for* them—indeed, they themselves are earning their livelihood by caring for the employers' homes and children. They do, however, want employers who care *about* them.

The realm of indignity is also affected by dominant views of job standards. How can we impose standards and evaluate job productivity without further dehumanizing the work and its objectives? Deborah Stone, who has written about productivity and care work, offers one answer; though her analysis applies less well to housecleaners, it addresses many of the concerns of nanny/housekeepers who care for children. Stone argues that squeezing paid care work into a model of productivity based on industrial manufacturing is ill-advised. The old model gauges inputs and outputs, seeking to gain productivity by minimizing the former and maximizing the latter. Clearly, this calculation cannot adequately assess the work of caring for another human being. Instead, she urges a model that valorizes affiliation, affection, and personalism, recognizing the care worker as someone with her own concerns and relationships. In addition, we need to make caring work less unidirectional, so that the care recipient (or, in the case of nannies, the parent of the child) shares the emotional burden of care. As suggested above, such a shift requires not the actual work of caring for so much as caring about and recognizing the employee as a person. This social recognition is a basic human need, and domestic workers deeply feel its absence in their jobs.

Advocating bidirectional caring and social recognition in this venue is controversial. On the one hand, the approach may seem politically incorrect: enhanced personal ties, in the context of an extremely asymmetrical relationship, could bring us back to employer maternalism and exacerbate exploitation. On the other hand, some employers may balk at the suggestion that paid nanny/housekeepers be accorded compassion and caring—the very qualities that they are paying for. Yet paid domestic workers and care workers need to be given scope to assert the terms of their own employment. Dignity and respect, their top demands, can be accorded only when social recognition and caring go both ways.

SIN ORGANIZACIÓN, NO HAY SOLUCIÓN (WITHOUT ORGANIZING, THERE'S NO SOLUTION)

As the list of the demands of the Domestic Workers' Association and the words of the women interviewed for this book make clear, domestic workers have many ideas on what areas in their jobs need improvement.[18] They want respect, better pay, equality, and job terms and benefits similar to those found in most other jobs in our society. Their attempts to effect these changes take many forms, ranging from deliberate, individual, informal efforts to upgrade working conditions at one particular house to collectively seeking legislative remedies aimed at improving the occupational landscape for all paid domestic workers.

Formal organizations and collective efforts focused on improving domestic workers' jobs have been rare in the United States, but they are not impossible undertakings. Virtually every Latin American nation has active domestic workers' associations and unions, and since 1988 many of them have met in inter–Latin American congresses.[19] In recent years, as Latina and Caribbean immigrants have swelled the numbers of women in the occupation in the United States, a plethora of innovative, community-based associations for Latina domestic workers, each one slightly different in form and focus, have sprouted on the East and West Coasts.[20]

Efforts to organize domestic workers in the United States began in the first half of the twentieth century, but those early groups were concerned less with advocacy for the domestic workers than with vocational training for them, so they might better serve employers.[21] The most notable exception in this regard is the National Committee on Household Employment (NCHE), which initially grew out of a 1928 Young Women's Christian Association–sponsored conference on domestic workers' wages and job hours, held in Washington, D.C.[22] The white middle-class women of the YWCA were more reformers than union organizers. At one point, Eleanor Roosevelt served as honorary chair. As the historian Phyllis Palmer has shown, the group at first tried to mediate between white housewives who wanted a supply of well-trained help and black women workers who wanted better wages and limited hours.[23] Although its members sincerely desired to remedy abuses in the occupation, the NCHE remained, in this early phase, a primarily white, middle-class, employers' organization, adamantly opposed to the imposition of written contracts and regulations.

After the NCHE reorganized in 1964 under the leadership of the National Council on Negro Women, it began affiliating with and receiving support from other groups. During this period, the NCHE became a more militant advocate, organized by and for African American paid domestic workers. It worked to publicize the poor working conditions and lack of labor regulations in the occupation, to establish training programs to standardize job skills, and to open contracting centers for job placement. Training programs were implemented in eight cities between 1967 and 1971, assisted by mediators who helped individual domestic employees bargain with individual employers. The NCHE's biggest concrete achievement came in 1974, when domestic workers were finally included in the Fair Labor Standards Act. As noted above, private domestic workers had previously not been covered by minimum wage legislation. Although personal attendants (baby-sitters, nannies, and attendants to the elderly and infirm who do not clean) still lack minimum wage rights, the 1974 victory was significant. The NCHE has faded away, but it had a lasting impact on private domestic work.[24]

Organizing labor is not easy in any industry, and the obstacles to efforts in domestic work are particularly daunting. One of the biggest impediments is that many women who work as housecleaners and housekeeper/nannies find it difficult to see themselves as workers, for reasons that include the stigma attached to the job, its location in a private residence, and the tasks themselves—which, as we have seen, are associated with women's "natural" expressions of love and caring. Moreover, the structure and scheduling of the job arrangements, with nanny/housekeepers on call at all hours and sometimes forming close attachments with the children who are their charges, may encourage them to see themselves as part of the family, not as workers. As social life and work life blur, so does job identity. Housecleaners face different working conditions, but many of them also do not fully identify as domestic workers. As already noted, some find it challenging to piece together full-time employment in Los Angeles, while others deliberately try to limit their housecleaning in order to take care of their own families. Thus many of them clean only a few houses each week, and some housecleaners in Los

Angeles supplement these earnings, usually with informal vending or with factory work. Their other jobs and their own homemaker activities also discourage a strong worker identity as *domésticas*. And of course, those who have hired nanny/housekeepers and house-cleaners, reluctant to take on their own responsibilities as employers, generally do not treat domestic employees as workers.

Besides the job's low status, its low pay and the limits on upward mobility within the occupation also persuade many Latina domestic workers, especially young women, that they should leave it alto-gether. Often these women find that their alternative sources of em-ployment are no more attractive; but regardless of whether they ac-tually leave or not, their ambivalence about staying in domestic work lessens the likelihood that they will put their energy into collective organizing to make the occupation better.

Those who do seek to organize and upgrade domestic work find their efforts hindered by spatial and legal constraints. Because the work sites are spread through residential neighborhoods, there is no obvious place in which to begin organizing—no garment district or factory gates for organizers to target with leaflets and recruitment efforts. Moreover, paid domestic workers are not covered by the Na-tional Labor Relations Act of 1935 (NLRA), which declares that "The term employee shall include any employee . . . but shall not include any individual employed . . . in the domestic service of any family or person at his home" (section 152, provision 3). Domestic workers have no legal rights to organize, and therefore no protection from termination if they begin to organize.

Taken together, these obstacles are impressive but not insur-mountable, as Latina domestic workers *are* organizing in cities around the nation. In the next section, I describe the efforts of one group in Los Angeles that has organized neither as a job cooperative, which makes jobs available as a part of a service, nor as a union, which would pursue collective bargaining, but rather as an associ-ation that strives to upgrade the occupation.

THE DOMESTIC WORKERS' ASSOCIATION

The Domestic Workers' Association began in 1990 as an outreach and advocacy campaign under the auspices of CHIRLA. A group of women—activists, attorneys, and community organizers (including myself)—came together with the idea of arming live-ins, the most isolated and exploited workers in the industry, with information on workers' rights and legal resources. Initially, the key materials were *novelas*, inexpensive booklets with captioned photographs that tell an amusing story that are a popular form of mass culture in Latin America; they are typically aimed at urban working-class men and women. In this project, didactic *novelas* were specifically designed for paid domestic workers; they were handed out by four paid *promotoras de derechos* (rights advocates), who also distributed a series of more general *novelas*—on topics such as how to obtain emergency medical care, renters' rights, and so forth—that had been prepared for other CHIRLA projects. The *novelas* aimed specifically at domestic workers focused on wage and hour rights (figure 3), on how to negotiate with bosses, and on how to avoid subcontracting arrangements. One addressed a more immediate emergency, alerting domestic workers that a rapist was luring victims into his car by offering housecleaning jobs to women waiting at bus stops.

With a small grant from the Liberty Hill Foundation, in 1991 our advocacy group hired four Latina immigrant outreach workers, two Salvadorans and two Mexicans, and trained them to distribute these materials and talk to Latina immigrant domestic workers as they rode the public buses to work, as well as in certain Westside parks where nannies congregate with their young charges, their employers' children. Posters announcing the program were printed up and placed on over four hundred municipal buses that ran along east-west routes. The posters included tear-off sheets with the telephone number for a legal clinic specializing in employment issues. By sending the outreach workers to the streets and parks, with *novelas*, the campaign initiated face-to-face contact with workers in transit to and from their isolated work sites.

The project continued this way until 1993, when our small group began planning a series of leadership classes. In 1994, with the goal of eventually forming an association, we organized an eight-week leadership training seminar. Latina domestic workers were recruited by the outreach workers and also by local churches and community organizations. Each week's session focused on a different theme, beginning with an open discussion of the occupation. After a session on self-esteem, the participants considered how to negotiate with employers, their legal rights on the job, the history of paid domestic work in the United States, and practical matters such as how to do

You know what? If you work as a live-in domestic worker, you have legal rights regarding the hours you work and the salary you receive.

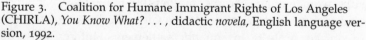

Figure 3.   Coalition for Humane Immigrant Rights of Los Angeles (CHIRLA), *You Know What? . . .* , didactic *novela*, English language version, 1992.

In the 1990s thousands of informative *novelas*, such as this one, were distributed to Latina immigrant nanny/housekeepers on buses and in public parks throughout Los Angeles.

outreach work, how to set an agenda, and how to run a meeting. These were exciting and spirited metings. The sessions included informal discussion and role-playing, and at the end of the series, certificates were presented at a graduation ceremony attended by friends and family members.

It was during this initial period that the "Super Doméstica" *novela* first appeared in print (figure 4). Five thousand copies were printed for free distribution. The comic book featured the story of a housekeeper who successfully learns to negotiate with her demanding employer, and the cover image became an important icon in Latino civil rights marches and labor protests in Southern California. The women in the group embraced the Super Doméstica icon, the product of a cartoonist's imagination, and literally made it their own, taking turns dressing as the domestic worker superhero when the group marched together in political rallies and protests or in neighborhood parades, or when they held special events, such as the graduation ceremony of the first leadership seminar. Political marches took on a festive aspect, and the costume—a red cape, a short skirt showing a spray bottle of cleanser and a feather duster attached to her thighs, and yellow rubber gloves on both hands—made the Domestic Workers' Association increasingly visible and drew many inquiries. The Super Doméstica icon was also featured on the organization's first T-shirts, and today, she stars in the popular community theater created by group members.

The image of Super Doméstica was not embraced by everyone. I distinctively recall the criticism leveled by another Latino community organization when she debuted: members charged that the small-waisted, pert-nosed woman represented an unrealistic, sexist, idealized physical figure. Women in the Domestic Workers' Association countered, "She's a superhero!" Like all superheroes, Super Doméstica is a hyperidealized fantasy image. She is inspired not by the superwoman image of career mothers but rather by Super Barrio, a caped and masked priest in Mexico City who became famous as he organized protests in squatter settlements. Interestingly, the women of the Domestic Workers' Association never considered using as an icon *la Virgen de Guadalupe,* an important feminine image used in many Chicano and Mexican organizations (e.g., the United Farm Workers). I believe this speaks to the diversity of the Latina immigrants in the association, who come not only from Mexico, where *la Virgen de Guadalupe* reigns, but also from El Salvador, Guatemala, Honduras, and Peru. Moreover, many of the women in the

Figure 4. Coalition for Humane Immigrant Rights of Los Angeles (CHIRLA), *Super Doméstica*, comic book/*novela* graphic, 1993. Artwork by Kelvin Manzanares.

When critics charged that "Super Doméstica" represented sexist imagery, the women in the Domestic Workers Association countered, "She's a Super Hero!" The image draws inspiration from "Super Barrio," a caped and masked priest in Mexico City who organized protests in squatter settlements.

Domestic Workers' Association are not Catholic. In fact, a large number of them, especially the Guatemalan women, were raised in or converted to Evangelical religions.

A group of about twenty domestic workers graduated from the initial leadership seminar. It was quite a festive event, with family members present, moving speeches from the women accepting their diplomas, media coverage, and plastic champagne glasses tied with ribbons on the tables covered with white tablecloths. After the graduation ceremony, participants continued to meet biweekly, with the idea that members would provide leadership and direction to other domestic workers, but sadly, attendance dropped off. Uncertain funding forced the group to cut back the hours of the outreach workers who were also helping to facilitate the meetings, personal conflicts arose among some of the members, and, as so often happens in grassroots efforts, the group's momentum ebbed.

In 1995 a paid organizer, Cristina Riegos, was hired, allowing the group to shift its focus to organizing and creating the building blocks for an autonomous association of domestic workers. Riegos, a recent graduate of Brown University, brought a new dynamism to the project, and she drew liberally on her experience with student and community organizing. Her strong, forceful personality enabled her to bring together a group of women diverse in both national origins (Mexico, El Salvador, Guatemala, Peru, and even Indonesia) and legal status. When Riegos passed away in 1998, Libertad Rivera, who had been hired as an outreach worker before the association was formed, took over as coordinator of the Domestic Workers' Association. By spring 2000, the association claimed 350 active members, although a much smaller core group attended the weekly meetings and took responsibility for committee work.

Members of the association are diverse. Some are naturalized citizens and legal permanent residents, many have temporary work permits, and others lack legal documents altogether. Their ages, class origins, and educational backgrounds vary, and, as we found with a simple survey, the majority entered the association without any history of political activism in their countries of origin. Most received an elementary school education in their countries, although some are functionally illiterate and others are university educated. Many are not currently married or residing with a male partner; those that are mothers either have young children "back home" in their countries of origin or adult children. Their freedom from heavy family obligations may be an important factor in their ability to participate in the association. Members reside in different parts of Los Angeles' sprawling metropolis; some drive and others take buses for two hours each way to attend the Sunday afternoon meetings. For many, Sunday is their only day off.

While some of the women hold live-in jobs that pay only $150 a week and others earn $500 a week, they share the same basic complaints about loneliness; lack of dignity and respect; lack of job security, health benefits, and sick days; and employers' failure to comply with withholding-tax laws. They also share everyday work problems—what to do when you are sick but must report to work or risk losing your job, or how to deal with an employer who routinely demands overtime without compensation. A deep sense of isolation draws the women together, and their common experiences with the daily indignities of paid domestic work provide a basis for solidarity. The association, through its monthly meetings and activities, creates a shared space for workers who otherwise lack such a space. That act of creation is one key to the association's successful organizing, for it makes possible the consolidation of worker identity both individually and collectively.

Today, the Domestic Workers' Association is an employee organization, but it is not a typical labor union. It plans expressive and social activities that solidify the group identity, and it arranges workshops and seminars directed at improving the occupation. The association focuses on upgrading and transforming domestic work by developing members' leadership skills and by creating a collective space—the monthly meetings—where the women can solve problems and plan strategy. The ongoing development of skilled leaders who advocate for improved job conditions and a group dynamic necessary for collective action are crucial to its organizing work. It follows neither the model of providing services to passive recipients nor the model of striving for one collective "win," such as a union vote, a particular contract, or a strike.

The service model obligates organization members to remain needy and encourages clientelistic relations between service providers and recipients. Conventional labor unions, whose members must show solidarity at the workplace and, if necessary, risk their jobs when a strike is voted, often develop bureaucracies and hierarchical structures within the organization. In the Domestic Workers' Association, there is no obligation for members to risk their jobs (they share no common employer); but they are required to demonstrate commitment to the association by paying dues, attending the monthly meetings regularly, and participating in group projects. Monthly dues were decided on by the members, and adhering to this requirement helps foster their sense of ownership and belonging. While professionals (a paid organizer, a staff attorney) and an elected governing board of members provide valuable input, the group operates, for the most part, collectively and democratically.[25]

A strong cooperative spirit prevails in the association as the domestic workers first identify an issue and then develop a long-term strategy around it. For example, many members consistently complained about the placement agencies specializing in domestic employment. They protested the high application fees—sometimes as much as a week's wages—jobs that never materialized, and the lack of refund policies. The group decided to file a lawsuit, selecting one particularly notorious agency as their first target. Two members of the association acted as plaintiffs in the suit, which sought injunctive relief and small monetary compensation (less than $200) for the women's losses. In their initial meeting, the attorney who was to litigate the case told the women not to expect a substantial financial gain from the case. Surprised that anyone would think they were motivated by the hope for individual gain, the women responded, "We're not doing this for the money. We are doing it for other women, so that what happened to us won't happen to them."

The Domestic Workers' Association also helps individuals upgrade the terms and compensation for their jobs, as Debora Zendeja's problem and its solution illustrate. Debora had worked as a live-in for a family for six years, earning $200 for a sixty-hour workweek. The latter three years had been marked by serious conflicts with her employers, and she had been fired and thrown out of the house on five occasions by her *patrona*. Each time, the *patron* coaxed her to return by describing how much the children needed her. Debora sought the advice of fellow association members, discussing her alternatives in long, tearful phone conversations, and she also sought the advice of the organizer. Everyone urged her to take direct action against the couple, and after consulting with attorneys at a labor legal clinic, Debora learned that she was owed more than $20,000 in three years' back wages. She filed a legal claim, and when her former employer tried once again to manipulate her into returning, she told him to speak with her attorney. She then reached a favorable settlement. Most important, in her new job she communicates with her employer; and if asked to work extra hours, she lets her new boss know that she expects overtime pay or compensatory time. As the saying goes, *se defiende.*

The association described here is just one alternative among many for organizing domestic workers, who can be served by organizations with a broad range of structures and purposes. At one end of the spectrum are domestic worker job cooperatives, such as Manos in San Francisco and Listo in Los Angeles, that typically make jobs available as part of a service but do not necessarily strive to change the conditions of work or raise the workers' consciousness (increasingly, however, job cooperatives are taking a more proactive approach to upgrading the jobs).[26] At the other end are unions negotiating collective bargaining agreements, such as the Service Employees International Union (SEIU), which in the late 1990s successfully organized home care workers in California. These workers contract with the state to offer elder care in private homes, and the union has won contracts that include health coverage, sick leave, paid vacation, and grievance procedures.[27] Similarly, office building janitors and hospital "housekeepers" have also successfully unionized. Unlike these home care workers, janitors, and cleaners, domestic workers employed in private residences do not share a common employer or work site, so they cannot engage in collective bargaining. The problem of not being paid at all or being paid subminimum wages is so endemic that one immigrant workers center, the Workplace Project on Long Island, launched an ultimately successful campaign to strengthen state laws on wage enforcement.[28] Filing for back wages is one strategy that the Domestic Workers' Association recommends to individual employees who have been paid below minimum wage; in the next section, I explore this procedure.[29]

USING THE SYSTEM: FILING CLAIMS FOR BACK WAGES

In the 1980s a group of public interest lawyers in Los Angeles saw that low-wage workers needed, among other things, a forum where they could seek help in claiming wages owed them by employers or former employers. In response to this need, attorneys affiliated with the Legal Aid Foundation of Los Angeles and the National Lawyers Guild opened a series of legal clinics focusing on employment.[30]

These walk-in evening clinics, held in various community centers located in poor, urban neighborhoods, soon became popular with many Latina and Latino immigrant workers. When I visited a couple of the evening clinics located in downtown L.A. and in the Pico Union neighborhood in the early 1990s, I saw dozens of Latino immigrants, many of them garment workers, assembly operators, and day laborers, waiting patiently, though visibly suffering from physical exhaustion, to speak with someone about their cases. I listened in on individual cases as law students and paralegals interviewed clients about horrendous abuses—grotesque workplace injuries, sexual harassment, appeals for unemployment benefits, and nonpayment for work performed. On one occasion a Honduran man, formerly an accountant in his country, broke down sobbing as he told me how his factory foreman had fired him after a forklift accident. Literally adding insult to his physical injury, the foreman had also issued him a bad check for his final payment.

Domestic workers who worked long hours at suburban, residential work sites far from downtown Los Angeles found it difficult to come to the evening employment law clinics. Still, it was primarily live-ins, the most spatially and socially isolated and the lowest-paid domestic workers, who came seeking help. "What motivates them to come is the indignity of having been fired," explained Sarah Cohen, an attorney who has represented many domestic worker cases. In fact, as we saw in chapter 5, most of these Latina domestic workers mistakenly believed they had been illegally fired. In California, an "employment at will" state, it is perfectly legal for an employer to dismiss an employee.[31] Yet an initial intake interview at the Labor Defense Network clinic would often reveal that a fired domestic worker had been paid below minimum wage and was therefore qualified to file a claim for back wages. As one attorney, Nancy Cervantes, told me, former employees were sometimes owed vast sums. "I mean underpaid," she said, "as in people working, let's say, a twelve- to sixteen-hour day, five, six, maybe seven days a week and being paid $125 a week." She quickly did some basic math, using California's minimum wage laws, and noted that if such employment arrangements had continued for years, "people may be owed, you know, $50,000 or more. It's shocking to hear that," she added, "but it's because they've been so grossly underpaid for so many years."

Many domestic workers never pursue their legitimate claims for back wages. While some eventually recognize the legal merits of their cases, they may not proceed with a legal action out of a sense of shame, or out of allegiance to the family for whom they worked. Even if their job ended with a blowup, former nanny/housekeepers may feel they are betraying the employer's children, whom they may have come to love, by suing their parents. Others fear that they will lose references for future jobs or become otherwise tainted in the job market, or that they will call attention to their status as undocumented immigrants. Many prefer to just move on and start fresh in a new job, sparing themselves the considerable time, risk, and emotional energy that a legal action typically involves.

Filing a back wage claim is a long, difficult, and often tedious process. To build a case, the attorney and client must reconstruct all the hours worked and assemble in minute detail the tasks completed, the breaks that were or were not taken, and the payments received for services rendered. Many office employees would have difficulty reconstructing what they had done on the job for the past week, and the nature of domestic employment makes this task even harder for nanny/housekeepers. Because of the diffuse and multiple tasks involved in caring for homes and small children, the flexible, nonregimented scheduling of many of these tasks, the blurred lines between "work" and "nonwork" life, and the long periods of time to be reconstructed, only plaintiffs with the most acute memories or meticulous record keeping will withstand the rigorous tests of the courts. "It's hard," said Sarah Cohen, who had spent many hours interviewing clients about their work histories, "to remember everything, every speck of dust, where it came from, and what you did with it."

"The ideal plaintiff is someone who has paid attention," noted Cervantes. "This would be somebody who kept track of hours they've worked, what kinds of jobs they did, when they were paid, how they were paid, kept copies of the checks if they've been paid by check, when they've had to do unusual things like stay late, or stay overnight, come in on their day off, or not been allowed to take sick days." Cohen concurred: "You want people who are good historians, who have good memories, who don't exaggerate. You would want somebody who would have very good records and documentation of what they did, how long it took them, and how much they got paid. That's ideal."

When the attorneys have collected the facts, they write a demand letter to the former employers, outlining the facts of the case and making the demand for payment of back wages. The typical reaction of the former employers is disbelief, say the attorneys. The employers may claim that supplying room and board compensated for the wages, or that the nanny/housekeeper spent long portions of the day watching television, gabbing on the phone, or taking long breaks. "She was like family" or "we gave her everything" are also common responses. Some employers become antagonistic and lash out with accusations of their own, claiming that their former employee broke or stole household items. Others go further and make threats. "It's very common for them to threaten contact with the INS" during initial negotiations, said Cohen. "They assume they're undocumented, but oftentimes, they don't even know for sure."

If the employers refuse to negotiate a monetary settlement, the case generally moves either to Small Claims Court or to the California state labor commissioner. Only claims of $5,000 or less are eligible for Small Claims Court; though plaintiffs rarely get everything they ask for in this legal arena, the procedure has the advantages of being faster and not requiring an attorney. Self-help videos in Spanish, produced by Sarah Cohen and other colleagues at the Los Angeles Legal Aid Foundation and featuring actors from the old television series *L.A. Law*, guide people through this process.

Larger claims typically go to the California state labor commissioner and begin a two-step process. First, the labor commissioner hearing officer confers with the two parties. If the commissioner believes there is sufficient evidence to continue, a formal hearing is scheduled. At this stage, it is common for the attorneys to encounter surprise and skepticism from the authorities. "With domestic worker cases, in almost any forum, there's an attitude of disbelief by the hearing officer, or the judge," explained Nancy Cervantes. "The judges think, 'What could this person have been doing for twelve hours a day?' It reflects the attitude that a lot of women encounter with their husbands if they're housewives, which is, 'What did you do all day? How could you possibly be tired?' " Once again, we hear the familiar theme: domestic work, the work of caring for children and cleaning homes, is not real work. More shocking is the attorneys' report that many judges in Small Claims Court, as well as labor commissioners and defense attorneys, seem surprised to find that domestic workers are entitled to earn minimum wage. Labor commissioners are civil servants, and the domestic workers' attorneys find, as one put it, that they must "do a lot of legal education with them." "They're people who worked their way up the bureaucratic, civil servant ladder," explained one attorney. "It's not to say that nonlawyers don't run good hearings. There are some exceptions. But for the most part, it's not the kind of background you need to conduct a hearing and afford people their due process rights."

The domestic workers' attorneys find equal lack of competence in their courtroom adversaries: the former employers often come to court in a state of outrage fueled by deep feelings of betrayal, accompanied by the family attorney, who is typically not familiar with labor law. While frustrating, this can also prove advantageous. "Most private lawyers don't know anything about wage and hour practice," noted Sarah Cohen. "So that's always our upper hand, and how we settle cases." Still, she finds the obstacles staggering: "We're working against a hostile state, a hostile court, judges that probably have domestic workers themselves and don't pay them minimum wages and overtime." Another attorney that I interviewed condemned the California Labor Commissioner's Office even more forcefully: "We no longer recommend people go to the labor commissioner, because they've gotten so bad over the years. They are hostile toward low-wage workers, who they see as just making more work for them, and there is no review system. They don't get reprimanded for not following the law."

Law and facts are the key elements in legal cases, and facts require proof. Documentation and witnesses can help establish credibility, but few paid domestic workers can supply them. Most live-in nanny/housekeepers work alone, or spend the day primarily in the company of small children. Neighbors, gardeners, other nannies who work in the neighborhood, and delivery people may be useful witnesses, but they are often reluctant to become involved. Gardeners and nannies, for instance, fear that testifying will jeopardize their own employment status, and neighbors or relatives of the employer often align themselves with that employer. "It's always an employer's word against a domestic worker's word," sighed Nancy Cervantes. "And you may have two employers, a husband and wife versus one worker."

The subordinate status of the domestic employee may also tarnish her credibility in court. As a poor, foreign-born, Spanish-speaking Latina immigrant, she may be viewed as inherently undeserving, disreputable, lazy, and incapable of hard work. These images were accentuated in California during the mid-1990s, when proponents of Proposition 187 drew heavily on stereotypical images of Mexican immigrant women as lazy, welfare-dependent drains on society. Michele Yu, who successfully won a $48,000 judgment for an Indonesian live-in domestic worker in Los Angeles, believes that her client's good English established courtroom credibility and helped win the case. "During the trial, the judge commented how impressive Yuni's English had been," noted the attorney. "By testifying in English, and saying that she never spoke a word of English before she came here, well, that basically demonstrated what a hard worker she is. That impressed the judge a lot." Language, as various commentators have noted, is intensely racialized in California; increasingly, Spanish is vilified while English is sanctified. Although Yuni Muliyono is a brown-skinned, undocumented immigrant, her English-language facility and the fact that she is not Latina may have contributed to her legal victory. Yuni Muliyono's command of English showed her to be an "American," and this racialization and acquired national identity then enhanced her credibility. Legally, of course, a worker is entitled to receive minimum wage regardless of knowledge of English, race, or nationality, but in reality judges use multiple indicators—dress, demeanor, race, and, in this case, language—in profiling plaintiffs and defendants and ultimately in rendering their decisions.

Winning judgments—here, payment for back wages and employer penalties—is difficult, and collecting them involves yet another major legal procedure. In many instances, the cases are settled confidentially. "We had one case," recalled Nancy Cervantes, "that involved a very, very big celebrity and confidentiality was one of the agreements of payment and settlement, and this is very typical. These people were very worried about bad press." She told me of another case that involved a very large judgment for back wages and penalties that a domestic worker won against her Guatemalan godmother, who had virtually enslaved her as an unpaid live-in. It proved to be Pyrrhic victory, however, as the employer, in this instance, was almost as poor as the employee. "She was judgment-proof," explained Cervantes. "She was probably ten cents richer than her goddaughter."

Not all domestic workers who pursue claims for back wages are interested primarily in the money. Many of them go to court out of a genuine wish to improve the occupation. Sarah Cohen noted that among many of her past clients, "There's a sense of, 'We're in this to vindicate our rights.' They don't want people who follow in their footsteps to be confronted with this same kind of problem." I certainly noticed this sense of solidarity and esprit de corps among members of the Domestic Workers' Association of CHIRLA; it was less evident, however, among the more randomly selected group of domestic workers that I interviewed.

A LEGAL VICTORY: YUNI MULIYONO

In 1996 Yuni Muliyono, an Indonesian undocumented immigrant who had worked as a live-in domestic worker in Southern California, made front-page news in the *Los Angeles Times* when she won a judgment for $48,000 in back wages.[32] Represented by Michele Yu, and buoyed by the support of her Latina co-members of the Domestic Workers' Association and by her Mexican friend Marcos Rodríguez, who had first told her about wage rights when the two met in ESL classes, the shy and soft-spoken Yuni Muliyono had overcome an impressive range of obstacles to win her case.

The legal victory was especially striking in that Yuni Muliyono was an undocumented immigrant. Her employers, an ethnic Chinese woman from Indonesia and her U.S.-born husband, had brought Muliyono to work as a domestic in their Los Angeles home; once in California, they had confiscated her passport. According to Muliyono, she found herself working eleven hours a day on Monday through Friday, four hours on Saturday, and six hours on Sunday, caring for the employers' home and their two children. During the two years and nine months she worked for them, she never received direct payment of wages. The employers told her they were sending money "back home" to her brother—which they did, but only seven times. In spite of these conditions, Yuni Muliyono was initially reluctant to bring suit against her employers. Like many live-in domestics, she felt grateful to her employers. As she put it, "For me this was a chance to better myself and to do more for my daughter and my brothers and sisters." She proudly noted that her earnings, modest and erratically paid out as they were, allowed her three siblings to finish high school, an opportunity she had not enjoyed.

Like many live-in employees, she had an extraordinarily isolated existence in the employer's home. But many Central American and Mexican live-in domestic workers, despite their extreme isolation during the workweek, see friends and family on the weekends. Even if they do not see them regularly, most of them do know other Mexican and Central American immigrants. But Yuni Muliyono and other women who are not members of immigrant groups numerous enough to form a community are much more alone. It was only several years after arriving in Los Angeles, when she began attending a Saturday ESL class, that she made a good friend, Marcos Rodríguez, who would eventually encourage her to leave her live-in job and seek assistance from the Domestic Workers Association.

Perhaps the most critical legal obstacle faced by this domestic worker was the defendants' claim that she was not an employee but simply a young "guest" from Indonesia whom they had benevolently invited to stay with them. "It was," acknowledged Michele Yu, "a very effective strategy for the employers to claim there was no employer-employee relationship." Although the plaintiff and her attorney provided evidence to the contrary, Yu attributes their victory in court largely to the credibility that Muliyono won from the judge because of her English-language skills, as discussed above, and the testimony of a particular expert witness. In both instances, the embodiments of linguistic, racial, and citizenship categories worked in favor of Yu's case.

Yu had called as witness a white U.S. citizen, a lawyer with Ivy League credentials, who had worked in Indonesia. He had taught English there and had observed firsthand the relations between domestics and their well-to-do employers. He testified that in that country, Indonesians of ethnic Chinese descent (such as the defendant) constitute a wealthy capitalist class and do not socially mingle with Javanese Indonesians (such as the plaintiff). Ethnic Chinese would never host Javanese as "guests" in Indonesia, he said, but they were quite likely to employ them as domestics. This testimony, perhaps in part because it came from someone so different from a low-wage,

Latina or Asian immigrant domestic worker, helped convince the judge of the implausible nature of the employer's defense. An expert witness who physically embodied racial and class privilege and the plaintiff's language skills were apparently decisive.

In recent decades the United States has once again become a nation of immigrants, including many highly educated members of the middle class. Coming from diverse countries throughout Asia, Latin America, and the Middle East, many of these professional and entrepreneurial newcomers were previously accustomed to households run by servants, and some of them seek to reestablish these arrangements in the United States. Some of the more privileged may even "import" domestic workers from their own countries of origin, as is common, for example, among Indians on the East Coast and Indonesians in Los Angeles. Yuni Muliyono's importation made possible the abuses by her employers. "They wanted to have a similar lifestyle to what they were enjoying in their country," noted Michele Yu, "but they couldn't really afford to do that."

When immigrant women are brought by conationals or coethnics to work as live-in domestic workers in the United States, they often remain extremely isolated and never learn about their other options and their labor rights under U.S. law. Particularly when there are relatively few of their immigrant group in this country, such women seem to be at risk for especially intense job exploitation. By contrast, Mexican or Central American immigrant women in Los Angeles are likely to have access to well-developed social networks that may be brimming with information and job alternatives. In 1980 a Bolivian live-in employee who had worked ten to twelve hours a day, seven days a week, without any pay for a Bolivian family won $56,000 in unpaid wages and penalties, perhaps the highest such court award to any live-in housekeeper in the United States.[33] More recently, in 1999 a Thai employer was found guilty of eleven criminal charges involving her abusive treatment of Thai undocumented immigrants whom she enslaved in her Southern California home; in testimony, one of the plaintiffs fell to her knees to demonstrate for the court how she had been forced to serve food and scrub floors.[34] The highly publicized case of Claudia Garáte, a Chilean live-in domestic worker in northern California who testified before the California labor commissioner in 1993 about her enslavement, provides another striking example of how the lack of an immigrant community exacerbates social isolation and leaves domestic workers vulnerable to almost unthinkable types of employer abuse.[35]

PAYING FOR CARE

The organization of work is today very different than it was at the beginning of the twentieth century, the heyday of monopoly capitalism and the industrial factory system. Monopolies are still with us but in a new form, as a series of corporate networks, offices, and factories stretched across the globe; and domestic workers, like other immigrants, travel thousands of miles for their jobs. Capital and labor mobility define the new globalization, demanding both national and local responses to social problems. As we face this emergent future, social justice will depend increasingly on our ability to imagine and implement global solutions.

Employment is increasingly decentralized and fluctuating. Work stability is a thing of the past, and popular magazine and newspaper articles regularly remind us that the average American worker can expect to change employers and even careers on many occasions throughout a lifetime. Everywhere, it seems, the proliferation of subcontracting, flexible employment, and part-time and temporary jobs makes less stable the relationship between employer and employee. The rigid hierarchy of yesterday's corporation has been called into question; in some cases, it has been replaced with employee participation and horizontal governing councils. At the same time, the meanings of work are no longer certain. For some lucky people, work is "fun"; for those at the bottom of the occupational hierarchy—prison workers, women conscripted into jobs through welfare reform, and many new immigrants holding service jobs—work is not even acknowledged as work. Up and down the occupational hierarchy, employers appear to be shedding their responsibility as employers. In this respect, they seem to be disappearing.

Divisions between formal- and informal-sector work seem fuzzier than ever. Looking at paid domestic work, we are immediately reminded that the informal sector is no longer—if it ever was—somewhere "out there" in downtown sweatshops, on freeway off-ramps, or on the corners where day laborers gather.[36] It looms in the kitchens and bedrooms of some very high income Americans. In Los Angeles, middle- and high-income citizens routinely engage and depend on informally organized, unregulated, untaxed, and unrecorded remunerated services. In fact, the manner in which these relatively privileged members of society organize care for their dependents and for their homes *creates* private, informal-sector employment for Latina and Latino immigrant workers.

As a result, the pathways leading to the homes of the affluent now lead many new immigrants to their workplaces. As we have seen, in Los Angeles it is predominantly Mexican and Central American immigrant workers who cross these thresholds. Housecleaners and nanny/housekeepers are not the only ones going off to work in private homes. They are joined by Latino gardeners, now ubiquitous in almost any Los Angeles neighborhood; pool cleaners, who arrive on regular, weekly schedules; and painters, handymen, furniture movers, and tree trimmers who might be hired from a day laborer corner or from flyers advertising their willingness to do modest-sized, one-time jobs.[37] Like the varieties of private paid domestic work, these occupations are differently organized, but they are all service-producing activities, typically performed for and purchased by residential "customers."

Increasingly important to the incorporation of Latina and Latino immigrant workers in the United States is their employment in and around private homes. A little-recognized social fact is that private homes today serve as major economic points of entry for many of these immigrant workers. How well new immigrants and their families fare in the United States depends not only on the educational and financial resources with which they enter the country but on the economic sector in which they locate. Scholars who study immigrant incorporation have looked closely at the inner workings of various sectors—for example, at enclave businesses where immigrants hire coethnics, and at immigrant-reliant industries, like the garment industry, where immigrants of different nationalities overlap but occupy distinct job niches. The long-term effects of economic incorporation in private residences will be revealed only with time, but they will hinge on the quality of these jobs. And the quality of these jobs will depend, in part, on the employers and their abilities to fulfill their obligations as employers.

When I informally chat about paid domestic work with other middle-class people, many of them wonder why Latina immigrants who are dissatisfied with their jobs don't simply look for other types of work in Los Angeles; or failing that, why they don't just "go home." Aren't they ambitious? Don't they aspire to something better? Some Latina domestic workers do try to leave the occupation, but they find the alternatives scarce. Among the most common and easily accessible jobs for them are informal vending, janitorial work, and factory work, often in the garment sector. But garment industry jobs in Los Angeles have deteriorated in recent years. Of the estimated 120,000 garment workers in Los Angeles, the majority are Latina immigrant women and many of them now earn less than the state minimum wage at jobs that present serious health and safety problems.[38] And as more immigrant women have turned to vending, competition has increased and shaved already slim profits even further. Office cleaning has opened up as a source of employment for Latina immigrants, but there too job terms and wages have deteriorated, although new organizing efforts by the Service Employees International Union (labeled "Justice for Janitors") are now reversing this downward trend in Los Angeles. Even Latina domestic workers who have all of their legal papers, who have years of experience in the United States, who have received some higher education, and who are totally bilingual have few options. The kinds of jobs they might get as cosmetologists, secretaries, or bank tellers, they say, would require high investment in work clothes and would still bring in low earnings. Legal work authorization and English literacy skills do not automatically open promising avenues of employment.

The bad news is this: there are no ladders of upward mobility leading out of paid domestic work today, as there were for European immigrant women in the early twentieth century. We live in a society that is increasingly characterized by an occupational hourglass, without a booming industrial sector for Latina domestic workers or their husbands to latch onto in the United States. While some of them hope to retire in El Salvador or Mexico, their possibilities for sustainable employment in their countries of origin have lessened with globalization, the North American Free Trade Agreement, and the economic aftermath of civil wars.

Many Latina domestic workers would like to have better jobs, but their options and their opportunities for advancement are slim. Upgrading their current occupation is one solution to their dilemma. How to achieve that, however, is less clear.

One step involves formalizing and regulating domestic jobs. Though government regulations covering employment verification, minimum wage, and withholding tax are in place, they remain, as we have seen, obscured, ignored, and unenforced in paid domestic work. Domestic workers are legally entitled to receive and employers are required to provide minimum wage and overtime, Social Security and Medicare payments, and in some instances unemployment insurance and workers' compensation. While most housecleaners earn well above minimum wage—with most earning more than the $7.25 an hour set by the Los Angeles Living Wage Ordinance—the same cannot be said of nanny/housekeepers, especially those working in live-in arrangements, who continue to earn below the legal minimum.[39] Live-in work remains the arena where the most egregious labor violations occur. Many of these workers face nonpayment and underpayment of wages. As noted above, all parties use the inclusion of room and board to justify the low wages of live-in work, but this practice is legally permissible only when there is a written agreement and when food and lodging is adequate—conditions that are rarely met. Nearly all nanny/housekeepers and housecleaners work without written contracts. California and other states could also take inspiration from New York State, which in 1997 (through the efforts of Latina immigrant workers) passed what is reputed to be the toughest wage enforcement law in the country, the Unpaid Wages Prohibition Act.[40]

Strengthening the formal employment standards is not enough, however. Widespread compliance with those standards will require a program of public education and outreach directed at middle-class and upper-middle-class employers, as well as enforcement of the laws that apply to them. Employers, regardless of their own mixed feelings about domestic work arrangements, must learn to act as employers with particular obligations rather than as consumers of domestic services. Instead of relying on employee certification or licensing (as "professional nannies") to upgrade the occupation, a strategy that would always exclude some and create a subcaste of unlicensed workers, we must look to the treatment of the least skilled who labor in the worst jobs. To that end, the behavior of employers must be changed.

Public acknowledgment of paid domestic work is necessary to achieve reform. In March 2000, California state assembly member

Gilbert Cedillo authored and received overwhelming assembly approval to recognize March 30 as Domestic Worker Appreciation Day. According to Victor Narro, worker rights project director at CHIRLA and sponsor of the resolution, "March 30 is celebrated [as an international day of appreciation for domestic workers] throughout Latin America. This declaration is an important first step in promoting labor protection for domestic workers." I attended the press conference and festive celebration at CHIRLA, but sadly, representatives from the mainstream English-language media—those who could do the most to get the word out to employers—were in scant attendance. Still, the resolution is an important symbolic step.

Improving the occupation will also require collective organizing by and for domestic workers. In spite of the many obstacles that Latina domestic workers face in undertaking such a project—the lack of union consciousness, the reluctance to identify as domestic workers, the job isolation, and the impossibility of setting up a collective bargaining unit—they *are* organizing in major cities around the country. The Domestic Workers' Association in Los Angeles, just one example of these associations, provides a site for domestic workers to give and receive social recognition, to seek job advice, and to pursue new occupational skills (e.g., how to do CPR, serve at a seder, or file income taxes); and when necessary, it helps its members pursue claims for back wages. Organized more as community-worker associations than as trade unions, these groups may find that their efforts are facilitated by their members' social needs and social abilities. An important point of strength for them is that unlike factory owners who can ship their factories and their union jobs overseas, American families are unlikely to move to Sri Lanka in search of cheaper domestic services: domestic workers' jobs are firmly anchored in place.

Recall that when the members of the Domestic Workers' Association listed their job demands, dignity and respect topped the list. Clearly, some aspects of the job need improvements that, unlike wages and hours, cannot be legislated. Given the structure of the occupation, with employer networks governing recruitment and hiring, those networks themselves appear to provide an important site of reform. The social connections among employers, currently the primary hiring mechanism, might also facilitate education and outreach. Organizations aiming at improving the terms of paid domestic work, such as the Domestic Workers' Association, might take a page from strategies used in the garment organizing campaigns of the 1990s, which targeted consumers and consumers' consciences with their "No Sweat" labels and National Day of Conscience.[41] Domestic workers could similarly target their employers.

Indeed, the employers have good reason to change: they and their family members who are cared for by Latina nannies will benefit greatly if the occupation is upgraded. They stand to gain better child care and other domestic services, greater length of service by those they employ, and perhaps even a fuller sense of humanity. We might ask ourselves what kind of society we wish to create for ourselves and our children. Do we wish to continue current arrangements, whereby many Latina and Caribbean immigrant women in nanny/ housekeeper jobs must forfeit their own family and community lives, leaving their own young children in their countries of origin? Is transnational motherhood and a form of domestic apartheid what we want? Should the costs of care be borne so disparately? Or can we imagine and design domestic jobs so that, like other forms of employment, these can accommodate and allow for employees' own social and family lives? While we cannot legislate caring about employees, we can strive for public education and social acknowledgment that paid domestic work is work, that it is an integral part of how our society is organized today, and that the Latina immigrant women who do the work are people with their own families, communities, and concerns.

Notes

1. The filmmakers are Sergio Arau and Yareli Arizmendi. The U.S.-born Mexican American population in Los Angeles includes many who hold low-skill white-collar and middle- to high-skill blue-collar jobs, as well as some who work as entrepreneurs, managers, and professionals. The Mexican immigrant population in Los Angeles, however, is overwhelmingly concentrated in low-paying, low-skill occupations, among them the "servicing" jobs I discuss. For a comparison of the economic status of Mexican immigrants and Mexican Americans in Los Angeles, see Ortiz 1996.

2. The 1993 Senate confirmation hearings for attorney general, the highest judicial post in the United States, led to a virtual media circus when nominee Zoë Baird, a corporate lawyer and mother, was discovered to have employed two Peruvian household employees who lacked legal work authorization, and for whom she did not report federal withholding tax as required. Dubbed "nannygate" by the media, the televised debacle became a defining point in shaping the first Clinton presidential administration; subsequent executive appointees, even men, had to pass the so-called Zoë Baird test. Kimba Wood, another nominee for attorney general, could not assume the post because she had hired an immigrant housekeeper who lacked work authorization. Wood had done so prior to 1986, when employer sanctions went into effect; while she had acted lawfully in hiring and had paid her employee's Social Security taxes, public outcry against the employment of undocumented immigrant workers prompted her to withdraw her name from consideration. These incidents were followed by revelations in California that two politicians who had based their electoral campaigns on anti-immigrant platforms, Governor Pete Wilson and U.S. Senate candidate Michael Huffington, had also employed undocumented immigrant domestic workers for whom they had not paid employment taxes.

3. Katzman 1981; Glenn 1986.

4. In fact, this particular Chilean family saved my mother's life, long after she had left their employ and come to the United States, when their personal connections ensured the best in South American brain surgery for her aneurysm. Whether I like it or not, that relationship probably influenced my thinking about personalism between domestic employees and employers.

5. I interviewed more employers than employees for three reasons: the study began as a study of employers, the interviews of employees (but not employers) were supplemented with a survey of 153 other Latina immigrant

women working as private domestic workers, and I needed fewer employee than employer interviews to reach a point of saturation in my findings. Of the employees, twenty were Latina immigrant women, and three (two white women and one Chicana, all of them in their twenties) were U.S.-born citizens with recent experience in paid domestic work.

6. See Momsen (1991) for an excellent overview of migrant women working in paid domestic work in the Americas, Europe, Africa, and Asia. Even in countries where paid domestic work is not performed by migrant women, the occupation has drawn increasing interest, as exemplified by a special issue of the leading feminist journal in Mexico City (see Lamas 2000).

CHAPTER 1. NEW WORLD DOMESTIC ORDER

1. In 1974 the sociologist Lewis Coser pointed out that the job of domestic servant is atavistic, based largely on ascribed status; requires the performance of nonspecialized, diffuse menial tasks; and relies on particularistic rather than universalistic relations between employer and servant. With the commodification and fragmentation of private household services (such as "take-out" food and laundry services) and the introduction of new household technology, Coser predicted the demise of this occupation. Similarly, David Chaplin (1978) concluded that domestic service occupations would decline as nations underwent modernization and industrialization. That these 1970s prognostications were made by men is not incidental. These scholars underestimated not only the compatibility of modernization and socioeconomic inequality, but also the seemingly endless activities required to maintain households and care for children. They also failed to recognize that household technologies, together with rising standards of hygiene and of middle-class child rearing in the twentieth century, have often extended, rather than reduced, the number of hours of domestic work. For analyses of how household technological innovations have often failed to contribute to reductions in domestic labor time, see Vanek 1974; Cowan 1983.

2. Child care centers in the United States evolved out of the poorhouses and settlement projects, and continue to be stigmatized as providing second-rate care (see Clarke-Stewart 1993; Wrigley 1995). Many parents don't like to take young children out of the home; and many Americans express a strong cultural preference for familial care, or for the one-on-one attention received in a private home and not in an institutional setting, for virtually all types of care giving (see Stone 1998).

3. Wrigley 1995.

4. The Harvard-affiliated economist Juliet B. Schor estimates that between 1969 and 1987, the average employed American added an extra 163 hours on the job annually, the equivalent of a month a year (1992:29–30). This estimate is based on calculations of annual hours of paid employment. According to Schor, work hours have risen for employed Americans in all income categories. See also Yates 1994; Hochschild 1997. For an analysis of

the "second shift" of housework that falls disproportionately to employed women, see Hochschild 1989.

5. Ruth Milkman, Ellen Reese, and Benita Roth (1998) use 1990 census data for the 100 largest metropolitan areas in the United States to show that income inequality is a significant predictor of the proportion of the female labor force employed in domestic work.

6. In 1997 the California Department of Finance released information showing that the strong growth in personal income tax revenue, collected from the unprecedented number of individuals enjoying soaring stock dividends, bonuses, or profits in business partnerships, had far exceeded the expectations of state finance experts, pushing tax receipts almost $1 billion ahead of what had been anticipated for fiscal year 1996–97 (Flanigan 1997). Already by 1996, California's postrecessionary economy was producing what one reporter called "a bumper crop of new millionaires" and new entrants to the $100,000+ income bracket (L. Gordon 1998:A1). Stock options and capital gains drove up the number of California tax filers with adjusted gross incomes of $1 million or more from about 9,000 in 1994 to 15,000 in 1996. In the same period, Californians reporting incomes between $100,000 and $1 million increased by 32 percent, to 777,000 (L. Gordon 1998:A20).

7. Saskia Sassen, in her pathbreaking book *The Global City* (1991), identifies London, Tokyo, and New York as the major centers for coordinating and controlling the global economy; but many have noted that Los Angeles belongs on this list, not as a center of high finance so much as an economy of entrepreneurial companies intimately connected to world markets.

8. Waldinger 1996.

9. See Waldinger and Bozorgmehr 1996:14–15.

10. According to one estimate, 144,415 Latina immigrant workers arrived in Southern California in the 1980s, and 142,827 before 1980. These figures, which include Latina immigrant workers ages 25 to 64 in 1990, were calculated by Dowell Myers and Cynthia Cranford (1998), using the year of immigration from the 1990 Census PUMS. It is widely acknowledged that the census routinely undercounts poor, minority, and immigrant populations who do not speak English; and when women are employed in "invisible" jobs—as private domestic workers, as vendors in the informal sector, or in sweatshop assembly—they are even less likely to be counted.

11. For research on Mexican immigration and social networks, see Massey et al. 1987; Hondagneu-Sotelo 1994a. On Mexican women's labor force participation in Mexico, see Beneria and Roldan 1987; and de Oliveira 1990.

12. For 1994 estimates, see Jonas n.d.: n. 6. These high estimates continued to increase; by 1999 the *Los Angeles Times* reported that Southern California had become home to 750,000 residents with roots in El Salvador, and 500,000 first- and second-generation Guatemalans (Olivio 1999). See also Lopez et al. 1986; Ulloa 1998.

13. A survey of 300 Guatemalans and Salvadorans in Los Angeles and San Francisco, conducted after the peace accords were signed in El Salvador in 1992, found that only 9 percent had definite plans to return to Central

America, probably influenced by the perception of economic stability and economic advantages for their children in the United States, their ties to family, jobs, and other institutions in the United States, and continued economic decline in Central America. See Chinchilla and Hamilton 1997.

14. See Hagan 1994; Repak 1995; Mahler 1995; Lopez, Popkin, and Telles 1996; Menjívar 1999.

15. Leslie Salzinger (1991), in a study of Central American domestic workers and their job cooperatives, identified precisely these categories of employers in San Francisco—a California city with a much smaller Latina immigrant population.

16. As Romero explains (1992:21–23), the inability to recognize paid domestic work as real work is predicated on the dichotomous separation between "work" and "family." "Housework," she notes, "does not fit the definitions of work as productive labor, it does not produce values which can be exchanged in the capitalist marketplace" (21). Romero also observes that "the same 'unskilled' tasks that consume housewives' daily energy and time are indeed considered productive labor when performed as paid work in the labor market . . . [in] laundries, restaurants, and day care centers" (23).

17. In the introduction to their book published in 1869, Catharine E. Beecher and Harriet Beecher Stowe explained that they sought "to elevate the honor and remuneration of [domestic] employment" (13), in both its paid and unpaid forms.

18. Stone 1998.

19. As Judith Rollins (1985:48) notes, for early American settlers, "democratic ideas undermined comfort with the traditional paternalistic master-servant relationship," presenting "a contradiction between the value of egalitarianism and the actual class and caste stratification."

20. Rollins 1985; Kaplan 1987; Romero 1992.

21. The amnesty program allowed nearly 3 million formerly undocumented immigrants, mostly Mexican, to obtain legal permanent residency—what is colloquially called the "green card"; a huge upsurge in naturalization applications in the mid-1990s followed. For a discussion of U.S. immigration policies as they have affected Mexicans, see Baker et al. 1998.

22. For an analysis of legalization strategies among Salvadoran immigrants and advocates from the early 1980s to the late 1990s, see Coutin 1998. In the spring of 1999, President Clinton announced his support of legislation providing amnesty-legalization for Salvadorans and Guatemalans who can prove they have permanently resided in the United States since 1990. This legislation did not pass in 2000.

23. See Colen 1989; Hondagneu-Sotelo 1997b.

24. On the ideology of a "colorblind" society, see Gotanda 1991 (cited in Kim 1999); Omi and Winant 1994.

25. Katzman 1991:53, table 2-2; Milkman, Reese, and Roth 1998.

26. Census figures pertaining to paid domestic work are more useful in suggesting trends than in providing accurate numbers. As Rollins (1985:56) reminds us, "Underreporting in 'private household work' has always been

widespread and for some groups of workers it may be increasing. The living-out and day-work arrangements facilitate the hiding of work and income. And both employers and domestics have more motivation now than in the past to do so," because of their coverage by Social Security legislation (mandated in 1951) and minimum wage legislation (mandated in 1974), and because of immigration status. The increasing centrality of Latina immigrants to domestic work—especially Central Americans, the majority of whom are without legal permanent residence status—makes contemporary census figures even less reliable.

27. Katzman 1981:66–69; Sutherland 1981:4–6.

28. Katzman 1981:222, 278.

29. Glenn 1986:103; Katzman 1981:90.

30. The higher-status domestic positions, such as butler, majordomo, and men's personal valet, have been defined as "men's jobs." In Western Europe, men worked as household servants from about 1700 until the early twentieth century; and in many colonial societies (see Hansen 1989; Constable 1997: 42–44), male servants were preferred to female servants.

31. The rapid Anglo settlement and the gold rush led to shortages of both labor and women, so Anglos recruited Chinese "houseboys" and cooks—men who had formerly worked for the railroads—in the 1850s to work as domestics. According to Katzman (1981:55), "in 1880, California and Washington were the only states in which a majority of domestic servants were men." In the early twentieth century, according to Glenn (1986:106–8) "Japanese school boys"—who were often neither boys nor students—were also recruited in California as live-in domestics; they were followed by Japanese immigrant women and, later, Japanese American women.

32. As Glenn (1986:104) notes, "the Japanese took a path intermediate to that of European immigrant groups and that of blacks and Chicanas. Theirs was a three-generation (or perhaps a two-and-a-half generation) mobility process."

33. See Romero 1992:79–87; see also Garcia 1981; Deutsch 1987. The historian Albert Camarillo has described the occupational ghettoization of Mexicans and Chicanos (1979:80): "Regardless of nativity and regardless of whether one was a second-generation descendant of Mexican-born parents or a first-generation descendant of one of the earliest Mexican settlers in California, the likelihood of upward mobility was almost nil."

34. Romero 1992.

35. Rollins 1985:56; Glenn 1986:266 n. 21; Powers 1990 (cited in Repak 1995:57).

36. In a significant journal article, Glenn (1992) has referred to service jobs in institutional settings as commodified social reproduction. "Racial-ethnic women," she notes, "are employed to do the heavy, dirty, 'back-room' chores of cooking and serving food in restaurants and cafeterias, cleaning rooms in hotels and office buildings, and caring for the elderly and ill in hospitals and nursing homes, including cleaning rooms, making beds, changing bed pans, and preparing food. In these same settings white women

are disproportionately employed as lower-level professionals (e.g., nurses and social workers), technicians, and administrative support workers to carry out the more skilled and supervisory tasks" (20).

37. Liddick 1973a; see also Liddick 1973b.

38. Grant, Oliver, and James 1996:396, table 13.3.

39. Simon and DeLey 1984; Ruiz 1987; Solorzano-Torres 1987; Colen 1989; Trevizo 1990; Salzinger 1991; Hagan 1994; Hondagneu-Sotelo 1994b.

40. Elizabeth Clark-Lewis describes settlement experiences of Southern women migrating to Washington, D.C., between 1910 and 1940 in terms that could easily be applied to contemporary Latina immigrant women. "For more than half the women," she writes, "their work was providing (unpaid) child-care and household maintenance. . . . Subsequently, the women were expected to develop economically productive lives by extending the services they were already providing for their own kin" (1994:80–81).

41. Although immigrant women from Korea, Taiwan, the Philippines, Vietnam, Cambodia, and China have also entered the United States in great numbers during this period, they enjoy greater employment opportunities because of their higher (on average) educational status, and their access to jobs in family businesses in ethnic enclaves and in the professions.

42. See Chang 1994. In a 1995 article I argue that Latina immigrants and their children were targeted because they were perceived as nonworkers whose social reproduction needs drain the public welfare system. Notions of race, class, gender, and generation were central to this xenophobic legislative effort.

43. Wong 1994:69.

44. Parreñas 2000; Richmond 1994.

45. In 1981 Canada began the "Foreign Domestic Movement" (FDM), later renamed in 1992 the "Live-in Caregiver Program," to facilitate the recruitment of foreign domestics (Bakan and Stasiulis 1997). Bakan and Stasiulis argue that formal domestic labor recruitment programs, which mandate indentured servitude, diminish the citizenship rights of foreign domestic workers in Canada—a change that coincides with the racialization of the occupation. When Canadians recruited white British women for domestic work in the 1940s, the mechanisms used were far less controlling than those applied in recent decades to Caribbean and Filipina contracted, live-in domestic workers. In 1990, 60 percent of the new 10,946 recruits were Filipinas, and in 1991, 68 percent of the 7,716 total. They are far outnumbered by illegal immigrant domestic workers, however, whose 1993 number may have been as high as 25,000 to 30,000 in Toronto alone (Mitchell 1993:A5, cited in Bakan and Stasiulis:49 n. 7, 50 n. 10). See also Macklin 1994. On state-sponsored contract labor programs for migrant domestic workers in Singapore, see Yeoh et al. 1999.

46. Constable 1997:3.

47. Constable 1997:3. Today, www.Amahnet.com touts itself as "the first Internet marketing service for maids and other domestic helpers in Hong Kong." Prospective employers can check their preferences for the employee's nationality, marital status, age, cleaning experience, and available

start date. When I tried the search and clicked on a hypothetical job candidate, the text next to the Filipina job candidate promised this: "She is a hardworking person and can adjust herself easily."

48. I am indebted to conversations with the geographer James A. Tyner, who has extensively studied the worldwide, state-supported migration of Filipinas, for this observation.

49. Colen 1989, 1990; Repak 1995.

50. Arat-Koc 1997:54.

51. Among the authors who have emphasized that women employers act as contractors are Palmer (1989), Glenn (1992), Romero (1992), Parreñas (2000), and, in the context of Hong Kong, Constable (1997).

52. Laslett and Brenner 1989:383. In this foundational article, they stress not only that social reproduction is legitimate, important work, but that the gendered organization of social reproduction is dialectically intertwined with macrohistorical factors, at once shaped by these and in turn producing new macro formations. Glenn (1992) emphasizes the changing racial formations of social reproduction, especially as it has encompassed a host of commodified forms (e.g., convalescent homes, institutional child care, cafeterias). I and others such as Parreñas (2000) point to the intersections of social reproduction with global macrostructural forces and immigration.

53. See DeVault 1991 for an exposition of ways in which the work of daily sustenance constitutes "the family."

54. On the changing tactics of the aristocracy and the middle class to ensure their children's class standing, see Wrigley 1995. On contemporary ideologies and practices of "intensive mothering," see Hayes 1996.

55. For an in-depth discussion of the changing meanings of motherhood brought about by transnational motherhood arrangements, see Hondagneu-Sotelo and Avila 1997, on which portions of the discussion in this section draw.

56. On the cult of domesticity and feminist "rethinking of the family," see Thorne and Yalom 1992; Glenn 1994. For a broader discussion of how women in Latin America are affected by notions of family rooted in industrialization and urbanization, as well as by Mexican cultural controlling images of *la Virgen de Guadalupe, la llorona,* and *la Malinche,* see Hondagneu-Sotelo and Avila (1997).

57. I have not included in this research project domestic workers who work as "companions" or in elder care, in part because those working in this sector are primarily Filipina immigrants who have backgrounds in nursing or other health professions or are home care workers, contracted and paid not privately by individual employers but by the state of California, with funds from a mix of federal, state, and local sources. In Los Angeles I met very few Latina immigrants who had worked in elder care or as *damas de compañía,* but this occupation may be more concentrated in popular retirement centers. As baby boomers age, the demand in paid domestic work may soon shift from nannies to companions of the elderly. For research on Latina immigrants working in the latter domestic jobs, see Ibarra (in press).

For research on Filipinas working in elder care in Los Angeles, see Parreñas 2000. Women who work in for-profit cleaning firms are also omitted, because I have chosen to focus on private paid domestic work. For a study of the cleaning firms, see Mendez 1998.

58. Romero 1992.

CHAPTER 2. MAID IN L.A.

1. Glenn 1986:141.

2. Lacher 1997:E1.

3. One nanny/housekeeper told me that a *señora* had admonished her for picking a bag of fruit, and wanted to charge her for it; another claimed that her employer had said she would rather watch the fruit fall off the branches and rot than see her eat it.

4. Many Latina domestic workers do not know the amount of their hourly wages; and because the lines between their work and nonwork tend to blur, live-in nanny/housekeepers have particular difficulty calculating them. In the survey questionnaire I asked live-in nanny/housekeepers how many days a week they worked, what time they began their job, and what time they ended, and I asked them to estimate how many hours off they had during an average workday (39 percent said they had no time off, but 32 percent said they had a break of between one and three hours). Forty-seven percent of the women said they began their workday at 7 A.M. or earlier, with 62 percent ending their workday at 7 P.M. or later. With the majority of them (71 percent) working five days a week, their average workweek was sixty-four hours. This estimate may at first glance appear inflated; but consider a prototypical live-in nanny/housekeeper who works, say, five days a week, from 7 A.M. until 9 P.M., with one and a half hours off during the children's nap time (when she might take a break to lie down or watch television). Her on-duty work hours would total sixty-four and a half hours per week. The weekly pay of live-in nanny/housekeepers surveyed ranged from $130 to $400, averaging $242. Dividing this figure by sixty-four yields an hourly wage of $3.80. None of the live-in nanny/housekeepers were charged for room and board—and, as we will see in chapter 8, this practice is regulated by law—but 86 percent said they brought food with them to their jobs. The majority reported being paid in cash.

5. See, e.g., Employment Classified Section 2, *Los Angeles Times*, June 6, 1999, G9.

6. Clark-Lewis 1994:123. "After an average of seven years," she notes in her analysis of African American women who had migrated from the South to Washington, D.C., in the early twentieth century, "all of the migrant women grew to dread their live-in situation. They saw their occupation as harming all aspects of their life" (124). Nearly all of these women transitioned into day work in private homes. This pattern is being repeated by Latina immigrants in Los Angeles today, and it reflects local labor market opportunities and constraints. In Houston, Texas, where many Mayan Gua-

temalan immigrant women today work as live-ins, research by Jacqueline Maria Hagan (1998) points to the tremendous obstacles they face in leaving live-in work. In Houston, housecleaning is dominated by better-established immigrant women, by Chicanas and, more recently, by the commercial cleaning companies—so it is hard for the Maya to secure those jobs. Moreover, Hagan finds that over time, the Mayan women who take live-in jobs see their own social networks contract, further reducing their internal job mobility.

7. As noted in chapter 1, several factors explain the shift to day work, including urbanization, interurban transportation systems, and smaller private residences. Historians have also credited the job preferences of African American domestic workers, who rejected the constraints of live-in work and chose to live with their own families and communities, with helping to promote this shift in the urban North after 1900 (Katzman 1981; Clark-Lewis 1994:129–35). In many urban regions of the United States, the shift to day work accelerated during World War I, so that live-out arrangements eventually became more prevalent (Katzman 1981; Palmer 1989). Elsewhere, and for different groups of domestic workers, these transitions happened later in the twentieth century. Evelyn Nakano Glenn (1986:143) notes that Japanese immigrant and Japanese American women employed in domestic work in the San Francisco Bay Area moved out of live-in jobs and into modernized day work in the years after World War II.

8. Katzman 1981; Glenn 1986.

9. Wrigley 1995.

10. Keep in mind that the survey questionnaire was administered at three different types of sites: bus stops, ESL evening classes, and parks where nannies congregate with the children in their charge. Housecleaners who drive and have their own cars, and who speak some English, typically earn more money and are able to clean more houses per week. Because my survey is biased toward Latina domestic workers who ride the buses and attend ESL classes, those housecleaners earning higher wages are not taken into account.

11. Romero 1992.

12. In addition to the jobs of live-in nanny/housekeepers, live-out nanny/housekeepers, and weekly or biweekly housecleaners, an increasingly important and growing segment of the domestic workforce is engaged in elder care. That, too, is organized in different ways; and though the occupation lies beyond the parameters of this study (much of it is formally organized and contracted for by the state or medical organizations), some Latina immigrants are privately contracted for jobs as elders' companions and caretakers, as *damas de compañía.*

13. Smith 1973; McBride 1976.

14. The only news report of INS raids involving nannies working in private homes in Los Angeles that came to my attention as I did this research involved a nanny working for a top-ranking Latino INS agent, Jorge Guzman. In 1996 armed plainclothes INS agents illegally raided Guzman's home,

and allegedly fondled and made sexual advances toward the domestic worker. Guzman claimed that the raid was part of a ten-year program of internal anti-Latino harassment directed at him. After he filed suit, the U.S. Justice Department agreed to pay him $400,000 to settle (McDonnell 1999).

15. Personal communication, Cynthia Cranford, March 1999; and Cleeland 1999a.

16. Rollins 1985; Glenn 1986; Romero 1992. See Romero 1997 for a study focusing on the perspective of domestic workers' children. Although the majority of respondents in that study were children of day workers, and none appear to have been children of transnational mothers, they still recall that their mothers' occupation had significant costs for them.

17. Hondagneu-Sotelo and Avila 1997.

18. Central American women seem more likely than Mexican women to leave their children in their country of origin, even if their husbands are living with them in the United States, perhaps because of the multiple dangers and costs associated with undocumented travel from Central America to the United States. The civil wars of the 1980s, continuing violence and economic uncertainty, greater difficulties and costs associated with crossing multiple national borders, and stronger cultural legacies of socially sanctioned consensual unions may also contribute to this pattern for Central Americans.

19. Glenn 1986; Dill 1988.

20. The figures on Salvadoran and Guatemalan women are taken from an analysis of the 1990 census data by the sociologists David E. Lopez, Eric Popkin, and Edward Telles (1996); they also found that Mexican immigrants were only 2.3 times as likely as those in the general population to be engaged in paid domestic work.

21. See Salzinger 1991; Hagan 1994, 1998; Repak 1995.

22. Lopez, Popkin, and Telles 1996:298.

23. According to 1990 PUMS Census data, about 70 percent of Central American women between the ages of 24 and 60 in Los Angeles County are in the labor force, while only 56 percent of their Mexican peers are. Among this same group, 71 percent of Mexican immigrant women but only 56 percent of their Central American peers are married and living with a spouse. To put it even more starkly, 28 percent of Mexican immigrant women and 43 percent of Central American women report living with family members or adults other than their spouses.

24. Repak 1995.

25. Mahler 1995; Menjívar 2000.

26. Some studies estimate that as many as 50 percent of poor households in San Salvador were formed by "free unions" rather than marriage by law. This pattern is related not just to internal and intra–Central American labor migration but also to urban poverty, as there is no need to secure inheritance rights when there is no property to share (Nieves 1979; Repak 1995).

27. Countries with traditions of consensual marriages afford women more migration opportunities (Donato 1992).

28. A survey conducted in Los Angeles and Orange County in 1986 revealed that 45 percent of Korean immigrants were self-employed; many were business owners in the Korean ethnic economy (Min 1996:48).

29. Mar and Kim 1994.

30. Between 1966 and 1985 nearly 25,000 Filipina nurses came to work in the United States, and another 10,000 came between 1989 and 1991. Filipinas who were formally recruited through government programs then informally recruited their friends and former nursing school classmates (Ong and Azores 1994).

31. Parreñas, in press.

32. Wrigley 1995.

33. Palmer 1989:140.

34. Personal communication with UCLA professor Abel Valenzuela, fall 1998.

35. Bet Tzedek Legal Services; see chapter 8, n. 30.

CHAPTER 3. IT'S NOT WHAT YOU KNOW ...

1. Dudden 1983; Glenn 1986; Steinberg 1989; Clark-Lewis 1994.

2. Employer demand for housecleaning has expanded in recent years as its relatively low cost has made it affordable to working families, apartment dwellers, and even college students. Unlike in Houston, where a study conducted by Hagan (1998) found that it is difficult for Guatemalan Mayan women to move out of live-in jobs and into housecleaning, in Los Angeles housecleaning and a growing number of occupational niches—including factory employment and, increasingly, office cleaning—are filled by Latina immigrants.

3. Numerous domestic employment agencies do sell referrals to houses, typically charging the job seekers a fee—say, $60—for access to an employer who will pay $60 for a weekly or biweekly housecleaning. This practice, known as *comprando casas*, or "buying houses," is widely recognized among housecleaners as fraudulent. Many housecleaners report paying agency fees, assuming that the agencies will ensure steady, weekly employment at a particular house for one year but finding that they are hired to clean only once or twice. In those cases, a housecleaner may invest $60 and earn only $120 for ten hours of work. In 1997, according to Orly Lobel (2000:12), the International Labor Organization (ILO) adopted a new "Convention Concerning Private Agencies." Article 7 of the convention prohibits the agencies from charging workers any fees or cost and Article 11 requires countries to ensure adequate protection for the workers, including minimum wages, regulation of hours, and so forth. These ILO provisions appear to go wholly unrecognized in the United States (see Lobel 2000:12 n. 24).

4. Hondagneu-Sotelo 1994b.

5. Mendez 1998.

6. Rollins 1985; Castro 1989.

7. Romero 1992.

8. Rollins 1985; Glenn 1986; Romero 1992.

9. Granovetter 1973, 1985, 1992, 1995. See also Neckerman and Kirschenman 1991; Portes and Sessenbrenner 1993.

10. Romero 1992:164.

11. Rollins 1985; Glenn 1986; Romero 1992; Dill 1994.

CHAPTER 4. FORMALIZING THE INFORMAL:
DOMESTIC EMPLOYMENT AGENCIES

1. This and all other agency names, as well as personal names of individuals, are pseudonyms. In Los Angeles, the agencies typically use alliterative and pun-filled names such as "Mama's Maid to Order," "Maid in Heaven," and "Domestic Darlings." Other agencies emphasize the personal service provided and feature the owner's name as the name of the business (e.g., "The Eileen Powell Agency"). One agency owner told me that she had paid an expensive business name consultant to invent her firm's catchy name, "Custom Maid for You," because when she started the business, with her "office" only a card table in her bedroom, "stationery and my card were going to speak for my image."

2. The agency personnel unanimously report that the majority of their clients—80 to 90 percent—are seeking workers to fill live-in jobs, because the extended job hours give them round-the-clock service and flexibility. The employees see live-in jobs as the least desirable, and these positions are the most difficult to fill through the informal social networks; generally only women who have arrived recently and are poorly established in the United States are willing to take them. Many women who have worked in live-in jobs have had a major, explosive conflict with an employer, and swear they will never place themselves in those same circumstances again. Other women advise their newly arrived Latina kin and friends to avoid live-in jobs, where they may experience loneliness, lack of food, disrespect, dawn-to-midnight work schedules, six-day workweeks, and sexual harassment.

3. I interviewed people who own or work at agencies that are relatively well-established: with the exception of one subsidiary, all of the agencies had operated for eight to ten years, although not all of the interviewees had themselves been in the business that long. One respondent told me that one superpower firm dominated the Los Angeles market, and that the next largest market share was divided up more or less equally among ten agencies; he put the agency he owned and that of another respondent, each with a tripartite structure, in the "group of ten" relatively high-volume agencies. These agencies provide a sharp contrast to the many small domestic employment agencies that routinely emerge and wither in Los Angeles' market. Some agencies specialize exclusively in nannies, in combination nanny/housekeepers, or in high-end butlers and housemen. I interviewed personnel at four agencies that specialized in nanny/housekeepers, and one agency that placed only high-end "American" nannies.

4. For a study that included interviews with white nannies and their employers in Los Angeles and New York City, see Wrigley 1995. See also Macdonald 1998.

5. Reliance on the telephone is especially pronounced when dealing with the higher-paying, upscale clients. The most elite nanny agency in this study, "Maid in America," makes nationwide placements, so the agency manager may meet neither the nanny nor the employer client. Another owner of a three-tier agency reported that he personally drives to the home of the client at the conclusion of the placement process to sign the contract that sets out his fee and the client's ninety-day guarantee. He and other agency owners emphasized that in a competitive service business, clients expect convenience and personal touches.

6. Agency owners and personnel sometimes call the employers of domestic workers their "clients" because the employers pay the most (and it is the employers whom they are most eager to please), but the initial, primary contract is with the job applicant. Typically, no written contract is signed by the employer until the final placement has been made and it is time to collect the fee. One high-volume, well-known agency does not use a written contract with the employer client at all, preferring instead the efficiency of a verbal contract over the phone. The agency's owner explained, "There's so many agencies in this city, that to do a signed contract . . . you're losing a day's worth of work." The manager of a low-tier agency saw more stringent requirements as necessary for the low-end clients in which her agency specialized: "I make them [the employer-client] sign a paper that says they will not go behind the agency's back [by hiring the job seeker directly to avoid paying the agency fee], and if they do, we can sue them." Agencies may hold job applicants responsible if they accept a direct offer of employment from a client who used the agency, and then went outside the agency's auspices. Agencies also enforce these restrictions more tightly with the low-end, low-paying client than they do with the upmarket client.

7. The high-end placements for white nannies generally require the client to pay the agency the equivalent of 10 percent of the nanny's annual salary, the midrange placements typically cost the equivalent of one month's salary, and the lower-end placements may require a flat fee. Thus an employer who hires an upmarket nanny at $500 a week will pay the agency $2,600, a midmarket nanny/housekeeper at $350 a week brings an agency fee of $1,400, and a $150-a-week lower-end nanny/housekeeper will earn the agency $200. There is much more volume at the lower end of the scale, and the lower-tier agencies also charge the job seekers an application fee ($5–35), while the higher-tier ones charge only the employer clients. A single $10 fee is not exorbitant, but poor women may pay it many times to various agencies around town—and remain jobless.

8. One example of a new subsidiary business is "TrustLine," a California state-certified registry service that enables parents who plan to hire private child care workers to check the California criminal records of prospective

employees. The TrustLine registry began in 1993, and over the next six years it rejected about 4,000 prospective nannies who had records of convictions for serious criminal conduct. TrustLine provides little information on those who have committed crimes outside the United States or even California, however. The agency personnel know this—they agreed that TrustLine was effective in capturing only convicted child abusers who have Social Security numbers (thereby ignoring most undocumented immigrants) and whose convictions occurred within California. While not a very effective screening tool, it does help the agencies market their services. The agencies will generally fingerprint the applicants, but the employer clients are responsible for paying the $85 TrustLine fee and contacting the service. Currently, some advocates are trying to take the program to a national level (see Healy 1999).

9. Wrigley 1995.

10. At the agencies that I observed, Polaroid snapshots are generally taken of the job seeker and attached to the application. All of the agency personnel—with the exception of the manager of a lower-tier agency, who admitted to showing the photos to the prospective employers—told me that the photo is only to help remind them of who the applicant is, not for shopping around to the client.

11. Rollins 1985; Romero 1992; Dill 1994.

12. One agency owner did add, "You know as an agency, if you get a single dad, send somebody very cute."

13. It would be easy but too simplistic to see sexual harassment in every such case. When parents (including fathers) interact daily with someone who seems to truly love and care for their children, they may be attracted to that person.

CHAPTER 5. BLOWUPS AND OTHER
UNHAPPY ENDINGS

1. I make an effort to present the employers' perspectives, but few of the employers interviewed described these explosive confrontations.

2. Portes 1994:118.

3. Bates 1999.

4. Wrigley 1995:26.

5. Hirschman 1970.

CHAPTER 6. TELL ME WHAT TO DO,
BUT DON'T TELL ME HOW

1. In his important 1979 book *Contested Terrain*, Richard Edwards analyzes various methods that capitalist employers have historically used to transform "labor power" (Marx used this term to refer to one's potential to work) into "labor" (the actual, concrete behavior of work). Edwards contends that labor control under capitalism evolved from the simple, unconstrained, absolute power of foremen on the shopfloor to the technical control

of the assembly line in Fordist industry, where the speed of the conveyor belt regulates the labor process, and then to the bureaucratic labor control of monopoly firms, where impersonal company rules and regulations exhort employees to diligently work long hours. Edwards's book built on Harry Braverman's argument (1974) that the relentless pursuit of profit drove capitalists to deskill the labor process first by separating conception from execution and then by deskilling execution itself into numerous separate components. In Braverman's analysis, the process of accumulation drove these developments. In the private relations of paid domestic work, there is generally no accumulation of profit, so it is striking that though here conception and execution often remain intertwined, the occupation remains a generally undesirable one, widely regarded as a low-status, unskilled or low-skill job.

2. The employers who, according to nanny/housekeepers and housecleaners, shouted complaints and demands were invariably not white, middle-class, and U.S.-born employers but immigrants. These immigrant employers hailed from various countries (e.g., Iran, Israel, Korea, Colombia), but they all brought to their new domestic arrangements in the United States their customary approach to controlling and managing servants in their countries of origin. Many Latina domestic workers who have had negative experiences with one foreign employer try to steer clear of future jobs with other immigrant employers.

3. Judith Rollins argues (1985), based on her study of black housecleaners and their white employers conducted in the Boston area in the early 1980s, that employers use maternalism to extract from their employees both physical labor and the expression of deference. Expressions of maternalism reported to Rollins included "giving gifts, the loaning of money, explaining bills, demanding to meet and approve of friends, making business calls for the employee, making travel arrangements for her, and (in the South) interceding on her behalf with the legal system" (189). In contemporary Los Angeles, the employers most prone to maternalistic gestures were white, middle-class homemakers, older than the baby boomers. Even women who fit this profile, however, sometimes encountered resistance to their maternalistic offerings.

4. Wrigley 1995:14.

5. Wrigley 1995.

6. Although nanny/housekeepers are expected to do what Hochschild calls "emotion work"—in this case, to smile and exhibit genuine warmth, caring, and patience toward and affection for the children and perhaps other members of their employers' families—they are not systematically trained or instructed in this duty, as are flight attendants or any number of corporate service providers (Hochchild 1983). Instead, their ability to do emotion work is thought by employers to be part of their natural disposition as "warm," "patient," and "loving" Latinas.

7. Wrigley 1995:85.

8. Wrigley 1995.

9. Romero 1992.

10. Dill 1994.

11. Mendez 1998; compare Rollins 1985; Romero 1992.

12. The originator and chief proponent of scientific management in the workplace, Frederick Winslow Taylor (1911), promised that through the standardization of parts, tools, and tasks, the labor process would become more efficient and thus more profitable for manufacturers.

13. Romero 1992:57.

14. Dudden 1983:179.

15. Romero 1992.

16. On cleaning service agencies, see Mendez 1998. Nicole Constable (1987) reveals that Filipinas who work as contracted domestics in Hong Kong must sign "oaths" stipulating that they agree to follow a plethora of rules regarding not only work performance but also their own personal hygiene, spatial mobility, curfews and communication, and uniforms. Filipina women who do not sign these oaths at the agencies are not placed into jobs. On labor control of Filipina domestic workers in Taiwan, see Lan 2000.

17. Wrigley 1995:77.

18. I am indebted to Michael Buroway for this important observation.

19. Romero 1992.

CHAPTER 7. GO AWAY . . . BUT STAY CLOSE ENOUGH

1. See Katzman 1981; Rollins 1985; Romero 1992.

2. Rollins 1985; Glenn 1986; Romero 1992.

3. Castro 1989.

4. Dill 1994; Mendez 1998.

5. Dill 1994:85.

6. I use the term *personalism* rather than the Parsonian *particularism* because the latter tends to imply a set of relations associated with traditional societies, where people associate with members of the same social circle, kin group, tribe, or village.

7. Most employers of paid domestic workers are heterosexual couples; and while both women and men benefit from the service of their paid employees, the women usually hire, fire, communicate with, and pay the domestic workers. As previous research has shown, the relationship between these two women, the paid domestic worker and her female employer, can be highly charged. This pattern holds true in contemporary Los Angeles, as the drama of these relationships continues to unfold between the "maid" and the "mistress," with men only peripherally involved.

8. Mendez 1998.

9. Romero 1992:69.

10. Mendez 1998:122.

11. Romero 1992; Rollins 1995.

12. Stone 1998.

13. Katzman 1981:188.

14. Rollins 1985:208.

15. Rollins 1985; Glenn 1986; Romero 1992; Dill 1994.

16. Rollins 1985; Glenn 1986; Kaplan 1987; Romero 1992; Clark-Lewis 1994.

CHAPTER 8. CLEANING UP A DIRTY BUSINESS

1. According to a study cited in the *Los Angeles Times,* a family of three supported by one worker earning the federal minimum wage of $5.15 would have an annual income 30 percent below the official national poverty line. Since 1994, a movement has organized in nineteen U.S. cities to call for "living wage ordinances" covering employees in firms with which the cities have contracts. In 1999 the living wage movement advocated setting a standard of $7.50 an hour for eligible workers (Pollin 1999). Since then, labor advocates have sought to raise the minimum wage in California to $8.00 an hour. In the year 2000, full-time minimum wage earners in California made $5.75 an hour and $11,900 a year (Tamaki 2000).

2. My sense of what might constitute "improvements" primarily reflects changes proposed by Latina domestic workers themselves, especially those who have organized in a Los Angeles–based group to upgrade the occupation; but I also draw on the thinking and experience of policy analysts and of attorneys who have served as advocates for domestic workers.

3. "Law Threatens" 1977; "Repeal of Law" 1977. For a more general discussion of employer resistance to regulations, see also Martin and Seagrave 1985; Rollins 1985; Palmer 1989.

4. In an editorial, John F. Lawrence (1978) argues that elimination of the regulations would diminish cheating (there would be, after all, no regulations to break if domestic employers were exempt from compliance) and would also encourage more middle-income households to hire domestic help and thereby raise the employment rate.

5. According to Martin and Seagrave (1985:128–31), the proposal to include private domestic workers under federal minimum wage laws had also appeared in a 1973 bill that was vetoed by President Nixon, who argued that it would lead to inflation and increase unemployment among domestics. They believe that pressures from Watergate may explain Nixon's turnaround. For further information on more recent legislation, see "Appendix A: The Fair Labor Standards Act" in National Organization for Women 1997:22–24. See also Martin and Seagrave 1985; Rollins 1985.

6. It is important to both recognize the advances of the FLSA, which took a significant step toward public acknowledgment of paid domestic work as employment, and to underline the historical and political context in which domestic work was included. The National Committee on Household Employees (NCHE), whose role in the policy arena will be detailed later in this chapter, deserves ample credit for this advance. The amendment to recognize the labor rights of domestic workers passed only through the efforts of the NCHE and of a vociferous bloc of women representatives in Congress in the early 1970s. Their rhetoric differed strikingly from that heard in Washington today, for it framed the amendment as part of a national initiative to

fight poverty: they wished to include domestic workers under the FLSA so that domestic workers would be kept above poverty income levels and off public assistance. They wrote, "These women are struggling to make ends meet and keep their families together. They are proud hard workers who are doing their darndest to stay off the welfare rolls and are getting precious little help for their efforts. Let's provide some help for those who are trying to help themselves" (H.R. Res. No. 93-913, 93d Cong., 2d sess. 2842–2844; quoted in National Organization for Women 1997:2). This letter was signed by Representatives Shirley Chisholm, Marjorie S. Holt, Leonor K. Sullivan, Yvonne Brathwaite Burke, Patsy T. Mink, Julia Butler Hansen, Edith Green, Martha W. Griffiths, Ella T. Grasso, Bella S. Abzug, Elizabeth Holtzman, Barbara Jordan, and Patricia Schroeder.

7. According to Wage Order 15 of California's Industrial Welfare Commission (IWC), private, live-in domestic workers need be paid overtime only if required to work during the three scheduled off-duty hours that fall within the twelve-hour work span, without being given twelve consecutive hours off in a workday, or on a sixth or seventh consecutive day in a workweek. See Fair Labor Standards Act 6 (f), 7 (1), and 13 (b)(21), 29 C.F.R. § 552 (1974). According to sections 3(A) and (B) of Wage Order 15, live-in employees are entitled to time and one-half for the first nine hours worked on a sixth or seventh consecutive day and double time for hours in excess of nine on such days. See *Cardenas v. Mission Industries,* 226 Cal. App.3d 952, 958 (1991). I am deeply grateful to attorney Victor Narro for providing me with these citations and helping me make sense of the FLSA and IWC provisions.

8. See "Appendix B: State Laws" in National Organization for Women 1997:25–31.

9. Until October 1, 1996, the minimum wage in California was $4.25 an hour. The successful efforts of a statewide coalition led to its gradual increase to $5.75 in March 1998. In January 2001, California's minimum wage rose to $6.25, and in 2002, it will become $6.75 an hour (Tamaki 200:A3).

10. See note 7.

11. "Household occupations," as defined by this document, include "all services related to the care of persons or maintenance of a private household or its premises by an employee of a private householder." Personal attendants and independent contractors do not fall into this category.

12. The order forbids employers from making deductions from wages or seeking reimbursement from employees for cash shortage, breakage, or loss of equipment, unless "it can be shown that the shortage, breakage, or loss is caused by a dishonest or willful act, or by the gross negligence of the employee" (see 8. "Cash Shortage and Breakage"); and employers that require domestic workers to wear uniforms must provide and maintain the uniforms. In California today, few employers require their domestic workers to wear a traditional "maid uniform," but many employers do state clothing preferences for their employees. In all my interviewing, I found no employees who wore uniforms to work; only one employer required her employee, an Eastern European immigrant who worked as a live-out, daily housekeeper, to wear a uniform.

13. Employers may deduct $20 a week for a room occupied alone, and $16.50 for a shared room (it does not stipulate if this deduction is permissable when a nanny/housekeeper shares a room with young children, a common practice in Los Angeles). The amount charged for breakfast, lunch, and dinner may not exceed $6.40 a day. Each meal must offer "an adequate, well-balanced serving of a variety of wholesome, nutritious food." Thus a live-in employee who works a sixty-hour week, earning the minimum wage of $5.75 an hour for the first forty hours worked, and subsequently time and a half for her next twenty hours, should earn, before deductions, $420 a week. If meals and lodging meet adequate standards, and if there is a written agreement for meal and lodging deductions, her weekly pay should be no less than $361.60. A live-in nanny/housekeeper who works the relatively rare forty-hour, five-day workweek, and who has a written agreement for meal and lodging deductions, should receive at least $178 a week.

14. See Martin and Seagrave 1985.

15. In IRS Publication 937 of 1994, titled "Employment Taxes," twenty factors are listed as "common-law rules" to help determine whether an individual paid worker is an employee or an independent contractor (4–5). In general, if the worker is under the employer's direct control, if services are rendered personally, if the employer maintains the right to discharge the employee, if the employer supplies the tools for work, if there is a continuing relationship with the employer (even one recurring at irregular intervals), and if the worker works the hours specified, then that person is an employee. By these standards, most paid domestic workers qualify as employees. But some of the twenty factors might lead employers of weekly or biweekly housecleaners to conclude that their cleaners are not employees but rather independent contractors. If, for example, the domestic worker offers services to two or more unrelated persons at the same time, and if they are paid by the job—as are most weekly and biweekly housecleaners—instead of by the hour, week, or month, they may be categorized as independent contractors. Thus the law as it pertains to housecleaners is somewhat ambiguous.

16. The Social Security Domestic Reform Act of 1994 established that wages paid to domestic workers are subject to Social Security and Medicare taxes only for cash wages of $1,000 or more per year. Prior to this change, wages paid in a calendar quarter were subject to the taxes if the employee was paid wages of $50 or more in the quarter. By raising the ceiling on the amount of pay required before employer compliance is mandated, the federal government, in effect, reduced the number of employers who must comply with Social Security and Medicare. Medicare, the federal health care system for the retired elderly, is financed by a payroll tax of 2.9 percent, to be split equally between employer and employee.

17. When employers first hire an employee of any sort, they are required to verify that the employee is eligible for employment—that the employee has "legal authorization to work"—and they must keep records of his or her name and Social Security number. If employers fail to comply, they may be fined or otherwise penalized. These employer sanctions and regulations came about as part of the Immigration Reform and Control Act (IRCA),

restrictionist immigration legislation enacted in November 1986. Employer sanctions, the centerpiece of IRCA, imposed civil and criminal penalties on employers who knowingly hire immigrants unauthorized to work in the United States. Verification of work authorization must be accomplished by filling out the Immigration and Naturalization Service Form I-9. Employers are also required to view the employee's Social Security card. In many low-wage, immigrant-dependent industries, employers often comply with the letter of the law by asking to see documents before hiring employees, but they do not check the documents' validity—and the law does not require such verification. IRCA leaves little doubt: it is illegal for employers to knowingly hire immigrant workers who lack the proper documents. Yet it is also plainly illegal for employers to pay subminimum wages to undocumented immigrant workers.

18. Portions of this section are drawn from Hondagneu-Sotelo and Riegos 1997.

19. In 1988 domestic workers belonging to unions in Argentina, Bolivia, Brazil, Chile, Colombia, the Dominican Republic, Mexico, Uruguay, Paraguay, Peru, and Venezuela met in Bogota, Colombia, to form the Confederation of Household Workers in the Caribbean and Latin America (CONLATRAHO). Union representatives from Guatemala joined in 1991 and Costa Rica in 1995. In March 1999 they held their inter-American meetings in Mexico City with organized domestic workers from the United States, including representatives from the Domestic Workers' Association of CHIRLA. We must also remember that Latin America has many reactionary organizations sponsored by employers, governments, and the Catholic Church that aim at training and disciplining poorly educated young women to fill employer needs, as well as advocacy associations attempting to organize among domestic workers. See Galvez and Todaro 1989; Goldsmith 1989; Leon 1989; Prates 1989.

20. Some of these efforts have been chronicled in the mass media. See, for example, Schmidt 1991; Wilkinson 1992; Carvajal 1996.

21. Palmer 1989; Romero 1992.

22. The organization was initially called the National Committee on Employer-Employee Relationships in the Home, and was renamed the National Committee on Household Employment in 1933 (Palmer 1989:116).

23. Palmer 1984.

24. In 1971 the NCHE spun off the Household Technicians of America (HTA), a collective bargaining group, but both organizations eventually disappeared; Phyllis Palmer argues that the decline of the NCHE resulted at least in part from "the influx of new female immigrants, which has always kept domestic work resupplied" (1984:87). In fact, both events—the entry of Latina and Caribbean immigrant women and the decline of the NCHE—also coincided with the exodus from the occupation of African American women (especially young women) after the civil rights era. As we have seen, many U.S.-born women of color left private household work for jobs in cafeterias, offices (as janitors), hotels, and restaurants, jobs that Glenn (1992)

refers to as "public reproductive work." The cause of the demographic shift in the occupation, however, and its relationship to organizing, is ambiguous and complex.

The United Domestic Workers Organization is another important worker-based effort aimed at organizing workers in private homes. This organization began in San Diego, inspired by César Chávez and the UFW. Later, the organization pursued collective bargaining for home care workers who care for the elderly in private homes. The United Domestic Workers Organization, an affiliate of the American Federation of State, County, and Municipal Employees (AFSCME), lobbied in 1998 for state funds to train welfare recipients for jobs as home workers. As Grace Chang observes, this example illustrates the extent to which "a body that claims to be a labor organization will jump at the opportunity to capture federal and state money at the expense of disenfranchised workers under the guise of 'welfare reform' and even 'worker advocacy'" (Chang 2000:196).

25. Domestic employment agencies may indeed serve as important mechanisms for promoting better labor practices. "Employment agencies have the advantage of deeper pockets and more stability," argues Orly Lobel, a Harvard Law School student who has written about the role of these private intermediaries in the United States and in Israel. "Because they are more likely than parents to be repeat players," Lobel contends, "agencies also have a greater interest in learning the practices of the market and a greater stake with regard to reputation" (2000:11). The efficacy of the agencies as regulatory bodies, however, is limited by the relatively small proportion of Latina immigrant domestic workers they place, and in some instances, as we saw in chapter 4, by the profit motive.

26. Salzinger 1991. By spring 2000 a new domestic workers job cooperative, Dynamic Domestic Workers, was operating in Los Angeles. Funded by the Los Angeles Women's Foundation, and established as a limited liability corporation, this organization did seek to upgrade the conditions of work, as well as make job placements (personal communication with Rosanna Perez, March 2000). Similarly, the Domestic Workers Program, organized through the Hollywood Community Job Center during the spring of 1998, offers job placements together with free English classes and job support (Hunt 1998).

27. During the 1990s, the Service Employees International Union (SEIU), together with workers, clients, and religious organizations, targeted these home care workers for organizing; by 1999 home workers had voted to join unions in five California counties: San Francisco, Contra Costa, Santa Clara, San Mateo, and Los Angeles. Consumer groups representing the elderly care recipients in Los Angeles also supported the unionization of the 74,000 registered home care workers in Los Angeles County (Cleeland 1999b).

28. J. Gordon 2000.

29. Typically, domestic employees file claims for back wages only after they have left the job. It would be unwise and perhaps impossible to take legal action against a current employer.

30. In 1995 Republicans in Congress, led by Newt Gingrich, cut funding to all organizations providing legal services to undocumented immigrants. As a result, the Legal Aid Foundation could no longer advocate on behalf of undocumented immigrants, regardless of the legal issue. The Labor Defense Network clinics eventually closed. Attorneys at Bet Tzedek Legal Services, a Jewish-affiliated organization that offers free legal services to the poor in Los Angeles, then became the principal providers of legal services to domestic workers seeking help with back wage claims (personal communication, Victor Narro, October 1998).

31. Firing an employee may be illegal only when the employer can be shown to have discriminated against the employee—and even then, most paid domestic workers have no case. Title VII of the Civil Rights Act of 1964, which prohibits employment discrimination on the basis of race, color, religion, sex, or national origin, covers only employers with fifteen or more employees; some state laws, such as California's, expand antidiscrimination laws to employers of at least five employees. Thus very few paid domestic workers have any legal recourse. For a list of state civil rights laws as they pertain to paid domestic workers, consult "Appendix B: State Laws," in National Organization for Women 1997:25–31.

32. The case was filed with both the Labor Commissioner's Office and California Superior Court, but was tried in the latter.

33. The case is *Lopez v. Rodriguez*, 500 F.Supp. 79 (D.D.C. 1980), cited in *Yuni Muliyono v. Lina Nilam et al.*, Plaintiff's Arbitration Hearing Brief, for Superior Court of the State of California for the County of Los Angeles, Case No. TC 008 897 (1996).

34. See Rosenweig 1999a, 1999b.

35. Claudia Garáte testified before the California state labor commissioner in Sonoma County that at her employer's home, she was forced to sleep on the floor and work on call, around the clock, twenty-four hours a day and seven days a week for $50 a month. As in the case of Yuni Muliyono, the employers confiscated her passport (see Marinucci 1993; Chang 1994).

36. Private paid domestic work in Los Angeles remains an effectively unregulated, unrecorded, untaxed income-generating activity, part of the informal sector of the economy. Various commentators have underlined the ways in which informal economic sectors are linked to the formal economy, focusing particularly on the spatial concentrations of business and professional services in global cities. Paid domestic work provides a key illustration of these articulations.

37. In a Los Angeles street corner survey of 460 day laborers, most of them Mexican immigrant men, conducted by UCLA professor Abel Valenzuela (1999), 41.5 percent reported that the type of individual most likely to hire them is a private individual (rather than a subcontractor or an individual acting as a boss or the manager of a firm).

38. On wage levels of garment workers in Los Angeles, see Cleeland 1999a. The estimate of 120,000 garment workers in Los Angeles is for 1998 and derives from the calculations of Bonacich and Appelbaum (2000:169).

See their book *Behind the Label* (2000) for an analysis of the rise of sweatshop apparel industry in Los Angeles.

39. In 1997 the Los Angeles City Council voted to join a dozen other cities, including San Francisco and Baltimore, in passing a living wage ordinance for employees under city contract. The Los Angeles Living Wage Ordinance (171547) requires that a "living wage," defined at a minimum of $7.25 an hour, be paid to employees of service contractors of the City of Los Angeles and its financial assistance recipients. Private domestic workers in Los Angeles are not covered by the ordinance, which I cite because it gauges more accurately than does the state or federal minimum wage what it takes to meet the high cost of living in Los Angeles.

40. J. Gordon 2000.

41. See Ross et al. 1997.

References

Arat-Koc, Sedef. 1997. "From 'Mothers of the Nation' to Migrant Workers." In *Not One of the Family: Foreign Domestic Workers in Canada*, edited by Abigail B. Bakan and Daiva Stasiulis, 53–79. Toronto: University of Toronto Press.

Bakan, Abigail B., and Daiva Stasiulis. 1997. "Foreign Domestic Worker Policy in Canada and the Social Boundaries of Modern Citizenship." In *Not One of the Family: Foreign Domestic Workers in Canada*, edited by Abigail B. Bakan and Daiva Stasiulis, 29–52. Toronto: University of Toronto Press.

Baker, Susan Gonzalez, Frank D. Bean, Augustin Escobar Latapi, and Sidney Weintraub. 1998. "Immigration Policies and Trends: The Growing Importance of Migration from Mexico." In *Crossings: Mexican Immigration in Interdisciplinary Perspectives*, edited by Marcelo Suarez-Orozco, 81–109. Cambridge, Mass.: Harvard University Press.

Bates, James. 1999. "Disney Settles Up with Its Former Studio Boss." *Los Angeles Times*, July 8, A1, A10.

Beecher, Catharine E., and Harriet Beecher Stowe. 1869. *The American Woman's Home: or, Principles of Domestic Science, Being a Guide to the Formation and Maintenance of Economical, Healthful, Beautiful, and Christian Homes*. New York: J. B. Ford.

Beneria, Lourdes, and Martha Roldan. 1987. *The Crossroads of Class and Gender: Industrial Homework, Subcontracting, and Household Dynamics*. Chicago: University of Chicago Press.

Bonacich, Edna, and Richard P. Appelbaum. 2000. *Behind the Label: Inequality in the Los Angeles Apparel Industry*. Berkeley: University of California Press.

Braverman, Harry. 1974. *Labor and Monopoly Capital: The Degradation of Work in the Twentieth Century*. New York: Monthly Review Press.

Broom, Leonard, and S. H. Smith. 1963. "Bridging Occupations." *British Journal of Sociology* 14:321–34.

Camarillo, Albert. 1979. *Chicanos in a Changing Society: From Mexican Pueblos to American Barrios in Santa Barbara and Southern California, 1848–1930*. Cambridge, Mass.: Harvard University Press.

Carvajal, Doreen. 1996. "For Immigrant Maids, Not a Job but Servitude." *New York Times*, February 25, C1, C19.

Castro, Mary Garcia. 1989. "What Is Bought and Sold in Domestic Service? The Case of Bogatá: A Critical Review." In *Muchachas No More: Household Workers in Latin America and the Caribbean*, edited by Elsa M. Chaney and Mary Garcia Castro, 105–26. Philadelphia: Temple University Press.

Chaney, Elsa M., and Mary Garcia Castro, editors. 1989. *Muchachas No More: Household Workers in Latin America and the Caribbean*. Philadelphia: Temple University Press.

Chang, Grace. 1994. "Undocumented Latinas: The New 'Employable Mothers.'" In *Mothering: Ideology, Experience, and Agency*, edited by Evelyn Nakano Glenn, Grace Chang, and Linda Rennie Forcey, 259–85. New York: Routledge.

———. 2000. *Disposable Domestics: Immigrant Women Workers in the Global Economy*. Cambridge, Mass.: South End Press.

Chaplin, David. 1978. "Domestic Service and Industrialization." *Comparative Studies in Sociology* 1:97–127.

Chinchilla, Norma Stoltz, and Nora Hamilton. 1997. "Ambiguous Identities: Central Americans in Southern California." Working Paper 14, Chicano/ Latino Research Center, University of California, Santa Cruz.

Clark-Lewis, Elizabeth. 1994. *Living In, Living Out: African American Domestics in Washington, D.C., 1910–1940*. Washington, D.C.: Smithsonian Institution Press.

Clarke-Stewart, Alison. 1993. *Daycare*. Rev. ed. Cambridge, Mass.: Harvard University Press.

Cleeland, Nancy. 1999a. "Garment Jobs: Hard, Bleak, and Vanishing." *Los Angeles Times*, March 11, A1, A14–16.

———. 1999b. "Home-Care Workers Are Expected to Join Union." *Los Angeles Times*, February 24, C1.

Colen, Shellee. 1989. "'Just a Little Respect': West Indian Domestic Workers in New York City." In *Muchachas No More: Household Workers in Latin America and the Caribbean*, edited by Elsa M. Chaney and Mary Garcia Castro, 171–94. Philadelphia: Temple University Press.

———. 1990. "'Housekeeping' for the Green Card: West Indian Household Workers, the State, and Stratified Reproduction in New York." In *At Work in Homes: Household Workers in World Perspective*, edited by Roger Sanjek and Shellee Colen, 89–118. American Ethnological Society Monograph Series 3. Washington, D.C.: American Ethnological Society.

Constable, Nicole. 1997. *Maid to Order in Hong Kong: Stories of Filipina Workers*. Ithaca: Cornell University Press.

Coser, Lewis. 1974. "Servants: The Obsolescence of an Occupational Role." *Social Forces* 52:31–40.

Coutin, Susan Bibler. 1998. "From Refugees to Immigrants: The Legalization Strategies of Salvadoran Immigrants and Activists." *International Migration Review* 32:901–25.

Cowan, Ruth Schartz. 1983. *More Work for Mother: The Ironies of Household Technology from the Open Hearth to the Microwave*. New York: Basic Books.

de Oliveira, Orlandina. 1990. "Empleo femenino en México en tiempos de recesión economica: Tendencias recientes." In *Mujer y crisis: Respuestas ante la recesión*, edited by Neuma Aguilar, 31–54. Caracas: Editorial Nueva Sociedad.

Deutsch, Sarah. 1987. *No Separate Refuge: Culture, Class, and Gender on an Anglo-Hispanic Frontier in the American Southwest, 1880–1940.* New York: Oxford University Press.

DeVault, Marjorie L. 1991. *Feeding the Family: The Social Organization of Caring As Gendered Work.* Chicago: University of Chicago Press.

Dill, Bonnie Thornton. 1988. "'Making Your Job Good Yourself': Domestic Service and the Construction of Personal Dignity." In *Women and the Politics of Empowerment,* edited by Ann Bookman and Sandra Morgen, 33–52. Philadelphia: Temple University Press.

———. 1994. *Across the Boundaries of Race and Class.* New York: Garland.

Donato, Katharine. 1992. "Understanding U.S. Immigration: Why Some Countries Send Women and Others Send Men." In *Seeking Common Ground: Multidisciplinary Studies of Immigrant Women in the United States,* edited by Donna Gabaccia, 159–84. Westport, Conn.: Praeger.

Dudden, Faye. 1983. *Serving Women: Household Service in Nineteenth-Century America.* Middletown, Conn: Wesleyan University Press.

Edwards, Richard. 1979. *Contested Terrain: The Transformation of the Workplace in the Twentieth Century.* New York: Basic Books.

Flanigan, James. 1997. "State's Economy Booming Again—With a Difference." *Los Angeles Times,* May 18, A1, A31.

Folbre, Nancy. 1994. *Who Pays for the Kids? Gender and the Structure of Constraint.* London: Routledge.

Foner, Nancy. 1994. *The Caregiving Dilemma: Work in an American Nursing Home.* Berkeley: University of California Press.

Galvez, Thelma, and Rosalba Todoro. 1989. "Housework for Pay in Chile: Not Just Another Job." In *Muchachas No More: Household Workers in Latin America and the Caribbean,* edited by Elsa M. Chaney and Mary Garcia Castro, 307–21. Philadelphia: Temple University Press.

Garcia, Mario. 1981. *Desert Immigrants: The Mexicans of El Paso, 1880–1920.* New Haven: Yale University Press.

Gill, Lesley. 1994. *Precarious Dependencies: Gender, Class, and Domestic Service in Bolivia.* New York: Columbia University Press.

Glenn, Evelyn Nakano. 1986. *Issei, Nisei, Warbride.* Philadelphia: Temple University Press.

———. 1992. "From Servitude to Service Work: Historical Continuities in the Racial Division of Women's Work." *Signs* 18:1–43.

Goldsmith, Mary. 1989. "Politics and Programs of Domestic Workers' Organizations in Mexico." In *Muchachas No More: Household Workers in Latin America and the Caribbean,* edited by Elsa M. Chaney and Mary Garcia Castro, 221–43. Philadelphia: Temple University Press.

Gordon, Jennifer. 2000. "Immigrants Fight the Power." *Nation,* January 3, 16–20.

Gordon, Larry. 1998. "Economy's Rise Pulls the Richest Along with It." *Los Angeles Times,* June 27, A1, A20.

Gotanda, Neil. 1991. "A Critique of 'Our Constitution Is Color-Blind.'" *Stanford Law Review* 44:1–68.

Granovetter, Mark. 1973. "The Strength of Weak Ties." *American Journal of Sociology* 79:1360–80.

———. 1985. "Economic Action and Social Structure: The Problem of Embeddedness." *American Journal of Sociology* 91:481–510.

———. 1992. "The Sociological and Economic Approaches to Labor Market Analysis." In *The Sociology of Economic Life*, edited by Mark Granovetter and Richard Swedberg, 233–63. Boulder, Colo.: Westview.

———. 1995. "The Economic Sociology of Firms and Entrepreneurs." In *The Economic Sociology of Immigration: Essays on Networks, Ethnicity, and Entrepreneurship*, edited by Alejandro Portes, 128–65. New York: Russell Sage Foundation.

Grant, David M., Melvin L. Oliver, and Angela D. James. 1996. "African Americans: Social and Economic Bifurcation." In *Ethnic Los Angeles*, edited by Roger Waldinger and Mehdi Bozorgmehr, 379–411. New York: Russell Sage Foundation.

Hagan, Jacqueline Maria. 1994. *Deciding to Be Legal: A Maya Community in Houston.* Philadelphia: Temple University Press.

———. 1998. "Social Networks, Gender, and Immigrant Incorporation." *American Sociological Review* 63:55–67.

Hansen, Karen Tranberg. 1989. *Distant Companions: Servants and Employers in Zambia, 1900–1985.* Ithaca: Cornell University Press.

Healy, Melissa. 1999. "Lawmakers Respond to a Mother's Mission." *Los Angeles Times,* September 26, A3.

Hirschman, Albert O. 1970. *Exit, Voice, and Loyalty: Responses to Decline in Firms, Organizations, and States.* Cambridge, Mass.: Harvard University Press.

Hochschild, Arlie Russell. 1983. *The Managed Heart: Commercialization of Human Feeling.* Berkeley: University of California Press.

———. 1989. *The Second Shift: Working Parents and the Revolution at Home.* With Anne Machung. New York: Viking.

———. 1997. *The Time Bind: When Work Becomes Home and Home Becomes Work.* New York: Metropolitan Books, Henry Holt.

Hondagneu-Sotelo, Pierrette. 1994a. *Gendered Transitions: Mexican Experiences of Immigration.* Berkeley: University of California Press.

———. 1994b. "Regulating the Unregulated: Domestic Workers' Social Networks." *Social Problems* 41:201–15.

———. 1995. "Women and Children First: New Directions in Anti-Immigrant Politics." *Socialist Review* 25:169–90.

———. 1997a. "Affluent Players in the Informal Economy: Employers of Paid Domestic Workers." *International Journal of Sociology and Social Policy* 17(3/4):131–59.

———. 1997b. "Working 'without papers' in the U.S.: Toward the Integration of Legal Status in Frameworks of Race, Class, and Gender." In *Women and Work: Race, Class, and Ethnicity*, edited by Elizabeth Higginbotham and Mary Romero, 101–25. Beverly Hills, Calif.: Sage.

Hondagneu-Sotelo, Pierrette, and Ernestine Avila. 1997. "'I'm Here, But I'm There': The Meanings of Latina Transnational Motherhood." *Gender and Society* 11:548–71.

Hondagneu-Sotelo, Pierrette, and Cristina Riegos. 1997. *"Sin Organización, No Hay Solución:* Latina Domestic Workers and Non-traditional Labor Organizing." *Latino Studies Journal* 8:54–81.

Hunt, Tamara. 1998. "Maid to Be Equals." *Westside Weekly,* Friday and Saturday supplement to the *Los Angeles Times,* July 17, D1, D4.

Ibarra, Maria Luz. In press. "Mexican Immigrant Women and the New Domestic Labor." *Human Organization* (forthcoming fall 2000).

Jelin, Elizabeth. 1977. "Migration and Labor Force Participation of Latin American Women: The Domestic Servants in the Cities." *Signs* 3:129–41.

Jonas, Suzanne. n.d. "Transnational Realities and Anti-Immigrant State Policies: Issues Raised by the Experiences of Central American Immigrants and Refugees in a Trinational Region." Working Paper 7, Chicano/Latino Research Center, University of California, Santa Cruz.

Kaplan, Elaine Bell. 1987. "'I Don't Do No Windows': Competition between the Domestic Worker and the Housewife." In *Competition: A Feminist Taboo?* edited by Valerie Miner and Helen E. Longino, 92–105. New York: Feminist Press.

Katzman, David M. 1981. *Seven Days a Week: Women and Domestic Service in Industrializing America.* Urbana: University of Illinois Press.

Kim, Claire Jean. 1999. "The Racial Triangulation of Asian Americans." *Politics and Society* 27:103–36.

Lacher, Irene. 1997. "An Interior Mind." *Los Angeles Times,* March 16, E1, E3.

Lan, Pei-chia. 2000. "Global Divisions, Local Identities: Filipina Migrant Domestic Workers and Taiwanese Employers." Diss., Northwestern University.

Laslett, Barbara, and Joanna Brenner. 1989. "Gender and Social Reproduction: Historical Perspectives." *Annual Review of Sociology* 15:381–404.

"Law Threatens State Domestic-Chore Services." 1977. *Los Angeles Times,* January 6, A9.

Lawrence, John F. 1978. Editorial Viewpoint: "Household-Help Laws Discourage Hiring, Encourage Cheating." *Los Angeles Times,* September 17, C8.

Leon, Magdalena. 1989. "Domestic Labor and Domestic Service in Colombia." In *Muchachas No More: Household Workers in Latin America and the Caribbean,* edited by Elsa M. Chaney and Mary Garcia Castro, 323–49. Philadelphia: Temple University Press.

Liddick, Betty. 1973a. "A Critical Game of Hide and Seek: Plight of the Foreign Domestics." *Los Angeles Times,* June 8, B4.

———. 1973b. "The Domestics—A Quest for Clout." *Los Angeles Times,* March 19, B1.

Lobel, Orly. 2000. "Class and Care: The Roles of Private Intermediaries of the In-Home Care Industry in the United States and in Israel." Paper written for Harvard Law School seminar, spring.

Lomas, Marta. 2000. "Editorial: El Trabajo Doméstico." Special issue on "Intimidad y Servicios" (Intimacy and Service). *Debate Feminista* 22 (October).

Lopez, David E., Eric Popkin, and Edward Telles. 1996. "Central Americans: At the Bottom, Struggling to Get Ahead." In *Ethnic Los Angeles,* edited by Roger Waldinger and Mehdi Bozorgmehr, 279–304. New York: Russell Sage Foundation.

Lowe, Lisa. 1996. *Immigrant Acts: On Asian American Cultural Politics.* Durham: Duke University Press.

Macdonald, Cameron. 1998. "Manufacturing Motherhood: The Shadow Work of Nannies and Au Pair." *Qualitative Sociology* 21(1):25–53.

Macklin, Audrey. 1994. "On the Inside Looking In: Foreign Domestic Workers in Canada." In *Maid in the Market: Women's Paid Domestic Labour,* edited by Wenona Giles and Sedef Arat-Koc, 13–39. Halifax, Nova Scotia: Fernwood.

Mahler, Sarah J. 1995. *American Dreaming: Immigrant Life on the Margins.* Princeton: Princeton University Press.

———. 1999. "Engendering Transnational Migration: A Case Study of Salvadorans." *American Behavioral Scientist* 42:690–719.

Mar, D., and M. Kim. 1994. "Historical Trends." In *The State of Asian Pacific America: Economic Diversity, Issues, and Policies,* edited by Paul Ong, 13–30. Los Angeles: LEAP Asian Pacific American Public Policy Institute and UCLA Asian American Studies Center.

Marinucci, Carla. 1993. "Immigrant Abuse: 'Slavery—Pure and Simple.'" *San Francisco Examiner,* January 10, A1, A8.

Martin, Linda, and Kerry Segrave. 1985. *The Servant Problem: Domestic Workers in North America.* Jefferson, N.C.: McFarlands.

Massey, Douglas S., Rafael Alarcon, Jorge Durand, and Humberto Gonzalez. 1987. *Return to Aztlan: The Social Process of International Migration from Western Mexico.* Berkeley: University of California Press.

Mattingly, Doreen J. 1999. "Job Search, Social Networks, and Local Labor Market Dynamics: The Case of Paid Household Work in San Diego, California." *Urban Geography* 20(1):46–74.

———. 1999. "Making Maids: United States Immigration Policy and Immigrant Domestic Workers." In *Gender, Migration, and Domestic Service,* edited by Janet Henshall Momsen, 62–79. New York: Routledge.

McBride, Theresa. 1976. *The Domestic Revolution: The Modernization of Household Service in England and France, 1820–1920.* New York: Holmes and Meier.

McDonnell, Patrick J. 1999. "U.S. to Pay $400,000 to INS Agent in Bias Suit." *Los Angeles Times,* January 21, B1, B5.

Meagher, Gabrielle. 1997. "Recreating 'Domestic Service': Institutional Cultures and the Evolution of Paid Household Work." *Feminist Economics* 3(2):1–27.

Mendez, Jennifer Bickham. 1998. "Of Mops and Maids: Contradictions and Continuities in Bureaucratized Domestic Work." *Social Problems* 45:114–35.

Menjívar, Cecilia. 1999. "The Intersection of Work and Gender: Central American Immigrant Women and Employment in California." *American Behavioral Scientist* 42:601–27.

———. 2000. *Fragmented Ties: Salvadoran Immigrant Networks in America.* Berkeley: University of California Press.

Milkman, Ruth, Ellen Reese, and Benita Roth. 1998. "The Macrosociology of Paid Domestic Labor." *Work and Occupations* 25:483–510.

Min, Pyong Gap. 1996. *Caught in the Middle: Korean Communities in New York and Los Angeles.* Berkeley: University of California Press.

Mitchell, Alana. 1993. "New Rules Create Greater Nanny Shortage." *Globe and Mail*, January 23, A5.

Momsen, Janet Henshall, editor. 1999. *Gender, Migration, and Domestic Service.* New York: Routledge.

Myers, Dowell, and Cynthia J. Cranford. 1998. "Temporal Differentiation in the Occupational Mobility of Immigrant and Native-Born Latina Workers." *American Sociological Review* 63:68–93.

National Organization for Women. 1997. *Out of the Shadows: Strategies for Expanding State Labor and Civil Rights Protections for Domestic Workers.* New York: NOW Legal Defense and Education Fund.

Neckerman, Kathryn M., and Joleen Kirschenman. 1991. "Hiring Strategies, Racial Bias, and Inner-City Workers." *Social Problems* 38:433–47.

Nieves, Isabel. 1979. "Household Arrangements and Multiple Jobs in San Salvador." *Signs* 5:139–50.

Olivio, Antonio. 1999. "Salvadorans Stake Their Claim in Southland Political Game." *Los Angeles Times*, April 11, B1, B8.

Omi, Michael, and Howard Winant. 1994. *Racial Formation in the United States: From the 1960s to the 1980s.* 2d ed. New York: Routledge.

Ong, Paul, and Tania Azores. 1994. "Health Professionals on the Front Line." In *The State of Asian Pacific America: Economic Diversity, Issues, and Policies,* edited by Paul Ong, 139–63. Los Angeles: LEAP Asian Pacific American Public Policy Institute and UCLA Asian American Studies Center.

Ortiz, Vilma. 1996. "The Mexican-Origin Population: Permanent Working Class or Emerging Middle Class?" In *Ethnic Los Angeles,* edited by Roger Waldinger and Mehdi Bozorgmehr, 247–77. New York: Russell Sage Foundation.

Ozyegin, Gul. 1995. "The View from Downstairs: Place and Stigma in the Lives of Caretakers' Wives." Paper presented at the Habitat II Preconference on Housing Question of "Others." Bilkent University, Ankara, Turkey, November.

———. 2001. *Untidy Gender: Domestic Service in Turkey.* Philadelphia: Temple University Press.

Palmer, Phyllis. 1984. "Housework and Domestic Labor: Racial and Technological Change." In *My Troubles Are Going to Have Trouble with Me,* edited by Karen Brodkin Sacks and Dorothy Remy, 80–91. New Brunswick, N.J.: Rutgers University Press.

———. 1989. *Domesticity and Dirt: Housewives and Domestic Servants in the United States, 1920–1945.* Philadelphia: Temple University Press.

Parreñas, Rhacel Salazar. 2000. "Migrant Filipina Domestic Workers and the International Division of Reproductive Labor." *Gender and Society* 14:560–80.

———. 2001. *Servants of Globalization: Women, Migration, and Domestic Work.* Stanford University Press.

Pastor, Manuel. 1998. "Interdependence, Inequality, and Identity: Linking Latinos and Latin Americans." In *Borderless Borders: U.S. Latinos, Latin Americans, and the Paradox of Interdependence,* edited by Frank Bonilla, Edwin Melendez, Rebecca Morales, and Maria de los Angeles Torres, 17–33. Philadelphia: Temple University Press.

Pollin, Robert. 1998. *The Living Wage: Building a Fair Economy.* New York: Free Press.

———. 1999. Column Left Commentary: "Living Wage Gives a Boost to Demand." *Los Angeles Times,* April 1, B9.

Portes, Alejandro. 1994. "When More Can Be Less: Labor Standards Development and the Informal Economy." In *Contrapunto: The Informal Sector Debate in Latin America,* edited by Cathy A. Rakowski, 113–29. Albany: State University of New York Press.

Portes, Alejandro, and Julia Sessenbrenner. 1993. "Embeddedness and Immigration: Notes on the Social Determinants of Economic Action." *American Journal of Sociology* 98:1320–50.

Powers, Marilyn. 1990. "Occupational Mobility of Black and White Women Service Workers." Paper presented at the Second Annual Women's Policy Research Conference, Institute for Women's Policy Research, Washington, D.C.

Prates, Suzana. 1989. "Organizations for Domestic Workers in Montevideo: Reinforcing Marginality?" In *Muchachas No More: Household Workers in Latin America and the Caribbean,* edited by Elsa M. Chaney and Mary Garcia Castro, 271–90. Philadelphia: Temple University Press.

Repak, Terry A. 1995. *Waiting on Washington: Central American Workers in the Nation's Capital.* Philadelphia: Temple University Press.

"Repeal of Law to Insure Domestic Help Clears Panel." 1977. *Los Angeles Times,* January 4, A5.

Richmond, Anthony. 1994. *Global Apartheid: Refugees, Racism, and the New World Order.* Toronto: Oxford University Press.

Rollins, Judith. 1985. *Between Women: Domestics and Their Employers.* Philadelphia: Temple University Press.

Romero, Mary. 1992. *Maid in the U.S.A.* New York: Routledge.

———. 1996. "Life as the Maid's Daughter: An Exploration of the Everyday Boundaries of Race, Class, and Gender." In *Feminisms in the Academy: Rethinking the Disciplines,* edited by Abigail J. Steward and Donna Stanton, 186–219. Ann Arbor: University of Michigan Press.

———. 1997. "Who Takes Care of the Maid's Children? Exploring the Costs of Domestic Service." In *Feminism and Families,* edited by Hilde L. Nelson, 63–91. New York: Routledge.

Ross, Andrew, et al. 1997. *No Sweat: Fashion, Free Trade, and the Rights of Garment Workers.* Verso.

Rosenweig, David. 1999a. "Jury Convicts Woman of Exploiting Thai Workers." *Los Angeles Times,* August 13, B1–3.

———. 1999b. "Thai Illegal Immigrant Testifies in Slavery Trial." *Los Angeles Times,* July 21, B1.

Ruiz, Vicki L. 1987. "By the Day or the Week: Mexicana Domestic Workers in El Paso." In *Women on the U.S.-Mexico Border: Responses to Change,* edited by Vicki L. Ruiz and Susan Tiano, 61–76. Boston: Allen and Unwin.

Salzinger, Leslie. 1991. "A Maid by Any Other Name: The Transformation of 'Dirty Work' by Central American Immigrants." In *Ethnography Unbound: Power and Resistance in the Modern Metropolis,* by Michael Burawoy et al., 139–60. Berkeley: University of California Press.

Sassen, Saskia. 1991. *The Global City: New York, London, Tokyo.* Princeton: Princeton University Press.

———. 1998. "Service Employment Regimes and the New Inequality." In *Globalization and Its Discontents: Essays on the New Mobility of People and Money,* edited by Saskia Sassen, 137–51. New York: New Press.

Schmidt, Katharine A. 1991. "Domestic Workers Note Abuse, Low Pay." *Santa Monica Outlook,* November 5, A1, A3.

Schor, Juliet B. 1992. *The Overworked American: The Unexpected Decline of Leisure.* New York: Basic Books.

Simon, Rita J., and Margot DeLey. 1984. "The Work Experience of Undocumented Mexican Women Migrants in Los Angeles." *International Migration Review* 18:1212–29.

Smith, Margo L. 1973. "Domestic Service as a Channel of Upward Mobility for the Lower-Class Woman: The Lima Case." In *Female and Male in Latin America: Essays,* edited by Ann Pescatello, 192–207. Pittsburgh: University of Pittsburgh Press.

Solorzano-Torres, Rosalia. 1987. "Female Mexican Immigrants in San Diego County." In *Women on the U.S-Mexico Border: Responses to Change,* edited by Vicki L. Ruiz and Susan Tiano, 41–59. Boston: Allen and Unwin.

Steinberg, Stephen. 1989. "Why Irish Became Domestics and Italians and Jews Did Not." In *The Ethnic Myth: Race, Ethnicity, and Class in America,* 151–66. Updated and expanded ed. Boston: Beacon Press.

Stone, Deborah. 1998. "Valuing 'Caring Work': Rethinking the Nature of Work in Human Services." Typescript, Radcliffe Public Policy Institute, April.

Sutherland, Daniel. 1981. *Americans and Their Servants: Domestic Service in the United States from 1800 to 1920.* Baton Rouge: Louisiana State University Press.

Tamaki, Julie. 2000. "State's Minimum Wage to Increase to $6.75 by 2002." *Los Angeles Times,* October 24, A3–14.

Taylor, Frederick Winslow. 1911. *The Principles of Scientific Management.* New York: Harper.

Trevizo, Dolores. 1990. "Latina Baby-'Watchers' and the Commodification of Care." M.A. thesis, UCLA.

Tucker, Susan. 1988. *Telling Memories among Southern Women: Domestic Workers and Their Employers in the Segregated South.* Baton Rouge: Louisiana State University Press.

Ulloa, Roxana Elizabeth. 1998. "De indocumentados a cuidadanos: Caracteristicas de los salvadorenos legalizados en Estados Unidos." Typescript, Facultad Latinoamericana para las Ciencias Sociales (FLACSO-El Salvador).

Valenzuela, Abel, Jr. 1999. "Day Laborers in Southern California: Preliminary Findings from the Day Labor Survey." UCLA Center for the Study of Urban Poverty Working Paper Series, May 30.

Vanek, Joann. 1974. "Time Spent in Housework." *Scientific American,* November, 116–20.

Waldinger, Roger. 1996. "Ethnicity and Opportunity in the Plural City." In *Ethnic Los Angeles,* edited by Roger Waldinger and Mehdi Bozorgmehr, 445–70. New York: Russell Sage Foundation..

Waldinger, Roger, and Mehdi Bozorgmehr. 1996. "The Making of a Multicultural Metropolis." In *Ethnic Los Angeles,* edited by Roger Waldinger and Mehdi Bozorgmehr, 3–37. New York: Russell Sage Foundation.

Wilkinson, Tracy. 1992. "To Protect Those Who Must Serve." *Los Angeles Times,* February 2, A1, A12.

Wong, Sau-ling C. 1994. "Diverted Mothering: Representations of Caregivers of Color in the Age of 'Multiculturalism.'" In *Mothering: Ideology, Experience, and Agency,* edited by Evelyn Nakano Glenn, Grace Chang, and Linda Rennie Forcey, 67–91. New York: Routledge.

Wrigley, Julia. 1995. *Other People's Children.* New York: Basic Books.

Yates, Michael D. 1994. *Longer Hours, Fewer Jobs: Employment and Unemployment in the United States.* New York: Monthly Review Press.

Yeoh, Brenda, Shirlena Huang, and Joaquin Gonzalez III. 1999. "Migrant Female Domestic Workers: Debating the Economic, Social, and Political Impacts in Singapore." *International Migration Review* 33:114–36.

Index

Abzug, Bella S., 262n6
African American domestic workers, 8,
  15–17, 48, 56, 197, 252n6, 253n7
  organization of, 220
Agencies. *See* Cleaning service agencies;
  Domestic employment agencies
Amnesty program, 13, 248n21
Anaheim School Board, 24–25
Arat-Koc, Sedef, 211
Arau, Sergio, 245n1
Arizmendi, Yareli, 245n1
Asian immigrant women, 15, 54–55,
  197, 250n41
  see also Filipina immigrants
Avila, Ernestine, xviii, 50

Back wage claims, 228, 229–38, 265n29
  English as important in winning, 234,
    236
  Muliyono, Yuni, 234, 235–38
  process for, 231–33
  winning and collecting judgment, 234–
    35
Baird, Zoë
  uproar over, ix, xv, 21, 86, 215–16,
    245n2
Bakan, Abigail B., 250n45
Beecher, Catharine E., 9, 248n17
Bet Tzedek Legal Services, 266n30
Blowups, 114–28
  causes of, 125–27
  consequences of, 132–34
  as epiphany for nanny/housekeepers,
    122–25
  legal rights in, 127–28
  see also Job termination
Bracero Program, 7, 25
Braverman, Harry, 259n1
Brenner, Joanna, 23, 251n52
Burke, Yvonne Braithwaite, 262n6

California Industrial Welfare Commission Wage Order 15, 214, 262n7,
  262n11, 262n12

California Labor Commissioner, 12
Camarillo, Albert, 249n33
Canada
  government and domestic workers in,
    20, 21, 250n45
Care work, 23
  affiliation in, 10, 194, 218
  autonomy and authority in childrear-
    ing in, 153–58
  employee relations with children in,
    39–40
  employee values of, 39
  not covered by Fair Labor Standards
    Act, 212–20
  talking and listening in, 217–18
Caribbean immigrant women, 6, 13, 14,
  17–19, 24, 20, 48, 50, 219
  in Canada, 21, 48
Central American women, 7, 8, 13, 17–
  19, 64, 236
  children of, 25, 49–51, 97, 254n18
  dominance of in Los Angeles domes-
    tic work, 52–55
  see also Guatemalan immigrant women;
    Salvadoran immigrant women
Cedillo, Gilbert, 242
Cervantes, Nancy, 230, 231, 232, 233,
  234
Chang, Grace, 265n24
Chaplin, David, 246n1
Chávez, César, 265n24
CHIRLA (Coalition for Humane Immigrant Rights of Los Angeles), xv,
  221–22, 242
  see also Domestic Workers' Associa-
    tion
Chisholm, Shirley, 262n6
Civil Rights Act of 1964, 16, 266n31
Clark-Lewis, Elizabeth, 36–37, 250n40,
  252n6
Class
  downward mobility and personalism,
    198–203
  and employee relations, 188–93

Cleaning service agencies, 164–68
    sample checklist of, 166–67
Clinton, William Jefferson, 248n22
Coalition for Humane Immigrant
    Rights. *See* CHIRLA
Cohen, Sarah, 216, 230, 231, 232, 233,
    235
Collective organizing, 219–29
    see also Domestic Workers Association;
    Unionization
Constable, Nicole, 20, 251n51, 260n16
Coser, Lewis, 246n1
Cranford, Cynthia, 247n10

DeVault, Marjorie, 148
Dignity. *See* Social recognition
Dill, Bonnie Thornton, 171–72
Domestic employment agencies, 92–113,
    256n3, 2567n5, 265n25
    documentation requirements of, 99–
        100
    fees of, 95, 257n7
    grooming of applicants by, 109–13
    racial preferences and, 93, 100–103
    referrals and trust, 95–101, 109
    screening of employer clients by, 102–
        7, 257n6
Domestic suboccupations, 47–53
    see also Housecleaners; Live-in nanny/
    housekeepers; Live-out nanny/
    housekeepers
Domestic Worker Appreciation Day, 242
Domestic workers
    Central American and Mexican
        women's predominance as, 52–55
    demand for, xii, 4–22, 27
    employment status of, 9–12
    global trends in, 6–7, 17, 19–22
    racialization of. *See* Racialization of
        paid domestic work
    see also Employees; Housecleaners;
    Live-in nanny/housekeepers; Live-
    out nanny/housekeepers; Nanny/
    housekeepers
Domestic Workers' Association (DWA),
    xv, xix, 111, 215, 217, 235, 242,
    264n19
    demands of, 217, 219, 222, 227–29,
        242, 243
    Muliyono, Yuni, and, 235, 236
    novelas of, 222, 223 (fig. 3), 224, 225
        (fig. 4)
    organization of, 221–22, 224, 226
    Super Doméstica icon of, 224, 225
        (fig. 4)
Dudden, Faye, 168

DWA. *See* Domestic Workers Association
Dynamic Domestic Workers, 265n26

Earnings. *See* Wages and hours
Economic factors in demand for paid
    domestic work, 5–9
Economic incorporation of immigrants
    in homes, 1, 238–42
Edwards, Richard, 258–59n1
Elder care, 251–52n57, 253n12
Employees
    ambivalent worker identity, 9, 219
    complaints of work load increases
        without pay increases, 138, 148, 158–
        61
    concentration of Central American
        immigrant women, 8–9
    on employers, 40
    on employers' parent-child relations,
        40–42, 153–54
    isolation of, 237–38
    occupation of prior to U.S. migration,
        29
    racial preferences of, 56–60, 101–2
    social networks of, 65–76
    social recognition of, 11, 144
    social relations with employer. *See*
        Employer-employee relationship
    stigma of, 12, 220
    see also Domestic workers
Employer
    ambivalence of, xi, 10–11; about labor
        control, *see* Labor control
    class heterogeneity and occupation, 6,
        9
    directives of. *See* Labor control
    distrust of employees, 68–70
    immigrant, 237–38
    prejudices against child care centers,
        4
    racial preferences of, 56–58, 102–4
    reluctance to accept employer obliga-
        tions, 139
    social relations with employees. *See*
        Employer–employee relationship
    trust established through network re-
        ferrals, 76–80
Employer-employee relationship
    distance in, 11
    and employer class status, 188–92
    and employer preference of minimiz-
        ing social interaction, 171–73, 192,
        196–97
    among housecleaners, 180–86, 194,
        203–4
    maternalism in, xx, 10–12, 172, 207–9;

as mechanism of exploitation 171–201

personalism in, xx, 72, 207–9; and employees' downward class mobility, 198–201; employees' preferences for, 193–95, 201–5; among employers with jobs, 172–81; among homemaker employers, 181–87; shaped by care work tasks, 194–95

Employment agencies. *See* Domestic employment agencies

Employment regulations
California Industrial Welfare Commission Wage Order 15, 214, 262n7, 262n11, 262n12
Fair Labor Standards Act, 212–13, 220, 261n5, 261–62n6
on firing, 127–28
lack of effective, x, 213, 216, 241
and lack of written employment contracts, 241
laissez-faire approach to, 19–20
and limitations of federal legislation, 212
on room and board deductions, 214
state regulations of wage and hours, 213–14
on overtime, 214
on wages and hours, 211

Employment taxes, 86, 211, 215, 263n15
and Social Security Domestic Reform Act of 1994, 215, 263n16

"English Only" campaigns, 18

European immigrant women, 14, 56

Fair Labor Standards Act (FLSA), 212–13, 215, 220, 261n5, 261–62n6

Federal Insurance Contributions Act (FICA), 215

Filipina immigrants, 54–55
in Canada, 21, 48, 250n45
in Hong Kong, 20, 168, 251n47, 260n16
as nurses, 255n30

Firing, 114–28, 266n31

Food
labor laws and, 214
nanny/housekeepers on, 33–35, 39
women, family, and, 148

Garáte, Claudia, 237, 266n35

Gingrich, Newt, 266n30

Glenn, Evelyn Nakano, 15, 32, 249n32, 249–50n36, 251n51, 251n52, 253n7, 264–65n24

Globalization of paid domestic work, 6–7, 17, 19–22

González-López, Gloria, xviii

Granovetter, Mark, 90–91

Grasso, Ella T., 262n6

Green, Edith, 262n6

Griffiths, Martha W., 262n6

Guatemalan immigrant women, 6, 8, 53–54
in Houston, 252–53n6, 255n2
see also Central American women

Guzman, Jorge, 253–54n14

Hagan, Jacqueline Maria, 253n6, 255n2

Hansen, Julia Butler, 262n6

Hiring. *See* Recruitment.

Hirschman, Albert O., 133

Hochschild, Arlie, 175, 259n6

Holidays
expectations about, 108, 126

Hollywood Community Job Center's Domestic Workers Program, 265n26

Holt, Marjorie S., 262n6

Holtzman, Elizabeth, 262n6

Homemakers
housecleaners and, 181–82
maternalism of, 182–88

Hong Kong
migrant domestic workers in, 19–22, 168, 250–52n47, 260n16

Hondagneu-Sotelo, Pierrette, 50, 250n42

Hours. *See* Wages and hours

Housecleaners, 28, 43–47, 255n2, 255n3, 263n15
agencies of, 164–68
control of time by, 158–61
employed employers and, 180–81
employers' search for, 76–81
finding work, 70–76
homemakers and, 181–88
network referrals for, 46, 70, 78–80
on personalism, 194–95, 203–4
wages and hours of, 45–47, 51, 83, 241
work expected of, 156–68

Household Technicians of America (HTA), 264n24

Houston domestic workers, 252–53n6, 255n2

Huffington, Michael, 245n2

Immigration and Naturalization Service Form I-9, 264n17

Immigration Reform Act and Individual Responsibility Act (IRAIRA, 1996), 18

Immigration Reform and Control Act
  (IRCA, 1986), 13, 263–64n17
Immigrant women
  Asian, 15, 54–55, 197, 250n41
  Central American, 3, 8, 25, 52–53; *see
    also* Central American women
  employment of prior to migration, 29–
    30
  European, 14, 56
  Mexican, 7, 8, 13, 52–53
  undocumented, 18, 48–49
Immigration legislation, 7, 13–14, 18, 24–
    25, 263–64n17
  Bracero Program, 7, 25
  foreign contract labor programs, 20–
    22
Industrial Welfare Commission (IWC).
    See California Industrial Welfare
    Commission Wage Order 15
Informal economic sector, x, 211, 238–39
Internal Revenue Service
  on employment taxes, 216
International Labor Organization (ILO),
    255n3

Japanese immigrant women, 15, 249n31,
    253n7
Job task(s), xx, 22–24
  lack of standardization of, 23–24,138
  meal preparation as, 23–24, 148
Job termination
  through excuses, 128–32
  firing and quitting, 114–28, 266n31
"Job work," 157
Jordan, Barbara, 262n6

Katzenberg, Jeffrey, 128
Katzman, David M., 14, 197, 249n31
Korean immigrant women, 3, 54,
    255n28

Labor control
  and ambiguous job requirements, 138–
    53
  in child rearing, 153–58
  emotional leverage in, 149–53
  and employees' preference for auton-
    omy, 115, 139, 153
  and employees' preferences for direc-
    tives, 138, 142, 169
  and employers' desire for employee
    initiative, 141–44
  of full-time nanny/housekeepers, 141–
    56
  and housecleaners' autonomy, 156–58

  in live-in jobs, 145–47
  racially conferred, 148–49, 153–56
  routinization and rationalization of, in
    cleaning service agencies, 165–68
  surveillance and, 146–47
  Tayloristic, 168
  through time control, 139, 168–70
Labor Defense Network clinics, 266n30
Labor laws. *See* Employment regulation
Laslett, Barbara, 23, 251n52
Lawrence, John F., 261n4
Legal Aid Foundation of Los Angeles,
    229, 232, 266n30
Liberty Hill Foundation, 222
Listo (Los Angeles cooperative), 229
Live-in nanny/housekeepers, 5, 28, 30–
    37, 256n2
  as entry-level job, 49–50, 63
  and food, 33–36, 114
  isolation of, 30–33, 114
  sleeping arrangements of, 30–33, 142,
    145
  wages and hours of, 35–37, 50–51,
    145, 213, 241, 252n4, 263n13
  see also Nanny/housekeepers
Live-out nanny/housekeepers, 28, 37–43
  cleaning and child care by, 38
  relations of with employers and chil-
    dren, 41–43
  wages and hours of, 38, 51
  see also Nanny/housekeepers
Living Wage Ordinance (Los Angeles),
    241, 267n39
Lobel, Orly, 255n3, 265n25
Lopez, David, 52, 254n20
Los Angeles Women's Foundation,
    265n26

Manos (San Francisco cooperative), 229
Martin, Linda, 261n5
Marx, Karl, 258–59n1
Maternalism, 172, 182–88, 259n3
  vs. personalism, 172, 207–9
Medicare, 215, 263n16
Mendez, Jennifer Bickham, 164, 174–79
Mexican American domestic workers,
    15–16, 245n1
Mexican immigrant women, 6, 7, 8, 13,
    52–53, 245n1, 254n23
  children of, 24–26
Milkman, Ruth, 6, 246–47n5
Mink, Patsy T., 262n6
Muliyono, Yuni, 212, 234, 235–37,
    266n35
Myers, Dowell, 247n10

Nanny/housekeepers
   labor laws and, 212–14
   on personalism, 194–98
   tasks expected of, 141–56
   "white middle-class," 94, 102–3, 110–
      11, 148
   see also Live-in nanny/housekeepers;
      Live-out nanny housekeepers
Narro, Victor, 242
National Committee on Household Employment (NCHE), 212, 219–22,
   261n6, 264n22, 264n24
National Council on Negro Women, 220
National Day of Conscience, 243
National Labor Relations Act (1935),
   221
National Lawyers Guild, 229
Nixon, Richard, 261n5
Novelas
   for domestic workers, 222, 223 (fig. 3),
      224, 225 (fig. 4)

Occupational mobility, 239–42
Occupational upgrading. *See* Back wage
   claims; Collective organizing; Employment regulations

Palmer, Phyllis, 57, 219, 251n51, 264n24
Parreñas, Rhacel, 19, 55, 251n51
Personalism
   class distinctions among employers
      and, 188–92
   defined, 172
   downward class mobility and, 198–
      203
   employees' view of, 193–207
   employed employers and, 172–81
   homemakers and, 181–82
   maternalism vs., 172, 207–9
   particularism vs., 260n6
Pets
   nanny/housekeepers on, 39–40
Popkin, Eric, 254n20
Portes, Alejandro, 127–28
Proposition 187 (California), xv, 18, 24,
   60, 100–101, 193, 234

Racialization of language, 236–37
Racialization of paid domestic work
   and African American women, 15–17,
      197
   and Asian American women, 15, 197
   and Central American, Mexican, and
      Caribbean immigrant women, 13–
      19, 48–55

and Chicana/Mexican American
   women, 13–17, 197
and domestic employment agencies,
   94–111
employees' preferences in, 56–60, 101–
   2
employers' preferences in, 56–58, 102–
   4, 148–49
and Filipinas, 19–20
global, and immigration, 13, 19–22, 24
regional, in United States, xii, 13–19
and "white middle-class" nannies, 94,
   102–3, 110–11, 148
Racialized nativism, 17–20, 24, 208
Recruitment
   by domestic employment agencies, 92–
      113
   among housecleaners, 70–76
   newspaper advertisements for, 65, 92–
      94
   social network references in, xix–xx,
      17, 61–91
   wage rates in, 81–91
Reese, Ellen, 246–47n5
Regulations. *See* Employment regulations
Repak, Terry, 53
Research description, x, xv–xix, 29
Respect. *See* Social recognition
Richmond, Anthony, 19
Riegos, Cristina, 226
Rivera, Libertad, 226
Rodríguez, Marcos, 235, 236
Rollins, Judith, 28, 197, 248n19, 248–
   49n26, 259n3
Romero, Mary, 9, 16, 29, 91, 168, 170,
   175, 207, 248n16, 251n51
   on housecleaning, 45, 46, 157
Roosevelt, Eleanor, 219
Roth, Benita, 246–47n5

Salvadoran immigrant women, 6, 8, 53–
   54, 247n12, 247–48n13
   see also Central American women
Salzinger, Leslie, 248n15
Sassen, Saskia, 6, 247n7
Schor, Juliet B., 246n4
Schroeder, Patricia, 262n6
Seagrave, Kerry, 261n5
Service Employees International Union
   (SEIU), 229, 240, 265n27
Small Claims Court, 232
Social networks
   of employers, in labor control, 143
   in hiring, xix–xx, 17, 61–91

Social recognition, 11, 144–45, 217–18
Social reproduction, 22–27
Social Security, 215–16, 249n26, 263n16
    domestic workers on, 217
    employers' verification of card, 263–64n17
Social Security Domestic Reform Act
    (1994), 215, 263n16
Stone, Deborah, 10, 218
Stowe, Harriet Beecher, 9, 248n17
Stasiulis, Daiva, 250n45
Sullivan, Leonor K., 262n6
Super Doméstica icon, 224, 225 (fig. 4)
Surveillance, 140 (fig. 2), 146–47

Taxes. *See* Employment taxes
Taylor, Frederick Winslow, 260n12
Telles, Edward, 254n20
Time
    scarcity in employer families, 5, 172–78
    on task vs. on job, 147–49
    see also Wages and hours
Transnationalism
    motherhood and, 22–27, 48–52, 152–53, 243
    parallels with slavery and contract labor, 51
Tyner, James A., 251n48

Undocumented workers, 13, 18, 48–49
    children of, 24–25

coverage under Fair Labor Standards
    Act, 212
Unionization, 220–21, 229, 240, 264n19,
    264–65n24, 265n27
United Domestic Workers Organization,
    265n24
United Farm Workers, 224, 265n24
Unpaid Wages Prohibition Act (New
    York), 241

Valenzuela, Abel, 266n37
Vidal, Gore, 36
Virgen de Guadalupe, la, 224

Wages and hours, 3, 35–38, 47–52, 109,
    261n1, 262n7, 262n9, 263n13
    back claims. *See* Back wage claims
    as influenced by social networks, 81–91
Waldinger, Roger, 7
Williams, Robin, 110
Wilson, Pete, 245n2
Wong, Sau-ling C., 18
Wood, Kimba, ix, xv
Workplace Project (Long Island), 229
Wrigley, Julia, 4–5, 40, 56, 130, 146, 148,
    152, 153, 169

Young Women's Christian Association
    (YWCA), 219
Yu, Michele, 234, 235, 236, 237

Text: 10/13 Palatino
Display: Palatino
Composition: Binghamton Valley Composition
Printing and binding: Maple-Vail Book Manufacturing Group